It Happened in Mifflin County

American History with a Central Pennsylvania Connection

Forest K. Fisher

It Happened in Mifflin County

American History with a Central Pennsylvania Connection

Forest K. Fisher

Published by the
Mifflin County Historical Society
Lewistown, Pennsylvania

Published by The Mifflin County Historical Society
1 W. Market Street
Lewistown, PA 17044
Telephone (717) 242 - 1022
FAX: (717) 242 - 3488
E-mail: mchistory@acsworld.com

ISBN 0-9763433-0-4
Library of Congress Control Number: 2004114890

First Edition

ALL PHOTOS ARE BY THE AUTHOR
UNLESS STATED OTHERWISE.

Printed by

МECHLING
BOOKBINDERY
1124 Oneida Valley Road - Rt 38
Chicora, PA 16025-3820
www.mechlingbooks.com
1-800-941-3735

Dedication

This book is dedicated to my wife, Dot, who has endured my endless hours of research and my untold hours hunched over the computer, totally ignoring her! She put up with my droning discussions of historical minutia, as well as helping me proofread finished articles. She also chauffeured me around the county to cemeteries and historical markers while I jumped out to snap photos or to complete research. I couldn't have done it without her!

Acknowledgments

First and foremost, I'd like to thank the Mifflin County Historical Society's board of directors for giving me their support for this project. The board extended to me the latitude to write about local history in the society's newsletter over these past many years of which this book is the result. Their kind words of encouragement kept me going when the demands of writing seemed overwhelming.

I would also like to thank Dan McClenahen for generously sharing his wealth of knowledge on all things Mifflin County and suggesting that I put this collection together.

A special thanks to the historical society's research librarian, Jean Suloff, who aided me with invaluable and comprehensive material on local history, presented in an organized, coherent way, from the historical society's vast archives.

And to Karen Aurand, historical society secretary, who has been part of my proofreading department, helped with research and also encouraged me to put this book together.

Thank you all for your help and encouragement!

F. K.F.

Table of Contents

The Juniata River at McVeytown - 1858
Image from MCHS Archives

*F*rom the old inhabitants of the villages and wilds in this gnarled latitude, the curious and genial tourist may gather rich pages of Indian history and romance, which will give an irresistible charm to the waters, and islands, and rocks of the merry Juniata...

"THE JUNIATA"
by T. Addison Richards
Harper's New Monthly Magazine March, 1856

Introduction

Since I became the editor of the Mifflin County Historical Society's publication, *Notes from Monument Square* over seven years ago, I've had the opportunity to investigate our local history in some detail. One of my goals as editor is to contribute an article on local history in each edition of the newsletter. So I trolled the society's archives and library in search of interesting stories and anecdotes about our area's heritage, the kind of thing that causes one to stop and say, "I didn't know that!" To my surprise AND pleasure, I found numerous Mifflin County connections to American history. This book is a collection of many of the stories and episodes I found and wrote about.

Mifflin County's third hall of justice built in 1843. Today's historic courthouse on Monument Square, home of the Mifflin County Historical Society.
Image from MCHS Archives

In the strictest sense, not every event I've written about happened within the borders of Mifflin County. I also realize that history is not always what happened, but what someone wanted to have happened. I've made an attempt to specify traditional accounts, those stories handed down through generations by retelling or reprinting. I also cite original sources I found so the reader can weigh the information accordingly.

To give you an idea of just how connected Mifflin County's heritage is to national events, start at Monument Square. The town commons or Square in Mifflin County's county seat, Lewistown, was the hub of activity since the early days. Local boys would play the area's first football game there, farmers sold their produce, people picnicked and meetings were held in this central location. This all changed in 1906 when an imposing granite memorial was dedicated to the soldiers and sailors of the Civil War and the area was cleaned up and became a symbol of local civic pride. The monument was rededicated in 1969 to all who served and died in service to the country and is flanked on four sides by Civil War-era cannons.

The near by 1843 courthouse, third in a line of four seats of county government (shown at right in an 1876 cut),is located just across Market Street from Monument Square. Walk up the old courthouse steps and turn around. Notice a Pennsylvania Historical Marker, shown below, which reads: Mifflin County – *Formed September 19, 1789 from Cumberland and Northumberland counties, and named for Thomas Mifflin, Governor, 1790-99. County seat, Lewistown, was laid out 1790; incorporated 1795. Important in Pennsylvania's canal development and early iron industry.*

The Mifflin County Historical Society's video, *A Walk Through Lewistown's History,* makes the point that within one square mile of the monument, you would find an impressive list of people and events that influenced a broad cross-section of American history.

A partial list of prominent individuals born or who lived or worked in the Lewistown area includes: Notable American Indian leaders of the colonial period; six US generals; three defenders of the Alamo; the builder of the US fleet of the War of 1812; a US naval commodore who led a fleet in the Mexican War; the man who led the first soldiers to fight for the Union in the Civil War; 19 newspaper publishers; four Congressional Medal of Honor recipients; the women who started the school system in Panama; the wife of Lincoln's Secretary of the Navy, Gideon Wells; the parents of Robert Frost; composer Stephen Foster's wife; and one of the four WW II chaplains, George L. Fox, immortalized on a US postage stamp, who died on the torpedoed troopship Dorchester; the longtime voice of Penn State football, Fran Fisher and actor Joe Campanella, both worked at local radio stations.

In addition, a battle of the French and Indian War was fought and a riot that nearly brought down the young county occurred at the first courthouse where the Mifflin County Correctional Facility stands today, both within that same square mile. The only stone to ever be removed from Abraham Lincoln's tomb in Springfield, Illinois is here, too. A 1776 copy of the Declaration of Independence was kept in a box just a couple of blocks up Main Street. And Wisto, a local health drink with a secret recipe, which drew the famous from Hollywood prior to WWII, was concocted a block away.

Or venture out into one of the county's eleven townships and many villages, and you'll find a rich history abiding there, too. The county's first television signal was received and televised programs viewed near Vira in 1930, Alexander Caverns and Searay Cave, now long closed to the public, once drew tourists even during the Great Depression.

From the Seven Mountains to the west end of Kishacoquillas Valley, the verdant landscape was viewed by Presbyterian missionary Philip Vickers Fithian in the 1770s. The reverend's journal recorded some of the earliest accounts of the life and times of what would become Mifflin County.

THE JUNIATA RIVER IS WHERE IT ALL STARTED

The river set the stage for the emergence of Mifflin County. Near Victory Park, Kishacoquillas Creek empties into the Juniata River. The Shawnee village of Ohesson, established by Chief Kishacoquillas, existed at this location for perhaps 75 years. Ohesson was first described in an affidavit by James LeTort and Jonah Davenport in 1731. The two traders reported to Pennsylvania's provincial authorities on activity of French agents in the area. The French were attempting to gain goodwill by sending gunsmiths to the Juniata Valley's Indian villages to repair their rifles and hosting their leaders

Juniata in winter - 1920s
Kepler Studio Photo Collection

at Montreal. The affidavit, dated October 29, 1731, states: *Ohesson upon the Choniata (Juniata) dist. from Susgueh. 60 miles; Shawnees, 20 fam., 60 men, (Chief) Kissikahquelas.*

Kishacoquillas – meaning "the snakes are already in their dens" – and other Shawnee chiefs attended a 1739 conference in Philadelphia, according to colonial records. Called by provincial authorities as a result of the French activities, the Shawnees promised to remain neutral, provided the rum traffic between the traders and American Indians stopped.

Kishacoquillas remained a friend to the English during this period, even while English-France relations became strained. Tradition recounts that Kishacoquillas was a friend of Arthur Buchanan, first settler in Mifflin County. In 1749, Lewis Evans' map of the area shows a village at the mouth of Kishacoquillas Creek which he names, "Kishequochkeles." Whether the old chief was still in residence is not known. At the time of his death in August, 1754, he was living along the Susquehanna near Sunbury.

In 1754, the heirs of William Penn bought a large tract of central Pennsylvania for 400 pounds from the Six Nations of the Iroquois. Known as the Albany Purchase, this opening permitted European settlement. Prior to this time, settlers who squatted on these lands were forcibly removed by the authorities. The provincial government burned the homes and crops of any trespasser. Such action was taken in Fulton County, southwest of Lewistown, when violators were driven back east. That's how the village of Burnt Cabins got its name.

By the late summer of 1754, a Scotch-Irishman named Arthur Buchanan set out from Carlisle toward this newly opened land. He traveled northwest to what is now Port Royal, following old established trails along Licking Creek for twenty

13

miles. Buchanan turned northwest through Granville Gap and ran into the Juniata River, which he followed for a few miles, coming eventually to the juncture of Kishacoquillas Creek and the Shawnee village of Ohesson.

He was in a valley 28 miles long and averaging six miles wide. On the south side of the valley ranged the Blue Mountains, breached only where Buchanan crossed through Granville Gap. Northwest was Jacks Mountain with Kishacoquillas Creek making the only gap there for twenty miles. Running eastward through these parallel ranges was the Juniata River, pressing so close to its banks, in what is now called the Lewistown Narrows, to make travel impossible.

Dorcas Buchanan Grave, Old Town Cemetery Brown & Water Streets, Lewistown, PA

The 1768 journal of Rev. Charles Beatty paints a vivid picture of the Narrows. His 110 page diary was printed in London and the August 26, 1768 entry states: *We traveled the Juniata River eight miles to a place called the Narrows, where rocky mountains bound so close upon the river as to leave only a small path...at this time (the waterway) is greatly encumbered by trees fallen across it, blown by a great wind...we were obliged to walk...along the edge of the water.*

Rev. Beatty crossed the river at a fording and gathered in the woods with the settlers who came to hear his service. While he was speaking, a rattlesnake made its way among the gathering, and Beatty notes it "caused considerable confusion" before being killed.

Buchanan had found an ideal trading location. It was the only practical intersection for pioneer travel, the north-south and east-west routes through the mountainous region. With the additional paths that converged in the area. Buchanan was at a frontier crossroads.

Perhaps typical of the pioneer spirit that built the first European settlement here can be traced to Buchanan's wife, Dorcas Holt Buchanan. Dorcas immigrated from Ireland. The majority of Mifflin County's settlers of this period were Scotch-Irish. It is how she came that merits mention. She was born in Ireland. Dorcas met and fell in love with Henry Holt, but his family greatly disapproved of the match. In a plot right out of the movies, Henry's family had Dorcas kidnapped and stowed aboard a ship bound for America. Henry's love was strong and he followed her, married in Philadelphia and eventually settled in Carlisle. Henry, a silversmith, was called back to Philadelphia, and was never heard from again. Accounts vary, one says his ship was lost at sea on a return trip to England, another

14

has him killed in route to Philadelphia. We'll never know.

Dorcas persevered, raising her two fatherless sons for three years, before meeting and marrying the trader Arthur Buchanan. They made the arduous, three-week journey westward, over narrow paths with little food, eventually to settle near Ohesson. The Buchanan's built a cabin, establishing their trading post across from the village. Dorcas became the first European woman in the area.

During the French and Indian War, the Buchanan's moved back to Carlisle. Arthur died there in 1760 and Dorcas made a startling decision for the era – to return, a widow, to operate the trading post alone. She warranted Arthur's land in 1762 and as the decades passed, Dorcas Buchanan became a very successful businesswoman, eventually buying and selling land from which Mifflin County and Lewistown would be created.

Dorcas lived an adventurous life, as did many settlers of the era. A description of her states she was, "...a high spirited, determined woman, full of energy and fire and possessed of a nature easily aroused." She died in 1804 at the ripe age of 93. Her grave is in the first town cemetery at Water and Brown Streets in Lewistown. Buchanan Elementary School and Dorcas Street, also in Lewistown, are named in her honor.

A COUNTY WITH A RICH HERITAGE

Mifflin is a county with an compelling history, just waiting to be shared. When my fourth grade students learn about the life of Dorcas Buchanan, for example, these nine and ten year olds absorb her life's details like a dry sponge. They want to know more about our local history, and the stories of real people who made their home in this part of Pennsylvania.

It's not too great a claim to say that those same pioneers and the many others who immigrated to Mifflin County over the years have made an imprint on the very history of the United States, as their decsendants moved to all parts of the United States and beyond. Allow me to share some of the county's rich and diverse history through these pages and the stories that make up our Mifflin County heritage.

Reedsville, Pennsylvania   Forest K. Fisher
September, 2004

1 - Thomas Mifflin - Our County's Namesake

A **person's name** is more then just an arrangement of letters, it engenders ancestry, heritage or even pure whimsy. Parents name their children after a grandpa, a favorite aunt or uncle, or even a rock music star. Out of the multitude of choices, the founders christened our collection of townships after Thomas Mifflin. Who was Mifflin and what was his significance to have a county named in his honor?

If one seeks credentials of the highest order consider this: Thomas Mifflin was in fact the presiding officer of the United States government - one of fourteen men to serve as President of the United States in Congress Assembled prior to adoption of the U. S. Constitution. He signed the treaty ending the hostilities with Great Britain and accepted the resignation of George Washington as army commander-in-chief in 1783. But let's start at the beginning of his life in eighteenth century Philadelphia.

Thomas Mifflin - Pennsylvania's first governor under the new state constitution of 1790. He was a popular political figure whose final term ended in 1799. This image is from a print of a painting by Gilbert Stuart completed when Mifflin was 51 years old. - Image from MCHS Archives

HIS LIFE BEGINS IN PHILADELPHIA

Born in 1744 into a fourth generation Philadelphia Quaker family, Thomas Mifflin studied at a Quaker school and then at the College of Philadelphia (later part of the University of Pennsylvania), earning a diploma at the age of 16. Mifflin then worked for 4 years in a Philadelphia countinghouse. In 1764 he visited Europe, and the next year entered the mercantile business in Philadelphia with his brother. In 1767 he married Sarah Morris. Although he prospered in business, politics tempted him.

He knew the founding fathers: Adams, Franklin and Jefferson, to mention just a few. Greater fame was clouded by events involving a plot to remove George Washington. Mifflin was at the heart of the Philadelphia war effort in the 1770s and was made a major. Locals dubbed him "the soul" of the effort. "Let us not be bold in declarations and afterward cold in action. Let not the patriotic feelings of today be forgotten tomorrow...," Mifflin noted before the War of Independence.

John Adams thought he should have been the general, considering "he has been the animating sole of the whole." Mifflin mustered a drive for both men and material, even his fellow Quakers made up a company of light infantry, The Quaker Blues. But the Quaker fathers strongly disapproved of this activity. Mifflin's military preparation was reported at the Monthly Meeting of Philadelphia. That July the Meeting noted: "Thomas Mifflin of this city, merchant, having for considerable time past been active in the promotion of military measures, he hath separated himself from religious fellowship with us."

QUATERMASTER-GENERAL

In May, 1775, Mifflin was selected by General Washington to be his aid-de-camp. The majority of appointed officers, Mifflin included, had no army experience. Half the generals served their apprenticeship during the conflict itself, on the job training, as it were.

Mifflin did have experience in an area Washington would soon find useful, even vital. The distribution of supplies was dismal, so a new department was established with Mifflin at its head. As a merchant-soldier, Mifflin was named Quartermaster-general to the Army of the United Colonies. He administered this office with zeal and efficiency.

Rumors eventually swirled about him, including: Mifflin was enriching himself at the expense of the army; family and business associates were receiving lucrative contracts at inflated prices; Mifflin's fortune increased during his service as quartermaster. Today terms such as "conflicts of interest" might apply. It was customary to allow five percent on purchases of the department to go to the quartermaster-general to defray expenses. Yet Mifflin wrote privately and stated publicly he wanted no profits or commissions. He even placed his business while quartermaster under the control of his brother and cousin.

As the war proceeded, Mifflin did his job as quartermaster, gaining Washington's initial approval of the effort. Mifflin came to hate the job. He wanted action, thirsted for military glory but was tied to the supply desk, a millstone around his neck.

He became ill, despondent, even depressed in today's terms. (Chronic illness would plague him

The Conway Cabal - Several officers in Washington's command were discontented and privately criticized the commander-in-chief. There were even a few members in Congress who leaned that way, too...Thomas Mifflin's name was associated with the group and a cloud drew over him.

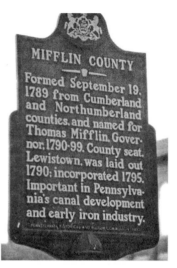

County Historical Marker - Located in front of Mifflin County's Historic Courthouse on Monument Square, Lewistown, the county marker was dedicated September 19, 1981. All 67 Pennsylvania counties have markers placed by the Pennsylvania Historical and Museum Commission. County markers are always located near the court house or other significant county building.

throughout his adult life.) His health finally broke in 1777 and he retired his position. It left the army AND Washington with no real choice for quartermaster-general. Washington had to do the job himself on several occasions, as Mifflin found his stock falling rapidly in the commander-in-chief's eyes. The Congress refused to accept his resignation, eventually he was appointed to a Board of War, retaining his rank and commission.

THE CONWAY CABAL
A faction of rebels within the rebellion created this episode that would haunt Thomas Mifflin for life. An event of pure intrigue, named for Colonel Thomas Conway, an Irish volunteer, it occurred at a time when the success of the American cause was in doubt.

It actually gives more credence to Conway and his fellows to call this episode a cabal. There was no master plan or effective group ever threatening Washington's overthrow, although in those troubled times, who could tell.

Briefly, it went like this: Several officers in Washington's command were discontented and privately criticized the commander-in-chief. There were even a few members in Congress who leaned that way, too. Into this mix was included the failed promotion of one of the principles, plus innuendo and bruised egos added for good measure. Inevitably, Washington found out and sent a terse letter to Conway.

Conway beat a path to Washington to protest his innocence. Accusation and counter accusation followed among the cabal members. Uninvolved officers were implicated. Challenges to settle points of honor were made, but only one duel actually materialized. Each, by letter or deed, rushed to Washington protesting innocence.

Modern historians find no "smoking gun" against Mifflin, but once associated with the episode, the suspect became tainted. Even with the advantage of hindsight, the true nature of the event is blurred. What can be said for sure is that Thomas Mifflin's name was associated with the group and a cloud drew over him. He vehemently denied any involvement, but Washington seemed to have an entrenched feeling against Mifflin. At the time, Mifflin was widely thought to be involved and it dogged him for the remainder of the war and his life.

Blood was shed as a result of the affair, Conway's. In a duel fought by Conway and an officer who accused him of cowardice, Conway took a bullet in the mouth, breaking teeth and his jaw. As he lay bleeding, the victor snorted, "I've stopped one...rascal's lying tongue..."

For a more complete discussion of the Conway Cabal, see John Hyde Preston's short history of the war, *Revolution 1776*, pages 265 to 270. Preston lays out the ineffective attempt to oust Washington. Also, Rossman's Thomas Mifflin, gives a detailed accounting of the political and military events and the fallout of the cabal episode.

POLITICAL CAREER

From 1778 until he died in 1800, Thomas Mifflin held office almost continuously. Despite the accusations of profiteering and the Conway affair, Mifflin was the most popular figure in Pennsylvania politics. The people loved him. He served in the Pennsylvania Assembly helping to overturn the constitution of 1776 which replaced the position of governor with an executive council. Eventually a new constitution would be adopted.

Mifflin was elected to Congress under the Articles of Confederation and became president of that body from 1783 to 1784. He was in fact the presiding officer of the government - one of fourteen men to serve as President of the United States in Congress Assembled prior to adoption of the U. S. Constitution. He signed the treaty ending the hostilities with Great Britain and accepted the resignation of George Washington as army commander-in-chief in 1783. He also served as a Pennsylvania Delegate to the U. S. Constitutional Convention and worked for Pennsylvania's ratification of that document in 1787.

Mifflin was elected to the Pennsylvania Supreme Executive Council and became its presiding officer, replacing Ben Franklin. He chaired the state constitutional convention held in 1789 - 1790 and became Pennsylvania's first governor under the newly adopted constitution in 1790. Mifflin's wide popularity in the state assured reelection, his final term ending in 1799.

His tenure was not a placid one. Mifflin faced a terrible Philadelphia yellow fever epidemic in 1793 and 1796. He called out the state militia several times, including during the Whiskey Rebellion in 1794, Fries Rebellion in 1799 and occasional Indian disturbances. (Fries Rebellion was an insurrection

Washington's choice - In May, 1775, Mifflin was selected by General Washington to be his aid-de-camp. The majority of appointed officers, Mifflin included, had no army experience. Half the generals served their apprenticeship during the conflict itself, on the job training, as it were.

19

over a direct taxation of land, houses and slaves.) The Erie Triangle was also acquired during his term as governor.

MIFFLIN'S FINAL DAYS

When he left the governor's office in 1799, he won a seat as state assemblyman from Philadelphia. He took that seat on December 20, 1799. By January 20, 1800, Thomas Mifflin would be dead. All his life he was plagued by "chronic illness." References to his condition appear in a number of sources, from diaries to official minutes. Mifflin was also known for his alcoholic consumption, but then many old war horses of the Revolution had liberal drinking habits. Society had a different standard toward use of liquor, especially as a medicinal, in the 1700s.

The exact nature of his illness isn't known. Perhaps it was malaria or some other chronic disease. Contemporaries variously refer to his condition as rheumatic trouble, ill health, as being too ill to receive friends, being much indisposed or gripped by his old complaint. His final illness was mercifully short. Sometime around the fourteenth of January 1800 he suddenly fell ill and died in the early hours of January 20. His wife proceeded him in death before he became governor. He left no lawful heirs, not that he had much to leave them.

Mifflin's "complaint" was not his only problem at the end. A life of high living drained the family fortune. In 1799, he left Philadelphia, never to return, driven by court action of creditors to recoup monies he owed them. Thomas Mifflin, did in fact, die penniless. Pennsylvania Senator Jonathan Roberts noted that Mifflin "was buried at public expense, it being uncertain if his property would have met it." His simple funeral was described as "the burial of a pauper."

Mifflin is buried at the Trinity Lutheran Church in Lancaster, Pa. In 1987, a bronze plaque was placed there in his memory by the Thomas Mifflin Chapter of the Daughters of the American Revolution from Mifflintown, Juniata County, Pa.

When our county was established in 1789, September 19 of that year to be exact, Thomas Mifflin became an obvious choice for a name. It was certainly politically correct in that era to honor this famous Pennsylvanian, soon to be the Commonwealth's first governor under the newly adopted state constitution.

Despite the impoverished end to a significant life, Thomas Mifflin was a man of his times, popular with most Pennsylvanians. His name should indeed be more then just a collection of letters to those of us who live here. "Mifflin" evokes the turbulent era of our nation's birth and the county's creation.

Thomas Mifflin chaired the state constitutional convention held in 1789 - 1790 and became Pennsylvania's first governor under the newly adopted constitution in 1790. Mifflin's wide popularity in the state assured re-election, his final term ending in 1799.

THE NAME LINGERS ON

Within Pennsylvania's borders, one can find the name "Mifflin" in various locals. Of course, there is our county and a few boroughs, so Mifflin if not a common name, is at least represented around the state. As for counties, there are no others in the United States with the name Mifflin. Even Texas, with more counties than it knows what to do with at 254, doesn't have a Mifflin County. Tennessee has a town called Mifflin, which has a connection to Mifflin Countians who settled there prior to moving to Texas prior to the siege of the Alamo.

The Pennsylvania Atlas & Gazetteer cites seven "Mifflin" examples, including: Mifflin and Mifflintown located in Juniata County; Columbia County has Mifflin Crossroads and Mifflinville, both near Bloomsburg; Mifflin Junction Station and Mifflin Mine Station are in Allegheny County, near West Mifflin. There is no North, South, or East Mifflin, however.

How about Pennsylvania townships named for Thomas Mifflin? Chances would seem pretty favorable, there are 1,548 townships in the state's 67 counties. Despite these odds, however, only Columbia, Dauphin and Lycoming have a Mifflin Township.

Pennsylvania roads, streets or avenues named Mifflin? Too many to recount here. There's a Thomas Mifflin Elementary School, opened in 1935 in the East Falls section of Philadelphia. And Governor Mifflin School District, with offices in Shillington, PA, is just southwest of Reading in Berks County.

Out-of-staters might guess that Mifflin Borough should be the county seat of Mifflin County. They would be wrong. Even the borough of Mifflintown wouldn't be correct, it is the county seat of Juniata. Lewistown is the county seat of Mifflin County, while Lewisburg is Union County's seat of local government. That leaves Uniontown the county seat of Fayette County. Wayne County's courthouse is located in Honesdale, while Waynesburg is the county seat of Greene County. Except for West Chester being Chester's county seat, all of the following counties have made it very easy. Their courthouse is located in the municipality of the same name. Beaver, Bedford, Butler, Clarion, Clearfield, Erie, Huntingdon, Indiana, Lancaster, Lebanon, Mercer, Philadelphia, Somerset, Warren, Washington and York.

Mifflin County and its history is a chronicle of the people - from the Shawnee and the settler to canal and railroad worker, the farmer or craftsman along with the wives and families who followed, the businesses that developed, prospered or failed - all struggling and enduring hardships to establish this county out of what was wilderness some 250 years ago. It is after all our name and part of this county's unique heritage.

"Notes from Monument Square"

To the reader: One of my jobs at the Mifflin County Historical Society is to write and edit *Notes from Monument Square*, the society's newsletter. The society's office and library are located on the square in Mifflin County's historic courthouse in downtown Lewistown, Pennsylvania. I include a variety of unusual, interesting or just plain silly bits of local Mifflin County historical trivia in every issue. The Mifflin County Trivia page has become a popular feature that readers anticipate. When I put the Thomas Mifflin article together in January, 2000, the bicentennial of his death, I had a number of interesting facts about our county's namesake unable to fit into the original piece. Thus, these questions appeared on the Trivia page and are here, too.

Thomas Mifflin Trivia

Thomas Mifflin
Mifflin County Namesake
Image from MCHS Archives

On Monday, December 2, 1799, Pennsylvania's first governor arrived in the new state capital, Lancaster. Mifflin was approaching the close of his tenure and five days later he delivered his last official address to the legislature. "An eloquent valediction" was how friends characterized his final executive remarks. He died January 20, 1800. He was an illustrious Pennsylvanian, and a significant figure of the War of Independence.

Try your hand at these questions based on our county's namesake, Thomas Mifflin. Answers are found on the following pages.

1. As recently as 1997, Thomas Mifflin and his wife Sarah made headlines in the Philadelphia press. In fact, generations after their passing, legalities concerning Thomas and Sarah reached the Philadelphia Orphans Court. Why were the Mifflins in the news?

[a] Distribution of a two hundred year old bequest from the Mifflin's estate was finally distributed to the Pennsylvania Philosophical Society.

[b] Ownership of a John Singleton Copely family portrait of the Mifflins was agreed to in Philadelphia courts.

[c] The placement of bronze statues of the Mifflins within Philadelphia's historic district was blocked by legal action of the city's preservation commission.

[d] A musical of the Mifflins' life set to open on Broadway was blocked on opening night by copyright problems.

2. Thomas Mifflin's son-in-law, Joseph Hopkinson, and his daughter Emily had a son they named Thomas Mifflin Hopkinson. The elder Hopkinson wrote the words to a

song in 1798 that became a national hit. The young nation was awash with patriotic passion, brought about by talk of war with France. What was this famous song that brought popular fame to Joseph Hopkinson?

[a] Hail, Columbia!   [b] Columbia, the Gem of the Ocean   [c] My Country 'tis of Thee   [d] Anacrion in Heaven

3. Another Mifflin namesake was George Mifflin Dallas, born in 1792, son of Thomas Mifflin's secretary, Alexander Dallas. George Mifflin Dallas went on to have a stellar political career of his own. Texans honored him by naming a county after him. Dallas County, Texas was named for George Mifflin Dallas because he was...?

[a] U.S. Minister to Russia, 1837-1839   [b]   Vice President of the United States, 1845-1849   [c] U.S. Minister to Great Britain, 1856-1861   [d]   All of the above.

4. Thomas Mifflin's signature can be found on many public documents. During his lifetime, his signature became one of the most recognized to many Pennsylvania citizens. Which of these public documents was NOT signed by Mifflin during his lifetime?

[a]   1763 - One of 150 signatures on a letter to Provincial governor John Penn

[b]   1776 - Declaration of Independence as a Pennsylvania delegate

[c]   1784 - Peace treaty with Great Britain ending the Revolutionary War

[d]   1787 - U.S. Constitution as a Pennsylvania delegate

[e]   1794 - Proclamation to prosecute and punish those involved in the Whiskey Rebellion in western Pennsylvania.

5. In 1987, Thomas Mifflin, soldier and politician, was named to a Hall of Fame. Which one?

[a]   The Quartermasters Hall of Fame as first quartermaster general.

[b]   Revolutionary War Soldiers' Hall of Fame for his service as Washington's first aide-de-camp.

[c]   The Pennsylvania Governors' Hall of Fame as the Commonwealth's first governor.

[d]   The Trap Shooters' Hall of Fame for introducing that clay pigeon sport to the gentry of Bucks County, Pa.

6. Fort Mifflin, located on Mifflin Road, near the Philadelphia International Airport, is a point of historical interest. The Fort was built on an island to protect Philadelphia from attack by the British during the Revolutionary War. It was renamed in 1794 after Thomas Mifflin, then Pennsylvania's governor, but during the war it went by another name. Originally, Fort Mifflin was called...

[a] Fort Swampy, for the low, swamp-like conditions surrounding the island.

[b] Fort Mud, for the island on which it was built.

[c] Fort Benjamin Franklin, who built a chain of forts through Pennsylvania.

[d] Fort Printz, for Swede Johann Printz, pre-English governor of the area.

7. As a privileged young man growing up in metropolitan Philadelphia in the 1700s,

Mifflin enjoyed many recreations. After returning from a trip to Europe, he and a number of his social equals organized an association devoted exclusively to a certain activity. This activity was...

[a] Skeet shooting - the first U.S. shooting of clay pigeons, then all the rage in England.

[b] Fox hunting - the first organized U.S. fox hunt, riders replete with special uniforms.

[c] Ice boat racing - the first winter "yacht" club in America located on the Delaware River.

[d] Mesmerism - the forerunner of hypnotism learned from Austrian physician Franz Mesmer who treated European elite.

8. Which of these offices or positions did Thomas Mifflin NOT hold in his service to the nation?

[a] Lamp-lighting Warden of Philadelphia

[b] Major-general in the Continental Army

[c] Governor of Pennsylvania

[d] Ambassador to Spain

[e] President of the United States

ANSWERS TO THOMAS MIFFLIN TRIVIA

1. [b] Ownership of a John Singleton Copely family portrait of the Mifflins was agreed to in Philadelphia courts.   The Historical Society of Pennsylvania – the portrait's owner – and the Philadelphia Museum of Art issued a joint press release in 1997, in part it said: *John Singleton Copley's Portrait of Mr. and Mrs. Thomas Mifflin (Sarah Morris), the premier colonial-era portraitist's only depiction of Philadelphia subjects, will have a new home in the city where it has been for over two centuries. The historic agreement has been unanimously approved at meetings of the respective boards of trustees of The Historical Society of Pennsylvania...and the Philadelphia Museum of Art. The Historical Society will be joined by the Museum in a petition to the Orphans Court in Philadelphia, seeking approval of the agreement.*

2. [a] Hail, Columbia! "The New Federal Song" was written in 1798 to the air of "Washington's March" and later renamed "Hail Columbia" by Joseph Hopkinson, Thomas Mifflin's son-in-law. The song honored John Adams and remained popular into the 1800s. A first edition of this song is housed in the Lester S. Levy Collection of Sheet Music, at Johns Hopkins University, in the Special Collections Division of the Milton S. Eisenhower Library. A letter by the song's author is also in the library. There are over 80 other editions of "Hail Columbia" in the collection. Hail, Columbia!, the last four lines...

> *When hope was sinking in dismay,*
> *When glooms obscured Columbia's day,*
> *His steady mind from changes free*
> *Resolv'd on death or Liberty.*

3. [b] Vice President of the United States, 1845-1849 – Dallas County, Texas was named for George Mifflin Dallas, vice president of the United States at the time of annexation. Dallas was all of the other positions, and more: mayor of Philadelphia, Pa., 1829; U.S. Senator from Pennsylvania, 1831-1833; Pennsylvania state attorney general, 1833; U.S. Minister to Russia, 1837-1839; Vice President of the United States, 1845-1849; U.S. Minister to Great Britain, 1856-1861. He died December 31, 1864 and is interred at St. Peter's Churchyard, Philadelphia. There are Dallas counties in Arkansas, Iowa, Missouri and Texas, all named for him.

4. [b] 1776 - Declaration of Independence as a Pennsylvania delegate

5. [a] The Quartermaster Hall of Fame as first quartermaster general. From *Quartermaster History & Tradition*: The Quartermaster Hall of Fame was established in November 1985, by MG Eugene L. Stillions, the Quartermaster General, as part of the Quartermaster Regimental honors program. On 12 June 1986, General Richard H. Thompson, Commander of the U.S. Army Material Command and MG Stillions opened the Hall of Fame in Mifflin Hall at Fort Lee. This permanent display of Quartermaster Hall of Fame inductees includes each inductees' name, their photograph and a narrative of their major achievements.

6. [b] Fort Mud, for the island on which it was built. – From the Fort Mifflin Visitor's Center: Fort Mifflin is located on Mifflin Road, near the Philadelphia International Airport. The Fort was built on Mud Island to protect the city from attack. It was originally called Fort Mud and was renamed in 1794 after Thomas Mifflin, an officer of the Revolutionary War and once governor of Pennsylvania. The Fort was also a federal prison during the Civil War and remained an active military installation until 1959. The Fort is open April 1 through November 30, Wednesdays through Sundays from 10 a.m. until 4 p.m. There is a small admission fee ($4.00 regular, $3.50 seniors, $2.00 children). Call 215-492-3395 for up-to-date information and admission cost.

7. [b] Fox hunting - the first organized U.S. fox hunt, riders replete with special uniforms. Wearing black velvet caps, their uniforms consisted of dark brown short coats with lapelled dragoon pockets, white buttons, frock sleeves, and buff waistcoats.

8. [d] Ambassador to Spain – This was sort of a trick question, but as a President of the Congress during the era of the Articles of Confederation, Mifflin was the head-of-state. *The Forgotten Presidents* by George Grant addresses this interesting situation. Grant's book is a collection of biographies of the Presidents and begins with the men who "are forgotten in the annals of American History, men who became Presidents of the United States before the acceptance of the Constitution."

2 - Artifacts Hint at County's Past

Picture this scene beside one of Mifflin County's popular trout streams, over two millennia ago ... Standing on the creek bank one late autumn evening, the young hunter looked down at the translucent water. Beneath the surface, gently holding their position, several large trout swim with heads upstream. The young hunter's gaze is fixed upon the fish. He holds the weapon in his right hand, while the fingers of his left hand unconsciously trace the edge of the stone point, a point he crafted himself and affixed with sinew to one end of a wooden shaft.

The feel of that edge triggers memories and the young hunter thinks of his grandfather. It was he who showed him the best stone for chipping. It was the grandfather who taught him to break large flakes from the rock with a hammer stone and to rough out a point's shape with a sturdy piece of antler and a stone hammer. It was the grandfather who guided his young hands with the antler tool to press off smaller flakes and form the notch. He treasured the few points he had, made by the grandfather's own hands, and remembered all that the grandfather taught.

The young hunter also remembered the point he lost in this same fishing spot. He cared for his points and hated loosing any to carelessness. With even breaths

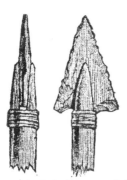

Stone points attached to an arrow shaft from the Smithsonian Institution's 1912 Handbook of American Indians - MCHS Collection

26

he raised the weapon and assured himself of the success to come as the shaft left his finger tips...

Fast forward twenty centuries. A much younger hunter wades in Honey Creek. The quarry: crawfish. The weapon: bare hands and a tin can. Feverish digging reveals a large water filled hole in the creek bed and ample muddy water. As another grandfather shouts from the creek bank, "What did you find?", the younger hunter looks down in the clearing water's flow and shouts back, "Grandpa, I found an arrowhead!"

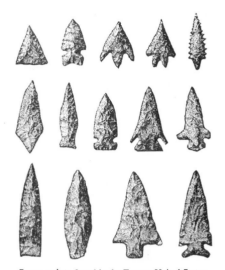

Stone points found in the Eastern United States, examples of which have been found in Mifflin County from the Smithsonian Institution's 1912 *Handbook of American Indians* - MCHS Collection

Many an adult first gained a lifelong interest in arrowheads by a chance find as a youngster. Literally hundreds of artifact hunters, from the avid collector to the occasional weekend hiker have combed the plowed fields and stream banks of Mifflin County in search of stone points and tools.

MIFFLIN COUNTY'S FIRST INHABITANTS

The Shawnee people were the last in a line of American Indians to live in what is now Mifflin County. Their predecessors were allowed into the area by the Iroquois nation, then concentrated in New York State. Who were the first local inhabitants?

County historians J. Martin Stroup and Raymond Martin Bell wrote about these "first people" in their extensively researched 1957 book, *Genesis of Mifflin County.* Stroup and Bell noted that the early inhabitants were known to Captain John Smith, through his contacts with other Indian groups. He referred to them as "Attaocks" on his 1608 map of exploration.

Through the middle 1600s, European settlers referred to the people

Points found by Sam Detweiler

of the region by various names, which eventually jelled into Juniata. Their emblem was a tall beacon stone placed vertically in the ground, thus the other name, "Standing Stone People."

As the traditional story goes, a ten year conflict with the Mohawks of New York eventually ended with the Juniata's defeat. The Iroquois claimed the interior of Pennsylvania by right of this conquest. William Penn is known to have acknowledged the Iroquois claim when he arrived in 1681.

The Iroquois described central Pennsylvania and the Kishacoquillas and Juniata Valleys as some of the best hunting areas and actively controlled the territory. It was in fact William Penn's policy of fair dealing with the American Indians, that prevented earlier settlement by Europeans in the Mifflin County area. As long as the land was used by the Iroquois or their protected groups, no settlements were allowed. Provincial authorities would keep white settlers out of this area, by force, if necessary.

The Tuscaroras from North Carolina were permitted by the controlling Iroquois to move through the Juniata Valley during first two decades of the 1700s. The Tuscaroras became part of the Iroquois Confederacy around 1723.

Around the same time, the Delawares of eastern Pennsylvania began a western migration. The Iroquois conquered this group, too, and affected active control over them. The Delawares were followed by the third group permitted into the area, the Shawnees.

Evidence of the earlier culture is well known locally. Stone projectile points and other artifacts of great antiquity are regularly discovered by farmers and hikers along the Juniata River even today.

LOCAL ARTIFACT COLLECTORS

Locally, several names are legendary, in the realm of artifact collectors: Jonas J. Yoder of McVeytown, Sam Detweiler of Allensville and Robert "Archie" Carolus of Lewistown. All three men not only preserved their finds, but each man shared the lore each carefully crafted point, knife or bowl had to tell.

Detweiler maintained a museum in his Allensville home, which he readily shared with visitors, until this past summer when his vast collection was sold at auction. Yoder and Carolus, now both deceased, each maintained comprehensive personal collections and often spoke to school groups or other gatherings and readily shared their extensive understanding of Indian culture. Each in turn was featured over the years in articles or stories by the local media or in area histories, like the late Raymond Harmon's *History of Mifflin County, Vol. 1* or in the Lewistown *Sentinel's* 1989 county bicentennial publication *All Aboard.*

IS IT AN ARROWHEAD AND WHY DO WE FIND THEM?

Archeologists remind us that the arrowhead is more correctly termed projectile point, as such points were commonly used with

Artifacts collected by Robert Carlous along Honey Creek, in Armagh Township, Mifflin County.

the atlatl or throwing stick and not with bows and arrows. (The throwing stick is a short shaft with a handle on one end and a hook that fits into the butt end of the spear at the other. In function, it artificially lengthens the throwers arm, enabling an increase in velocity.)

Based on archeological finds, the bow and arrow is roughly 2000 years old in the Northeast, so anything older cannot be an arrowhead, although that's what we call them. Also, some large points were used as knives, yet fall under that common term. Along the Juniata and its tributaries the common lithic materials, the stone used to manufacture arrowheads, are local flints and cherts and rhyolite. Sedimentary materials like mudstone were also used for larger tools.

Why do we find arrowhead and points anyway? Is it possible that the abundance of artifacts is due to Indian carelessness? Not likely. It seems more probable that many finds are simply used up points, discards. Other points bear evidence of being reworked after a break in use or through accident. Loss during practice and play must also be valid reasons for projectile point finds.

Cashed points have also been discovered, stored away for safe keeping and then forgotten due to death or other occurrences. This 19th century article from the Lewistown Gazette attests to that possibility.

Lewistown Gazette - May 10, 1871

INDIAN RELICS - We notice last week the finding of some curiosities in a stone quarry at Jack's Creek. They were discovered by Samuel Nightsinger and others in a natural cavity in the rocks, from which it would appear as if the boulder had been pitched about since the relics had been deposited. They were nearly fifty in number and neatly piled in. In our opinion,

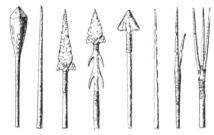

Diagram of arrows from the Smithsonian Institution's 1912 Handbook of American Indians -

since we have examined them, are not arrow but spear heads. The largest in our possession is over 3 and 3/4 inches long and 2 and 3/4 inches broad, regularly cut to a point, with scalloped edges; is composed of the hard brownish flint in such general use among Indians, none of which, so far as we know, is found this side of Lebanon County. A defective one, apparently broken in its manufacture, has a mark which many pronounce to be clotted blood, as if a finger had been cut. To the eye it bears that resemblance, but under a microscope looks like red porphyry. How the Indians with the rude instruments in their possession, succeeded in cutting these hard flints into shape, sharpening and scalloping the edges in a manner which would puzzle workers in stone at the present day, is a marvel which we have never explained. These things are worth preserving. Is there no association in town which will take charge of such curiosities?

DATING PROJECTILE POINTS

There are no tests that authentic stone artifacts can be subjected to for determining when they were made. This according to Gary L. Fogelman, author of Pennsylvania Artifact Series, a monumental set of books and booklets, in which Fogelman extensively describes Pennsylvania artifacts. The chart above was prepared by the Pennsylvania Historic and Museum Commission and shows a sequence of cultural stages suggesting a range of periods and point shapes used at those times.

McCoy House Exibit - Artifacts found after 1972 Flood along the Juniata River.

However, only artifacts found in a systematically excavated site with datable components, such as bones or charcoal, can be accurately dated. Locally, most artifacts are from non-stratified sites, that is there are no buried levels, the Indians lived on the same surface as we walk today. Since most area sites are located on farmland, the Indian's living surface has been plowed through many times, confusing the relationship of one object to another. Such artifacts can be found anywhere from the surface to as deep as the farmer's plow, perhaps twelve to eighteen inches.

ARTIFACTS AT MCCOY HOUSE

Finding arrowheads is still a chance proposition. Expert hunters rely on years of searching experience and a "trained eye." Highway construction, as in the case of the Route 322 Missing Link project through Mifflin County or floods can unearth long buried artifacts. In fact, artifacts turned up in 1972 as a result of the high water from Hurricane Agnes are on display at the McCoy House Museum, Lewistown. In addition, the museum also holds several Indian artifact collections which can be viewed and studied.

McCoy House Exhibit - Donated stone scrapers and arrow points on display.

Granted, these are just stones and everyone doesn't experience a feeling of reverence while holding an arrowhead or other artifact. Yet in a world obsessed with making alien contacts from distant stars, holding an arrowhead is a way to make contact of another sort. Touching the same surface, feeling the same edge create so long ago, hints at the county's rich American Indian heritage.

The next time you walk the byways of Mifflin County enjoying the seasonal landscape, remember to look down from time to time. History is at your footsteps, just waiting to be discovered.

3 - The Grasshopper War

*W*hen the first settlers *came to that part of Mifflin County that would later form Juniata County, the Indians in that area were friendly. They told the settlers about a famous battleground near Licking Creek. The Indians said that long ago there were two Indian Villages nearby. They were on opposite sides of the creek from each other. One day the children were out playing. They found a grasshopper. Children from both villages wanted the grasshopper. They began to argue about the grasshopper. Soon their mothers came and they began to argue too. Finally the men got involved and the argument turned into a battle. Hundreds of men, women and children died in the battle.*

The settlers thought that this was an interesting story but they didn't believe it. Some years later the farmers were plowing their fields on the spot where the Indians said the war had happened. They began to plow up many relics. The arrowheads, spear points, clubs, and bones showed signs of a fierce battle. It seems that a big battle had happened because people failed to agree over a little grasshopper.

Artist and author Patrick Reynolds produced a column in the 1980s on this topic in his popular *Pennsylvania Profiles* series.

The Grasshopper War is also included in the textbook, *Mifflin County Yesterday and Today,* an extensive history written in 1991 by local educators, as part of the fourth grade social studies curriculum in the Mifflin County School District.

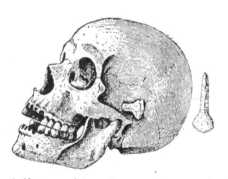

Artifacts can point to pre-European conflicts among American Indian groups, like the Grasshopper War. Skull and point from a burial mound in Illinois - Smithsonian Institution's 1912 Handbook of American Indians

Each day, thousands of travelers drive through the Reedsville Narrows on U.S. 322, in Mifflin County's Brown Township, unaware they pass beneath the visage of a giant stone bird. Known locally as Bird Rock, the massive monolith has guarded this break in Jack's Mountain for eons and is the object of an interesting local legend.

"Bird Rock" by Anne Kepler Fisher
(1925 - 1977) - Author's collection

4 - The Legend of Bird Rock

It was a time well before the first white settlers ventured into the verdant land, and the native people made a home out of the wilderness. Ample streams crisscrossed the land, wild berries grew in plentiful amounts, waterfowl abounded. The first people hunted elk, bear and deer amid the forested valley that one day would be known as the Kishacoquillas.

The first people were lead by a great chief. Since his own beloved wife's death, the chief treasured his only child, a daughter, more than life itself. The daughter, too, loved her widowed father and vowed never to displease him, but serve him always. To show his love the great chief bestowed upon this only child the finest adornments - bracelets, necklaces and rings for which he traded near and far. He granted her every wish.

The chief had but one demand, though, of his only child. She must not marry, save the one the chief himself approved. It soon became apparent to the daughter that she was doomed to perpetual maidenhood, for her father refused every request of marriage from her many suitors.

Just as winter follows fall, and summer the spring, the inevitable happened, she fell in love. Never wanting to go against the wishes of her father, whom she loved as dearly as life itself, she was thrust into a terrible dilemma- she knew her father would not agree to a union with her new-found love. Despite her impassioned entreaties, the chief refused her marriage request, he would not give way. Dolefully relating the news to her beloved, the warrior persisted as no other before him. Run away with him and leave the father. He would recover in time, the warrior told her, but she knew better. Her father would be heart broken.

She resisted and ran into the woods. Up the mountain she fled, the warrior close behind her. She pealed off bracelets, rings and necklaces, casting them to the ground behind her, hoping her pursuer would be diverted by the riches. To no avail. Hysterical and desperate, she found herself at the very edge of a mountain cliff. Disobey the beloved father? In despair she chose to leap from the cliff to her death.

The breathless warrior stood at the edge of the precipice and looked disbelievingly at the maiden's lifeless body on the rocks below. At this very moment, the Great Spirit who watched the events unfold from afar, instantly turned the warrior into a giant stone bird. He would now keep a perpetual vigil on the mountain for his lost love. To this very day, the hapless warrior still keeps his silent watch, and we know him as Bird Rock.

Bird Rock in the 1940s - Kepler Studio Collection

A TRADITIONAL STORY

The Legend of Bird Rock, to say the least, has an uncertain origin and appears from time-to-time in various versions. The version that appears here is adapted from one that appeared in the Lewistown *Sentinel*, January 8, 1969 and was reprinted in *Birds and Friends of Central Pennsylvania* by Ben and Hattie Meyers, 1973. This little privately published book is a collection of columns titled "We Notice That" by Ben Meyers. The Sentinel carried his column for 39 years.

When or by whom the Legend of Bird Rock was first told is not known, and will likely never be known, but over time the tale became a traditional legend with each retelling.

The Legend of Bird Rock is a tale not unlike those collected by Pennsylvania folklorist Henry W. Shoemaker, famous for his collections of state lore and legend titled, *Pennsylvania Mountain Stories, In the Seven Mountains, Susquehanna Legends* plus a dozen more. Shoemaker has been suspected of embellishing his stories to add interest, while championing our state. There are those who even term Shoemaker's brand of story, "fakelore." Who's to say? We remember Shoemaker today for the legends he helped promote, one was Centre County's "Nita-Nee," Indian princess for whom it is said Mt. Nittany is named.

Mankind devised stories to explain everything from the rising and setting sun to why the bear has a stubby tail, so why not a legend to explain how that geological feature we call Bird Rock came to perch in the Reedsville Narrows?

IT'S A CASE OF GEOLOGY

This area of Jack's Mountain is now called the Reedsville Narrows, earlier it was Mann's Narrows and even earlier, Logan's Gap. The convenient break in the mountain is frequented by geology students from Penn State studying the well exposed outcroppings of various rock types.

Roadside Geology of Pennsylvania by Bradford B. Van Diver notes that: "The gap is well profiled in both the northern and southern approaches, and the Tuscarora quartzite is exposed in several places along the ridge crest."

As to how, scientifically, that old rock came to rest on the side of Jack's Mountain, Ben Meyers speculated in his 1969 column:

Looking closer...one gets the view which indicates that there was a large gorge of the sandstone and a conglomerated ridge. Included was a stone which formed the basis for a sculptor to work on. This might have produced the basis for a big stone image. Seems as if the original rough rock was upended by water, frost and ice action and the rock in some unknown manner became balanced, quite close to its very source.

But what force produced the shaping of the rock? What unseen sculptor was busy here? Must have been ages of water, wind, frost and snow action at work.

Thus the forces rounded the head, shoulder and wings, creating a likeness as it now appears for sightseers to gaze upon.

Well...that is an interesting conjecture and Bird Rock likely formed that way. Yet it seems so poetic if that roving warrior was indeed turned into a stone bird by the Great Spirit. What do you think? As Ripley urged decades ago, "Believe it or not."

**Mann's Narrows in 1938, looking toward Yeagertown,
as old US 322 snakes its way through the gap.**
- Kepler Studio Collection

From the Pages of...

The Lewistown Gazette

July 20, 1893

"Bicycle Championship"

The bicycle race for the championship of Menno Township was one of the leading events this week. The contestants were John A. Webb, one of the proprietors of the Allensville Woolen Mill and Homer Zerby, one of the expert weavers of the same establishment. The latter carried the honors, passing the judge's stand two necks and a half ahead!

5 - In the Seven Mountains

Located in northern Mifflin County,
This area is a source of history, beauty, legends and
controversy... about the name.

Vintage Post Card ca.1940 of the Seven Mountains - Titled "The Seven-Mountains Roof Garden View" along US Route 322 between Bellefonte and Lewistown

The Seven Mountains and the respective names of the chosen seven has always been a topic of local discussion We've had some experience with this topic at the historical society that I'd like to share. It might start something like this...

The telephone rings at the Historic Courthouse on Monument Square.

"Mifflin County Historical Society"

"Yes, I hope you can help, we've been having an argument and would like to know the official names of the Seven Mountains. The list PennDOT gave us doesn't match the one someone saw in the Game News and the travel guide we have doesn't even mention them by name! Surely, you folks MUST know."

"We may have some information, but there is some disagreement on that subject. Would you like to stop by and we'll show you what we have?"

As the perceived official arbiter of all things Mifflin County, the Mifflin County Historical Society is often consulted in such matters. You know...all we have to do is just look it up in some ancient volume or consult a venerable map and disclose all the names, one through seven. Black and white, chiseled in stone, cut and dried. No ambiguity.

It does seem like a simple request, but in this case the line between fact and fiction begins to blur rather quickly. Let's consult some of the existing sources and see what's been written about the Seven Mountains and their respective names.

PRESBYTERIAN MISSIONARY
ENCOUNTERED THE SEVEN MOUNTAINS

Two aspects of this complicated sequence of northeast-trending mountain ridges, jointly referred to as the Seven Mountains, are not in doubt - their beauty and their danger. Motorists on US 322 between Milroy and Potters Mills acknowledge the natural splendor and magnificent views in autumn. Those same motorists know the winter snow-covered highway can be hazardous, even deadly. An eighteenth century traveler was extremely fearful of his journey through the then roadless forest on his way to spread the word of God to the settlers of early Mifflin County.

The Rev. Philip Vickers Fithian, Presbyterian missionary, journeyed through the Kishacoquillas Valley in August, 1775. His observations were recorded in his often quoted journal. Fithian's passage from Penn's Valley over the Seven Mountains lacked a "good wagon-beaten road." The first mountain he crossed was the highest he had ever traveled. On ascending it he found "On the top of this - O Another! - Another, & still higher!" He was astonished at the summit, "the rough romantic Prospect, the highest Tops of very Tall Trees are apparently, two or three hundred Feet below us & within Gunshot of us."

Fithian's constant apprehension: a miss step by his horse, "...which would be of more consequence than miswalking a Minuet." Warning those who might follow on this journey, he implored them to be "armed with an uncommon share of patience & perseverance, for if they are furious & hasty they may, like the Israelites of long ago, commit sin on these American high places & swear."

The journey of the missionary likely followed what has been described as Kishacoquillas Path, as he traveled from Eagle's Nest (Milesburg) to Lewistown. In fact, Fithian described the path as "blind and unfrequented." Another Indian trail, Logan's Path, coexisted with the Kishacoquillas Path from Potter's Mills through the mountains to Lewistown.

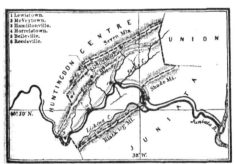

Does the Fithian journal further the search for the names of these mountains? The answer is no. Paul A. W. Wallace, in his book *Indian Paths of Pennsylvania*, does describe Fithian's journey and the Seven Mountains. Wallace's interpretation is that rather than seven separate ridges, the true name should be Seven Mile Mountain, "now more romantically but less accurately called the Seven Mountains," noted Wallace, being seven miles from Potter's Mills to Milroy.

1846 map of Mifflin County, prior to the formation of Snyder County, shows the Seven Mountains area. *State Book of Pennsylvania*, from which this map is taken, notes that a stage line called the North-Western Turnpike, commenced operation after 1817 and by 1828, three regularly scheduled stages a week between Harrisburg and Pittsburgh crossed through the Seven Mountain area. - MCHS image

THE SEVEN MOUNTAINS & THE TURNPIKE

The roadless plight of Rev. Fithian was corrected a few years later. In 1789, a route was laid out across Kishacoquillas Valley starting at Reedsville (Brown's Mill) following more or less old US 322 to Milroy, and due north to a gap in the Seven Mountains near Centre (then Northumberland) County. Referred to as the North-Western Turnpike in the 1846 *State Book of Pennsylvania*, a stage line commenced operation after 1817 and by 1828, three regularly scheduled stages a week between Harrisburg and Pittsburgh, crossed through the Seven Mountain area, but no specific naming of the mountains occurs in these references.

The *Historic Souvenir of Lewistown, Penna.* published almost eighty years ago, recalls a stagecoach-era episode from the Seven Mountains. The colorful tale describes a rollicking encounter with a highwayman and the stage driver, one Kernel Korn. Although no specific "seven" are mentioned, this excerpt reflects the local color of the mountain route.

"In a quiet and old-fashioned village located in the heart of the Seven Mountains of Pennsylvania, noted for their legends of Indian stories...there existed a stage-coach line, noted for its promptness in service. This early form of public transportation carried their passengers over a pike that was and is noted today for its natural beauty. Wild flowers and shrubbery, with a background of virgin timber formed a setting of scenery magnificent, that made each trip delightful and without monotony."

"Starting out from a point where Bellefonte now stands, this stage line wiggled and rolled over the Seven Mountains to the town of Milroy, usually stopping at the Duncan House, noted in those days for their four per cent, not a banking institution. Six horses dragged their burden over the rough roads, sometimes carrying a capacity crowd, and other times not a single passenger. True enough, it may have been a losing proposition...but the government had been helping to support the line by extending the privilege of carrying the mail post to post."

"As the story goes, the driver of the stage, a man of nearly sixty summers, but determined to stay with his coach until death should part, had the pleasure, if you want to call it so, of driving this coach, also acting as mail carrier along the route."

"At a certain place, midway between Bellefonte and Milroy, the company had constructed a small watering trough for watering the horses. It was the daily duty for Kernel Korn to stop at this receptacle and replenish the saliva of his faithful horses."

STATE FOLKLORIST, HENRY W. SHOEMAKER SUGGESTED THE SEVEN

Modern highways followed the stage line, but Henry W. Shoemaker encouraged hiking rather than motoring to best appreciate nature's beauty here. Consider Shoemaker's description of the vista of the Seven Mountains in his 1917 Eldorado Found - The Central Pennsylvania Highlands, A Tourist's Survey:

"The most impressive entrance to the scenic grandeur of Mifflin County is through the rocky gorge of Jack's Mountain north of Lewistown. Beyond this savage defile, there is a hill-girt valley, behind which loom the lofty camel-backs of the Seven Mountains, with Sample Knob in the foreground like a stalwart sentinel and, the entire scene culminating in Milliken's High Top, a height which seems to pierce the clouds."

Henry W. Shoemaker (1880 - 1959), publisher of the *Altoona Tribune* and the *Reading Eagle*, was Pennsylvania's first state folklorist, the first in the nation, and a tireless promoter of "selling Pennsylvania to Pennsylvanians." In addition, Shoemaker was an early chair of the Pennsylvania Historical Commission and an influential member of the State Forest Commission and State Geographic Board. He is responsible for the network of historical markers that dot

"Starting out from a point where Bellefonte now stands, this stage line wiggled and rolled over the Seven Mountains to the town of Milroy, usually stopping at the Duncan House..." *Historic Souvenir of Lewistown* - 1925

the highways and byways of Pennsylvania.

With such credentials, who could doubt Shoemaker's assertion that THE Seven Mountains are: Path Valley Mountain, Shade Mountain, Bald Mountain, Thickhead Mountain, Short Mountain, Sand Mountain, and Tussey Mountain. That would seem to put this matter to rest. But wait...where is Path Valley Mountain? With our state crisscrossed with trails originated by native people, the name "Path Valley" is found in Juniata, Union, Franklin, and Huntingdon counties. Two Shade Mountains are shown on a state topographical map, one in Juniata County and another in Huntingdon County.

Shoemaker's list seems to encompass much of Central Pennsylvania. Actually, mountain counting wasn't the purpose for Shoemaker's catalog of the Seven Mountains, rather his consuming passion for preserving Pennsylvania's natural and cultural heritage. He painted his interpretations with a broad brush.

Simon J. Bonner, Shoemaker biographer and author of *Popularizing Pennsylvania: Henry W. Shoemaker and the Progressive Uses of Folklore and History* explains, "Eldorado Found had the Seven Mountains at its heart, and by Shoemaker's definition included the source of the Juniata and West Branch of the Susquehanna, the two highest mountains in the state, and the Black Forest (North central Pennsylvania). Within its boundaries, animals and people have left a legacy of folklore and history...that adds...to the Keystone State's grandeur."

U.S. GEOLOGICAL SURVEY WEIGHS IN

If **Shoemaker's "seven"** remain more poetic than precise, what could be more bona fide and factual than the renderings of a division of the United States government, the U.S.G.S.?

The *Lewistown Sentinel* grappled with this concept in a 1964 article. Using topographical maps from the U. S. Geological Survey of the northern part of Mifflin County and the southern part of Centre County, the newspaper drew this major conclusion: Whoever named The Seven Mountains must have counted them!

Did German settlers bring the "Seven Mountains" to Pennsylvania? The 1700s saw the emigration of German settlers to Central Pennsylvania, many from the Valley of the Rhine, an area of legends, castles and awe-inspiring scenery.

The article draws a minor conclusion: They could have been called The Eight Mountains, because you don't have to strain very much to count eight mountains with names along Route 322 between Potters Mills and Milroy. The order then is, according to this *Sentinel* article:

"Beginning at Potters Mills and traveling south, the first mountain on the east side is Kohler Mountain, in Centre County. The other mountain on that side is Front Mountain in Mifflin County."

"On the west

All Seven Have Names:

Whoever Titled Mountains Titled Them With Care

Whoever named The Seven Mountains must have counted to Potters Mills you might try the mountains; them. picking out the mountains—Tries- That's the major conclusion ter, Long, Spruce and Little reached from a study of U. S. the left, and Kohler and Front Geological Survey topographical the right. maps of the northern part of Mif- There are many references to flin County and the southern part The Seven Mountains in the of Centre County where The Seven history of Mifflin County. Linn's Mountains are located. History, published in 1883, says

On your next trip from Milroy this in regard to the naming of try the mountains: "The mountains, in maps of on 1826 called 'Seven Mountains,' in on earlier maps are shown as continu- ations of Tussey(Mountain), and were so regarded and spoken of in acts of Assembly of an early date respecting the county bound- aries."

Lewistown Sentinel, Wednesday, April 1, 1964, notes the names of the Seven mountains, as seen along US Route 322. The article quotes *Linn's History*, published in 1883, that "The mountains, in maps of 1826 called 'Seven Mountains,' in earlier maps are shown as continuous of Tussey (Mountain), and were so regarded and spoken of in acts of the Assembly of an early date respecting the county boundaries."call it so, of driving this coach, also acting as mail carrier along the route."

side of the highway two mountains are in Centre County. They are First Mountain and Triester Mountain. In Mifflin County there are three, Long Mountain, Spruce Mountain and Little Mountain."

"There is a fourth mountain on that side - the last mountain before the flat leading to Milroy. It is called Straley's Knob and perhaps was not important enough to be called an extra mountain to make it 'The Eight Mountains'."

The article was written with thoughtfulness and, it seems, an eye to be acute, but the date is intriguing to say the least, April 1, 1964.

A GERMAN RHINELAND CONNECTION?

Agreement isn't easy to come by, but consider the possibility that the "seven" has no local origin at all. Sounds radical, but Jeffrey R. Frazier in his book, *Pennsylvania Fireside Tales (Origins and Foundations of Pennsylvania Mountain Folktales and Legends)* puts forth this very convincing proposition.

The 1700s saw the emigration of German settlers to Central Pennsylvania, many from the Valley of the Rhine, an area of legends, castles and awe-inspiring scenery. An ancient Germanic story of the Rhineland tells how seven principal hills in the Westerwald, today a nature preserve near Bonn, became known as the Siebengebirge or the Seven Mountains. The tale is fantastic, involving giants and superhuman feats, but is significant to that part of Germany, according to Frazier.

" With such a capacity to inspire as well as to capture a permanent place in a person's heart, it is not unreasonable to assume that the memories of the Seven Mountains were always present and clearly remembered in the heads of any early German pioneer who came from this area in Germany to settle among the Pennsylvania mountains we now know as the Seven Mountains. This area would have reminded these settlers of the familiar scenery they had known back home," Frazier explains.

Certainly an intriguing thought to those of us who live here now. This explanation focuses on the "mystery and romance" of legends in ascribing the name. However, early maps show the term "Seven Mountains" already in place prior to the greater influx of German settlers locally. The early area land warrants went to Scotch-Irish settlers. The 1790 census reveals seventy-five percent of the population locally were Scotch-Irish, with the other twenty-five percent either Welsh, English or German. Draw your own conclusions on the Rhineland connection.

SO WHAT ARE THE NAMES OF THE SEVEN?

Is there just one mountain seven miles long or are there seven - but which seven - or eight? Or does the name originate in Germany? We haven't even touched upon the Indian legends of the naming of the Seven Mountains promoted by Henry Shoemaker. I personally like the list from the '64 Sentinel, but other explanations could well be out there just waiting for us to consider. Suffice it to say, if you call the Mifflin County Historical Society to ask about THE names of the Scenic Seven Mountains please be patient with the society.

Regardless of the names or their origins, the Seven Mountains is an area of beauty and legend, frequented in our past by American Indians, wilderness hunters, settlers, lumbermen and even a reputed hermit. It's been the source of stories both fact and fiction, even ghost stories have these mountains as a backdrop. So, the next time you journey to State College on US 322, look around and appreciate this natural area, it's rich in our early history and is part of Mifflin County's colorful heritage.

From the Pages of...

The Lewistown Gazette
April 11, 1861

"Town Square Scene of Popular Activity"

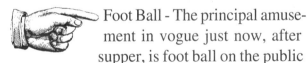 Foot Ball - The principal amusement in vogue just now, after supper, is foot ball on the public square, in which a large number of young men and boys daily participate. It is rather violent exercise, sore shins, falls, and scratches being quite common among those over anxious to get a kick at the ball.

Mifflin County Trivia
"Was it a kick by a horse?"

1. In 1875, James Harris of McVeytown, Pennsylvania had an unusual mishap, resulting in a distressing medical condition. In 1892, Harris made, what some might consider to be a miraculous recovery. What were the unusual circumstances of Harris' case?
[a] After an extremely rough stage ride over the Seven Mountains, he began to hiccup and didn't stop for 17 years.
[b] Kicked by his horse, lost his hearing, regained his hearing 17 years later when he was kicked by the same horse.
[c] Swallowed his false teeth, which lodged in his throat, then his stomach, finally passing the dentures 17 years later.
[d] The brown-haired Harris became completely bald following a gas explosion, spontaneously regrowing a full head of hair 17 years later, only it came in blonde.

2. What was unusual about the baseball game played in 1893 at Siglerville, Pa. between the Left Hand Club and the visiting Royals ?
[a] After a scoreless 25 innings, the game ended in a 0 - 0 tie.
[b] The Royals were a women's team and won.
[c] It was the first official all-county championship game in Mifflin County history.
[d] The umpire arrived in the county's first "horseless carriage," an 1893 Duryea.

3. In July of 1950 the operators of the Midway and Burnham Drive-in Theatres were blasted in the local newspaper with charges "...that this constitutes an attack at the very foundation of our democratic state." Both were arrested. Why?

4. In 1919, Mifflin County won the right to name a U.S. ship by contributing a record amount to the fourth Liberty Loan of WWI. What was the ship named?
[a] Thomas Mifflin [b] Chief Logan [c] Kishacoquillas [d] Dorcas Buchanan

5. At 5:55 p.m. one August day in 1873, something landed on the Oliver Township farm of Mr. G. Dunmire. This most uncommon happening

involved...

[a] a huge flock of sea gulls forced inland from an Atlantic hurricane.

[b] Mifflin County's first hang-glider attempt.

[c] a hot air balloon launched in Altoona.

[d] a large meteorite now at the Carnegie Museum.

6. What horticultural prominence did Henry Snyder of Granville Township attain that placed his name and achievement in the state Agricultural Report of 1890?

        [a] record potato harvest   [b]an apple variety

        [c] largest pumpkin   [d] sweet corn variety

7. Discovered during harvest season in 1862 by Abram Fultz of Allensville and improved upon by him, what agricultural commodity was named for Fultz and widely used?

      Was it... [a] corn [b] wheat [c] spelt [d] sugar beets

TRIVIA ANSWERS:

1. c The story of Harris appeared in Notes from Monument Square

2. b

3. Arrested for showing movies on Sunday in violation of Pennsylvania's Blue Laws.

4. c During the Liberty Bond drive of 1919

5. c

6. The Snyder apple, named for him. Snyder developed this apple variety.

7. Fultz developed this strain of wheat from three heads of wheat he saw at a neighbor's farm. He carefully saved those three and planted the grains next season. Over several years of planting and harvesting he eventually had a bushel, which he sowed in a field. Considered a sure crop in the 1870s and 80s, it was grown in this state and those south and west.

Chief Logan - Author's collection

His father was the Oneida chieftain, Shikellamy, the Six Nations overlord of the Shawnee, Delaware and other subjugated tribes of the Susquehanna Valley. Prior to 1728, Shikellamy came with his family to the Forks of the Susquehanna, now Sunbury, to maintain the interests of the Six Nations. The second son of Shikellamy was born at Osco Village, now Auburn, New York around 1725. His tribal name was Tal-gah-yee-ta. His father renamed him James Logan, after the esteemed Secretary of Pennsylvania's Provincial Council. Today, Mifflin County history remembers him as...

6 - Logan, Chief of the Mingoes

He built his cabin not far from the break in Jack's Mountain known formerly as Logan's Gap – the Reedsville Narrows, today. Logan made a living hunting and selling dressed deer skins to the traders. It's said his neighbors held Logan in high esteem.

Around this time a man came by the cabin and traded wheat for good deer skins. Logan soon found the grain to be spoiled and lodged a complaint with Judge William Brown. After questioning, the jurist found in Logan's favor, ordering full restitution. He liked the results of English law. Brown recalled Logan saying, "It makes the rogues pay." Yet Logan's faith in colonial justice would vanish and his peaceful ways would take a dramatic turn. His life would end tragically to our west.

Logan's Spring - 1843
Woodcut from Dey's 1843 *Pennsylvania Historical Collections*
MCHS image

LOGAN, THE MAN

In almost every account of Logan's life, authors felt the need to answer this question – What did he look like? Born a century prior to photography, Logan's appearance comes from personal descriptions in diaries, letters or oral recollections. No life portrait or paintings exist of Logan. "Logan was the finest specimen of humanity..." is how this often repeated description usually begins. It's been attributed to traders, settlers and trappers, but was spoken by one who knew him personally, Judge William Brown, early Mifflin County settler.

Norman B. Woods' 1906 *Lives of Famous Indian Chiefs* notes that the hunters and backwoodsmen of the era describe Logan's "splendid appearance, over six feet tall, straight as a spear-shaft, with countenance as open as it was brave and manly..."

Allen W. Eckert described Logan in his historical novel, *The Frontiersmen*, first of his "The Winning of America" series, published in 1967. Eckert presents the physical appearance of the somber, dignified Mingo in 1774 at the time of Logan's famous speech, lauded by Thomas Jefferson for its eloquence and later known as Logan's Lament.

"Logan stood before them silently, a figure commanding the respect of any who might look upon him. He was clad only in fresh doeskin leggings and high moccasins laced to mid-calf. At the back of his head he wore four white-tipped brown eagle feathers and on each wrist and his left upper arm were wide bands of beaten silver. He wore no weapon of any kind. Despite the primitive costume, his bearing was as regal as any king in royal garb."

"Most striking, however, was his strong face, etched by sadness, his deep dark eyes reflecting an inner pain beyond description. The expression did not change as he shook hands briefly with the three white men, nor did it alter to any appreciable degree as he began to dictate in a soft voice..."

TRADITIONAL LOGAN

The retelling of the encounters with Logan stem from the oral accounts of local settlers, the William Brown family, in particular. These are traditional stories standardized with the passage of over two hundred years. Starting as oral history, as you might ask your grandfather about his childhood, no better source of Logan's local presence exists, then the Brown family's recollections.

Logan and Brown meet from the 1906 *Lives of Famous Indian Chiefs* published by American Indian Historical Publishing Company
- Author's collection

The "wheat" anecdote is attributed to one of Judge Brown's daughters, who remembered the incident as a girl. She married John Norris, who came to Mifflin County in 1787 as a trustee appointed to lay out the county seat. He also served as a contractor for the court house erected in the public square.

Mrs. Norris elaborated on the incident some years later. Her recollection was that a tailor named De Young, living in Ferguson Valley, bought quite a large number of deer skins from Logan. Buckskin breeches were his stock in trade and wheat was bartered for the skins.

It wasn't until Logan took the grain to be milled, that De Young's ruse was uncovered. So spoiled and tainted with rodent droppings was the wheat, the miller refused to sully his mill with it. According to Mrs. Norris, Logan was chagrined at being deceived, returned to the tailor and demanded the return of the skins, without much success. Logan next turned to Judge Brown, who questioned him about the exact quality and character of the grain. Logan found it difficult to express in English, the exact adulteration of the wheat, only to say it resembled in appearance the wheat itself.

As the true nature of the problem became clear, Brown noted, this isn't wheat, "...it must be cheat!" Logan thought that was a good name

50

for the tailor, too.

Brown presented Logan with a writ to be given to the constable, which the justice assured him, would bring Logan his skins or an equal amount of money.

By what power could this piece of paper, compel the tailor to return his skins? If the tailor refused, what magic did it possess that could make this happen? Logan did not understand the concept, according to Mrs. Norris. Judge Brown took his royal commission from the wall, with the arms of the king clearly, boldly upon it. He explained the basic principles of civil law to Logan. It is here that the Norris account asserts that Logan noted, "Law good, makes rogues pay."

Another recounting of this story tells that Logan was fully prepared to make his position prevail and intended to accomplish this demand for the skins by force, but acquiesced to Brown's entreaties to let the law take its course.

FIRST MEETING REMEMBERED IN 1842

The *Pittsburgh Daily American* of March 21, 1842 printed a letter from the Honorable R. P. McClay of the Pennsylvania Senate to the Honorable George Darisie, also of the Senate. McClay was responding to a letter that appeared in the paper the previous March 17 to correct some inaccurate details of Logan's first meeting with white settlers in Mifflin County.

Sen. Maclay asserted that the person surprised at the spring, called Big Spring, four miles west of Logan's Spring, was William Brown – the first actual settler of the Kishacoquillas Valley. McClay related a narrative from Judge Brown himself, while on a visit to McClay's brother, who owned and occupied the Big Spring farm at the time.

McClay quoted Brown:

"The first time I ever saw the spring, my brother and I, accompanied by

Logan leaves the longhouse illustration from *Logan, Mingo Chief,* 1976 by Mifflin County artist Anne Kepler Fisher (1925 - 1977) - Author's collection

51

Logan - illustration from *Logan, Mingo Chief,* 1976 by Mifflin County artist Anne Kepler Fisher - Author's collection

James Reed, wondered out of the valley in search of land and finding it very good, we were looking for a spring. About a mile from where we started, we came across a bear. We separated to hunt."

"I was traveling along looking for rising ground to better spot the bear, when I suddenly came upon a spring. Being pretty dry, I more rejoiced at finding water, than killing a dozen bear. I set my rifle down and bent to drink. As I put my head to the water's surface, I saw reflected in the water on the opposite side the shadow of a tall Indian."

"I sprang for my rifle, when the Indian gave a yell, I knew not for peace or war...but upon me facing him with my rifle, he knocked up the pan of his gun, threw out the priming and extend an open palm, I took as a token of friendship."

"After putting down our guns we again met at the spring and shook hands. This was Logan, the best specimen of humanity I ever met with, either white or red. He could speak a little English and told me there was another white hunter...and offered to guide me to his camp. There I first met your (R. P. McClay's) father."

A FRIENDLY COMPETITION

The aged Judge Brown remembered going with the elder McClay to Logan's camp, near the spring named for Logan. McClay and Logan shot at a mark for a dollar a shot, Brown said. Logan lost four or five rounds and conceded the match. Brown explained,

"When we prepared to leave, Logan entered his hut and returned with deer skins equal to the lost dollars. He handed the skins to McClay, who refused them, saying we were Logan's guests, not intending to rob him and that the shooting match was just a friendly competition. "

Brown reminisced that Logan persisted, it was a point of honor to him. Both men shot their best and Logan said he would have taken McClay's dollars if he had lost. McClay was obliged to accept the skins or risk an affront to this new friend. Logan refused even a horn of powder offered by McClay in return.

52

Judge Brown continued, "The next year, I brought my wife up and camped under a big walnut tree on the bank of Tea Creek until I built my cabin, near where the mill (Reedsville Mill) now stands." Sen. McClay recalled the tears streaming down the old man's face as he said, "Poor Logan soon went to the Allegheny...and I never saw him again."

LITTLE MARY'S SHOES

Mrs. Norris recounted another Logan story, involving her younger sister, Mary, who in later life would become the wife of General Potter, of Potter's Mills, Centre County.

Logan visited the Brown's cabin when Mary was just learning to walk. Her mother expressed her regret that she didn't have a pair of shoes that would give Mary's first steps more firmness. Logan heard this comment, but said nothing.

Some time later, Logan asked Mrs. Brown if little Mary could come and spend the day with him at his cabin. With Judge Brown away, she wasn't sure, but felt her husband would approve. She allowed Mary to go with Logan, "while the cautious heart of a mother was alarmed at the proposition."

The hours of the day grew longer as the sun began to set and little Mary wasn't home. Mrs. Brown grew more concerned, until she heard the sound of footfall on the path. In the next moment, "the little one trotted into her mother's arms, proudly exhibiting a beautiful pair of moccasins on her little feet, the product of Logan's skill."

Other stories are more legendary. One depicts a full length figure brandishing a war club, hand carved by Logan on the trunk of a giant oak near present-day Huntingdon.

LOGAN DEPARTS THE VALLEY

In 1770, Logan left Mifflin County and moved west, where Beaver Creek empties into the Ohio River, according to C. Hale Sipe's *Indian Chiefs of Pennsylvania*. While there, Logan was visited in 1772 by Moravian missionary, John Heckewelder.

Heckewelder recounts a

Logan and Brown - "A Friendly Competition" illustration from *Logan, Mingo Chief,* 1976 by Mifflin County artist Anne Kepler Fisher - Author's collection

53

I had even thought to have lived with you, but for the injuries of one man. Col. Cresap, the last spring, in cold blood, and unprovoked, murdered all the relations of Logan, not sparing even my women and children.
- Logan's Speech - *"Trouble on the Frontier"* illustrationson from Logan, Mingo Chief, *1976 by Mifflin County artist Anne Kepler Fisher* - Author's collection

conversation, where Logan admits having trouble holding his young men in check. They want to make reprisals of blood on white settlers, who were encroaching on their territory, in a cycle of attack and revenge.

Indeed, it will be Logan's own family who will fall victim of a revenge attack in 1774. That terrible act results in his own bloody spree and a famous speech. Logan's dramatic utterance, one of the earliest documented examples of Mingo text, will be immortalized by Thomas Jefferson, "Its eloquence...so admired, that it flew through all the public papers of the continent."

During his stay in Mifflin County, Logan was the settlers' friend, but brutality and murder in the Ohio Valley drove him to vengeance, vowing to kill ten for every one of his murdered family.

Yet Logan would save a famous frontiersman from death at the stake a few years later. Beset by addiction and depression, his own life would end tragically in 1781.

I have been three times at war... but all the Indians are not angry, only myself... – Logan, 1774

During a short, but bloody series of frontier attacks between colonials and Shawnees, known as Lord Dunmore's War, terror and devastation spread through southwestern Pennsylvania. The path of Logan's life took a deadly and tragic turn at this time, transforming the amicable chief into a vengeful fury.

Hale's *The Indian Wars of Pennsylvania*, cites three causes of this conflict which began in 1774:
1. The settling of Virginians upon land claimed by the Shawnees.
2. The murder of peaceable Shawnees at the mouth of Captina Creek.

3. The murder of the family of Logan, Chief of the Mingoes.

A deadly cycle of attack and reprisal ensued when a band of Shawnees fired upon a survey party from Virginia in 1773. Resenting the intrusion into their territory by the land-grabbing settlers, several surveyors were captured by the Shawnees and two Indians were killed.

In 1774, Lord Dunmore, Governor of Virginia, sent a force to protect his settlers. Locals took matters into their own hands before the troops arrived and declared war on the Shawnees, killing non-hostiles at will. Logan's openly peaceful family was slaughtered in one of these raids at their camp at Yellow Creek, on the upper Ohio, April 30, 1774.

The horrendous scene is described in stark detail by Allen W. Eckert in his historical narrative, *The Frontiersmen*. This heinous act is credited with sparking Lord Dunmore's War.

HIS FAMILY MASSACRED

At the end of April, 1774, Logan was away hunting, when a group led by Daniel Greathouse arrived in the vicinity and arranged an apparently friendly shooting match with Logan's brother and others. Liquor was freely given and the Indians were invited to shoot first, out of courtesy.

With weapons discharged, and the confusion created by intoxication, Greathouse and his men brutally murdered Logan's family, including his mother, sister and brother and sister-in-law, scalping the dead and dying.

Theodore Roosevelt, in his Winning of the West wrote of the death of Logan's family, "The whole party was plied with liquor, and became helplessly drunk, in which condition Greathouse and his associate criminals fell on and massacred them, nine souls in all. It was an inhuman and revolting deed, which should consign the names of the perpetrators to eternal infamy."

With the awful image of his murdered family

"Trouble on the Frontier" illustrations on this and facing page from *Logan, Mingo Chief*, 1976 by Mifflin County artist Anne Kepler Fisher

55

seared into his mind, Logan is known to have killed settlers in reprisal. The traditional story recounts Logan vowing to kill ten white settlers for every one of his murdered family. Logan erroneously blamed Captain Michael Cresap for the atrocity, as he would later state in his famous speech. Cresap, appointed a captain of a frontier militia, had ambushed, killed and reportedly scalped, friendly Shawnees prior to the Logan massacre.

General hostilities erupted across the territory, with Logan taking a lead. In one incident, Logan and seven other warriors raided a settlement, capturing two prisoners. Logan delivered the hapless pair to a nearby village for eventual death at the stake.

Norman Woods' *Lives of the Famous Indian Chiefs*, recounted Logan's change of heart: "Logan...cut the cords of one of the prisoners, named Robinson, who was about to be burned at the stake and saved his life at the risk of his own."

It seems Logan had another purpose for Robinson, however. He had the former prisoner write a note that was later tied to a war club and placed at the site of a settler attack. It read: *Captain Cresap: What did you kill my people on the Yellow Creek for? The white people killed my kin at Conestoga, a great while ago, but I thought nothing of that. But you killed my kin again on Yellow Creek, and took my cousin prisoner. Then I thought I must kill too; and I have been three times at war since; but all the Indians are not angry, only myself.*

**Logan, the Orator or
TAL-GA-YEE-TA**

A melodramatic and idealized illustration of Logan from the 1906 *Lives of Famous Indian Chiefs* published by American Indian Historical Publishing Company - Author's collection

In time, those living on the frontier, whites and Shawnees alike, knew Greathouse and company were responsible for butchering Logan's family. In 1791, Greathouse himself would suffer an even more gruesome fate at the hands of the Shawnees. As Allen Eckert observed, "The Shawnees reserved special forms of slow death for their greatest enemies."

LOGAN'S ELOQUENCE
The death of Greathouse was of little comfort to Logan, who

would die ten years earlier. In the autumn of 1774, a disillusioned Logan was advised of a peace conference aimed at ending Lord Dunmore's War, but Logan refused to attend. Emissaries would instead come to Logan and transcribe his words.

The stage was set for Logan's famous speech. Three representatives of Dunmore arrived at his camp. The trio consisted of translator Simon Girty, Simon Kenton, friend of Logan, and John Gibson, who served as scribe.

Girty has a Mifflin County connection himself. A young Simon Girty was captured in 1756 by the French and Indians after the fall of Fort Granville,

Logan, The Indian Chief - Engraving that appeared in *Pictorial Sketch Book of Pennsylvania* - 1852 - Author's collection

along with his mother, brothers and stepfather. Raised as an Indian who gained a renegade's reputation, Girty would serve the British during the Revolution.

Simon Kenton was a friend of Daniel Boone and Logan. He led an adventurous frontier life, escaping death at the stake more than once. Logan would use his considerable influence to intervene on one occasion, just long enough to alter the course of events and prevent Kenton's fiery death in 1778.

John Gibson, veteran frontier trader, owned a small trading post in the Ohio country. He knew the territory and the American Indian language. Were the words of Logan taken down accurately? Gibson was described as an honest backwoodsman, very unlikely to have "doctored" Logan's words for the better, rather recording them literally.

The meeting began at Logan's little camp, "under a spreading elm tree, along the south bank of Congo Creek." (An eastern tributary of the Scioto River in south-central Ohio.) Logan dictated in a deliberate, yet soft voice, as John Gibson wrote:

I appeal to any white man to say, if ever he entered Logan's cabin hungry, and he gave him not meat; if ever he came cold and naked, and he clothed him not. During the course of the last long and bloody war, Logan remained idle in his cabin, an advocate for peace. Such was my love for the whites, that my countrymen pointed as they passed, and said, "Logan is the friend of the white men." I had even thought to have lived with you, but for the injuries of one man. Col. Cresap, the last spring, in cold blood, and unprovoked, murdered all the relations of Logan, not sparing even my women and children.

There runs not a drop of my blood in the veins of any living creature. This called on me for revenge. I have sought it: I have killed many: I have fully glutted my vengeance. For my country, I rejoice at the beams of peace. But do not harbor a thought that mine is the joy of fear. Logan never felt fear. He will not turn on his heel to save his life. Who is there to mourn for Logan? - Not one.

The writer of the Declaration of Independence and future U. S. president, Thomas Jefferson, commented on Logan's words:

"I may challenge the whole of the orations of Demosthenes and Cicero, and indeed of any more eminent orator – if Europe, or the world, has furnished more eminent – to produce a single passage superior to the speech of Logan..."

McGuffey's Reader, the American educational icon of the 1800s, first published in 1836, further spread Logan's words decades after his death. The classic reading book printed Logan's famous speech in its fourth edition.

A MAN OF INFLUENCE

Allen Eckert makes the case that Logan wielded considerable influence on the frontier, among both Indians and white settlers. His support was sought by each side, as peacemaker and arbiter.

The episode of Simon Kenton, condemned to burn for actions against the Shawnees in the Ohio territory, is an example of this influence. A beaten and injured Kenton was being taken by his captors to Upper Sandusky for execution. The party stopped for the night near Logan's winter camp. Logan greeted the guards and saw his friend Kenton.

He told the Shawnee captors he had quarters for them and that he would house Kenton with him that night. They were reluctant, but this was Logan and they could not refuse. Logan had Kenton's injuries treated that night.

Logan was a Mingo, and held no official rank among the Shawnee people and couldn't just free his friend Kenton, but his standing was impressive. A plea from Logan could not be ignored.

Today, we would portray what happened next as "behind the scenes diplomacy" or "spending political capital" in lobbying for Kenton's very life. Runners were sent to Upper Sandusky by Logan and influence exerted. Kenton was spared. Eckert ex-

Simon Kenton and Logan -
Harper's Monthly, Feb., 1864 -
Author's collection

tensively describes the details
in *The Frontiersmen.*

THE DEATH OF LOGAN

In this politically correct age,
we're often pressured to rede-
sign historical accounts to con-
form to our times. Certainly,
historians of the last century
spoke with a different tone then
today.

Teddy Roosevelt referred
to Logan "...who drank deeper
and deeper, becoming an impla-
cable, moody and bloodthirsty
savage, yet with noble qualities... at last he perished in a
drunken brawl."

Samuel Drake wrote in the

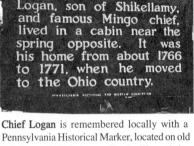

Chief Logan is remembered locally with a
Pennsylvania Historical Marker, located on old
US Route 322, between Reedsville and the
Church Hill Cemetery. - MCHS photo

1850s, "He was himself a victim of the same ferocious cruelty that ren-
dered him a desolate man...a party of whites murdered him on his way
back to Detroit."

There are several accounts of his death, that involve a chronic alcohol addiction as a contributing cause of Logan's demise in September,
1781. Logan had gone over to the British side in 1780, helping in several
raids in Kentucky. After those raids, he went to Detroit for a council of
chiefs. When he was refused whiskey, Logan was overheard declaring,
"If the British won't give me whiskey, maybe the Americans will." Fear-
ing his influence might sway the Mingoes against the British, he was murdered on the trail back to Sandusky.

The traditional account of Logan's death has him striking his wife a
near mortal blow while in a drunken rage. Pursued by her relatives, Logan is killed on the trail, variously by ambush, while sleeping or shot
climbing from a horse. But in 1999, anthropologist and historian Anthony
F. C. Wallace wrote *Jefferson And The Indians: The Tragic Fate Of The
First Americans* which details Jefferson's ambiguous relationship with Native Americans. Wallace recounts the murder of Logan:

*Logan's murderer was a nephew, chosen and deputized to execute
his uncle because, as the victims closest relative, he would be immune
from obligatory revenge. Years later he told a white visitor on the Allegheny River why the council ordered the killing: "Because he was too
great a man to live...he talked so strong that nothing could be carried
contrary to his opinions, his eloquence always took all the young men
with him...He was a very, very great man, and as I killed him, I am to fill*

his place and inherit all his greatness." By a twist of fate, the eloquence that earned Logan immortality led also to his death.

In 1927, Henry W. Shoemaker wrote about Logan's remains in *Indian Folk-Songs of Pennsylvania.* Shoemaker quoted Jesse Logan, great-nephew of Chief Logan during a visit to the Pennsylvania Reservation (1) prior to Jesse Logan's death in 1917, according to Shoemaker, at "well past the century mark."

The aged descendant recounted how he retrieved his ancestors remains in Ohio, "I have told you," said Jesse Logan, "of the time when I went to the Muskingum and found the bones of my great-uncle James Logan, the Mingo orator, and carried them on a pony sewed up in an elk's hide to the Wolf Rocks in the Seven Mountains and buried them there."

LOGAN'S LEGACY

Regardless of how he died, others share our admiration for Chief Logan. Mifflin County has its historical marker recognizing Logan's presence near Reedsville and local organizations proudly share his name, as did a local school, Chief Logan High School.

Counties and townships in Ohio and West Virginia are named for Logan and his Mingo people. Logan County, the city of Logan, and Chief Logan State Park are all named in his honor.

An Ohio marker remembers Logan's Elm, located in Pickaway County, Ohio. The marker is at Pickaway Township Elementary School, Circleville, Ohio. It states: *Mingo Chief Logan settled with his family on the Pickaway Plains in 1770. He was a longtime supporter of peace between Native Americans and white men until his family was murdered at Yellow Creek. Logan went on the warpath and raided settlements in Pennsylvania, West Virginia and Tennessee. Logan made a powerful speech on Indian-white relations during negotiations following Lord Dunmore's War. The speech was inscribed on the Chief Logan Monument, in the Logan Elm Park, which was dedicated in October 1912.*

Logan's Spring - Located on private property in Brown Township along old US 322 near Reedsville, Mifflin County, Pa. Marble marker, above, was placed in 1981, marking the oldest landmark in the community founded by William Brown. - MCHS photo

Considered to be one of the largest elms in the U. S., the tree stood 65 feet tall, with a trunk circumference of 24 feet and foliage spread of 180 feet. It died in the 1960s from damage by blight and storms. The tree's former location is marked by a plaque. Logan Elm Memorial is five miles south of Circleville, in Pickaway County, one mile east of U.S. Route 23 on State Route 361.

"Who Mourns for Logan - A touching tale of love and loss on the Ohio frontier" appeared in the Fall 2002/Winter 2003 issue of *Ohio State Parks Magazine* written by editor Jean Backs. Backs observed, "Logan's legacy of hope lives on in

Logan's Spring - Located on private property in Brown Township along old US 322 near Reedsville, Mifflin County, Pa. - MCHS photo

a bustling town, a serene historic site, and two scenic natural areas named in his honor. The City of Logan in Hocking County was named for the great Mingo chief by its founder, Colonel Thomas Worthington, the Father of Ohio Statehood. Nearby Lake Logan, the centerpiece of Lake Logan State Park, was also named in Logan's memory. Mount Logan, the crowning peak in Great Seal State Park, was reputedly the location of a cabin where Logan stayed when visiting the Shawnee town nearby."

Even after two hundred years, Logan's story teaches us the qualities of honesty, friendship and survival in this frequently violent colonial period. Traditional accounts of Logan's life mingle with historical facts, and recent academic writings. Yet Logan and his contemporaries were real, living, breathing human beings, who survived on the stage of history and added humanity to the story of our Mifflin County heritage.

Mifflin County Trivia
"Is it buffalo or grizzly bear?"

1. Auto racing is a popular spectator sport today, with many Mifflin County residents following NASCAR, for example. The Port Royal Speedway in Juniata County is a popular area raceway. Although auto races were staged at the Mifflin County Fair in Lewistown over the years, Mifflin County once had an auto race track within its borders in the 1940s. Name the race track?
[a] The Siglerville Raceway
[b] The Reedsville Speedway
[c] The Ryde Rumble
[d] The Burnham Bump'n Race Track

2. The Greater Lewistown Shopping Center in Burnham was not always as we know it today. A succession of stores - Town & County, W. T. Grants, Jamesway, Weis Market - occupied that piece of real estate. What commercial enterprise first occupied the property now known as The Greater Lewistown Shopping Center? (Not including farming.)

3. Mifflin County's fire companies are always looking for ways to raise money for new equipment. Fifty-five years ago, Thomas Janison of the Burnham Fire Company bought a thousand pounds of something unusual, with plans to make sandwiches out of it and sell them to benefit the company. What did Janison buy in 1944?
[a] a buffalo   [b] a grizzly bear
 [c] two five hundred pound ostriches   [d] an elk

4. The first fire code in the U.S. colonies is adopted in 1653 in Boston; The first fire proof building is built in 1854 in New York City of concrete and steel; Franklin Roosevelt gives his first fireside chat in 1933. When were the first fire hydrants installed in Lewistown, the county seat?
[a] 1823 [b] 1833 [c] 1843 [d] 1853

5. In 1851, the Singer Sewing Machine was patented, the first chapter of the YMCA opened in Boston, the first baseball uniforms were worn by the New York Knicker-bockers and the clock was installed in the Mifflin County courthouse tower in Lewistown. It began striking in June of that year. How much did it cost?

[a] $300   [b] $600   [c] $1,300   [d] $2,000

TRIVIA ANSWERS:

1. Reedsville Raceway ran cars on a track located in Lumber City, near the KVRR track along Kishacoquillas Creek.

3.   [d] an elk The Lewistown *Sentinel* - 9/44

4.   [c] 1843 - *History of Lewistown,* 1970, p.6

2. According to a series of Lewistown *Sentinel* articles from July, 1950, The Burnham Drive - In Theatre opened July 1, 1950. The Mid-Way Drive-In in Mifflintown opened May 18, 1950.   An estimated 600 cars containing 1800 people, attended the opening at the Logan Boulevard lo-cation. - 1960 image from *Burnham Jamboree* first program

5.   [a] $300   - *History of Lewistown,* 1970, p.6

7 - Tales of Fur, Hoof and Claw:

Hunting in Mifflin County

When **William Penn** stepped from the good ship *Welcome* in 1682, he found his colony to be a land of bountiful natural riches. As settlers moved into Penn's Woods, hunting and trapping became a necessity of daily life. Penn soon proclaimed that the inhabitants of Pennsylvania could "fowl and hunt upon the lands they hold and all other lands not enclosed." And hunt they did. Deer hides became a monetary standard of trade in the Pennsylvania frontier. A buck today is one dollar, but in those early days a buck was literally a buck's skin.

THE LURE OF HUNTING

In what became Mifflin County, Pennsylvania settlers found black bear and white-tailed deer, much as today, but other animals lived here, too. Early accounts tell of elk, and beaver dams were seen along creeks and streams, as were otters. The grandchildren of early settlers even recounted stories told by their ancestors of the "vast herds" of

Pennsylvania bison hunted in Central Pennsylvania. Modern authorities cast doubt on the veracity of such claims, but the mental image of a buck skin-clad hunter leveling his Pennsylvania rifle at a bison roaming the Seven Mountains caught the fancy of later storytellers.

Predators such as timber wolves and mountain lions were found in the area and provided cash through the state approved bounty system. In 1915, McVeytown native and noted conservationist Dr. Joseph T. Rothrock, wrote about his experiences with the mountain lion in Armagh Township's Treaster Valley.

The abundance and variety of animals drew a profusion of hunters to pursue them and Mifflin County had its share. If one believes all the tales of hunting prowess, these early local Nimrods rivaled the likes of Daniel Boone and Davy Crockett. Bear Jacob Miller of Mattawana, reputedly shot and killed almost thirty bruins in his ninety-six years. Kishacoquillas Valley's "Major David" Zook who in just ten consecutive shots took eight deer and one bear. In the 1890s, Clement F. Herlacher reportedly shot the last panther in Mifflin County.

Or Andrew Swartzell, pioneer descendant and keeper of wild "varmints" in Armagh Township near Milroy, made one of hunting's longest shots locally in those pre-magnum days of the early 1800s. However, these hunters had nothing on The Huntress of the Juniata. She used no gun at all, just here bare hands!

Venison vanisheth down the vale,
With bounding hoof and flaunting tail.

This verse is a quotation from Theodore S. Van Dyke's classic work on the white-tailed deer, *The Still-Hunter*, published in 1882, yet still illustrates the nature of the hunters' quest. Mifflin County fields thousands of hunters each year, for sport and recreation. But in the context of that basic need, food, hunting was a part of Mifflin County's rural life in the 18th and 19th centuries. And one might argue the point even into the 21st century, in some quarters of the county.

AMERICAN INDIAN HUNTERS

In the days prior to the arrival of European settlers, American Indians in Pennsylvania considered hunting important. However, in The Pennsylvania Game Commission's *100 Years of Wildlife Conservation*, author Joe Kosack said that Indian groups placed no greater emphasis on hunting than farming chores or social duties. Kosack writes, "Because game was so abundant, Indians rarely walked more than a day to reach hunting grounds." There are indications Mifflin Countys earliest inhabitants sought game in the area. Moravian missionary John Heckewelder wrote in the 18th century that, "...The Iroquois had a path leading

directly to a settlement...(on the Juniata River)...The Indians said that the river had the best hunting ground..."

FIRST SETTLERS AND HUNTING

In January, 1684, William Penn wrote to a friend in England, "The food the woods yield, is your elk, deer, raccoons, beaver, rabbets, turkeys, pheasants, heath-birds, pidgeons and partridges innumerably; we need no dogs to ketch, they run by droves into the house in cold weather."

Bounties on animal skins soon became a method of control. A year earlier, Penn established a bounty on wolves, at 10 and 15 shillings. Over the next 200 years, the wolf bounty would be in effect at various times. But the colony's squirrel bounty was a failure from the start. It seems that as lands were cleared in Penn's Woods, the squirrels began to feast upon the farmers crops. By 1749, the colony placed a three cent bounty on the rodents, only to have to pay out on more than 640,000 squirrel scalps. They cut the bounty to a penny and a half in 1750! The *Colonial Record* noted that "...the farmers complained this year...for the laborers, instead of helping them with the harvest, had taken up their guns and gone to hunt squirrels."

THE MOUNTAIN LION IN MIFFLIN COUNTY

Bounties were, from time to time, placed on panthers or mountain lions. As early as 1802 in the Commonwealth, an adult cat brought in $8.00. Pennsylvania and Mifflin County had their share of big cat hunters from the 19th century.

Two hunters shot mountain lions in Mifflin County in 1916, according to Henry W. Shoemaker in his 1917 book, *Extinct Pennsylvania Animals*. The favored hunting area of the big cat, was Armagh Township's Treaster Valley, near a spot aptly named Panther Cliffs. John Treaster, namesake of Treaster Valley, shot a mountain lion in his valley in 1875, according to Shoemaker.

Over and Under Pennsylvania Rifle - Part of the Mifflin County Historical Society's collection at McCoy House Museum, 17 N. Main Street, Lewistown, PA. Third from the top, octagon barrels marked "Worly" at the breech. This gun was owned by John Treaster of Milroy and was said to have killed one of three panthers shot in Mifflin County.

However, a full-fledged hunt for the Pennsylvania mountain lion by John Treaster and company is described in detail in the 1925, *Historical Souvenir of Lewistown, Penna.* That hunt took place in

1856, resulting in the quarry escaping. The same panther, according to the story, was eventually killed and the nine foot (nose to tip of tail) skin was given to Andrew Swartzell of Milroy.

The Mifflin County Historical Society received John Treaster's double over and under rifle a number of years ago. The weapon is on display at the McCoy House Museum, with the notation, Octagon barrels marked "Worly" at breech. This gun was owned by John Treaster of Milroy and was said to have killed one of three panthers shot in Mifflin County.

Shoemaker's Mifflin County record contained these additional entries: February 27, 1872, John Swartzell shot a mountain lion, also in Treaster Valley, and another on New Years Day, 1882; John Reager and William Dellett together, shot a large lion in 1869, as did John Orr in 1876. Perhaps the last confirmed mountain lion killed in Mifflin County, by Shoemaker's count, was a cub shot by Clement F. Herlacher in 1893, again in Treaster Valley.

McVeytown's native son, Dr. Joseph T. Rothrock, conservationist and founder of the Pennsylvania Forestry Department, wrote in 1914 about the cry of a mountain lion, he encountered in the 1890s. Rothrock wrote, "...It would not be an adequate reply if I said it sounded like the wail of a child seeking something. A cry distinct, half inquiry, half temper...I heard it one evening in Treaster Valley repeated so often that I could recognize it as coming from an animal moving along the rocky slope of the mountain where no child could have been at that hour and was told by those residents in the region, *Oh, it's the painter's cry.*"

An interesting note about place names: a Mifflin County location that takes its name from the Pennsylvania panther or "painter" as Rothrock quoted, is Paintersville, on the Back Maitland Road, Decatur Township.

TALES OF THE WHITE-TAILED DEER

From the earliest days, this native of Pennsylvania, and our state animal, was a favorite of local hunters. Deer were the object of the state's first game law, enacted by Colonial Governor Sir William Keith in 1721. From January 1 to July 1 "...buck, doe, fawn or any sort of deer whatsoever" were protected. Penalty for violation of this act was 20 shillings. Indians were exempt. About a hundred twenty years after the first game law, a rapid dwindling of wildlife was evident. Many counties, enacted various protection laws. Mifflin County banned deer hunting with dogs in 1848, as did nine other counties. The Civil War lessened the pressure on the game population.

The *Lewistown Gazette*'s January 22, 1873 edition reported on the hunting success of a party in Menno Township. The paper noted, "A party...who hunted together the past season killed fifteen deer, one turkey, one fox and trapped two bears."

Within twenty years, shooting a buck was rare, seeing deer tracks in the snow was an occasion for a hunters' gathering. Eventually, deer season would be closed for a few years. As white tails became scarce in the area, the few that remained took on almost mythical proportions.

In the Seven Mountain area, several famous "big bucks" were shot in the later 1890s. Henry W. Shoemaker reported in his 1912 edition of *Pennsylvania Deer and Their Horns*, a twenty-six point white tail of Titanic proportions was brought down in that area by hunter S. Strohecker, possessing fifteen points on the right and eleven on the left antler. Its antlers measured 31 inches in total length, and 21 inches at the widest. Such hunting successes were rare. It was common for a party to pack into Mifflin County's back country during this era and camp in tents for two or three weeks, with no hunting success at all. Perhaps the card playing was better in the 1890s. However, according to the pages of Mifflin County's newspapers, there were a few legendary local hunters in the later 1800s, some would have put Crockett or Boone to shame.

S. Duane Kauffman's 1991 *Mifflin County Amish and Mennonite Story*, details the hunting exploits of some sturdy members of that community. Kauffman notes, "During the winter when farm work slackened, the men and boys often devoted time to hunting ...Recreation and ego fulfillment were fringe benefits, but the primary motivation was meat for the table or hides for supplemental income."

BRATTON TOWNSHIP'S ELI STAYROOK

The *Lewistown Gazette* reported in 1892, that Eli Stayrook, a "Dutchman for luck all the time," had a successful fall hunting season. The publication described the year's results as eight deer, five turkeys, twenty-seven rabbits, fifty squirrels, and several pheasants. Stayrook's favorite rifle was a thirty-eight calibre Winchester, "the best gun made," according to the Bratton Township resident.

"EXCITING TIME IN UNION TOWNSHIP"

The hunting prowess of a Kishacoquillas Valley hunter, "Major David" Zook, was the topic of a report in the Lewistown *Gazette* years earlier. The newspaper, under the heading listed above, retold the events of Zook's 1870 hunting season in the November 22 edition.

It seems that a bear of large size was harassing local livestock in the valley, toward Huntingdon Co. Traps were set, but the rogue bruin tore loose from the steel jaws. Zook tracked down the marauder, trailing it to the crest of Back Mountain in Union Township. The *Gazette* further explained, that Zook "...brought down the 240-pound beast with one shot."

"Mr. Zook is one of those marksmen whose aim on game seldom fails, and is probably unequaled in this part of the state. Of the last ten shots he has fired, eight deer and one bear attest his skill." Seven years later, in December, 1877, the *Lewistown Gazette* ran a report that cast aspersions upon the venerable Zook record, at least on the marksmanship part. While hunting with his son, Samuel. the paper averred, the elder Zook accidentally mistook the son for a deer and shot through Samuel's coat. Within a week, the newspaper retracted the report, noting Zook had shot a deer, not the son, saying the report was "...concocted by jealous and blind hunters who couldn't hit the side of a barn door, except by accident, at a hundred yards."

MATTAWANA HUNTER, JACOB MILLER, KNOWN AS "BEAR JACOB"

Although David Zook had a considerable hunting record, he couldn't hold a candle to the man known as "Bear Jacob." Jacob Miller came to Mattawana from Berks County as a child, sometime around 1805. The *Lewistown Gazette* wrote in November, 1887, "Jacob Miller...though in his eighty-seventh year, still goes hunting occasionally. He killed twenty-six bears along Jack's Mountain...having earned the title of 'Bear Miller' by which he is generally known. He says his father, the original "Bear Miller" killed in all, ninety-nine bears, eighty wolves, and so many deers (sic) that he never kept an account of them, but he knows that he killed one hundred in four fall seasons."

Jacob Miller lived to the venerable age of 96.

"ONE OF THE LONGEST SHOTS" - A. SWARTZELL

The *Democratic Sentinel* of Lewistown recounted this episode in its September 18, 1879 issue, under the line, "Armagh Reminiscences." The writer interviewed Andrew Swartzell, at the time retired and living in Milroy, asserting that he saw and held the very rifle that made the extraordinary shot, noting, "Its without any ornament whatever, only distinguished from hundreds like it by its great weight."

Swartzell, descendent of one of the early settlers of the area, recalled the day he jumped a deer while hunting, and before he could fire, "...a long distance intervened" between hunter and quarry. Never dreaming that a shot would find its mark, he let go with a blast from his rifle. To his surprise, the deer came to a complete stop.

While reloading, Swartzell kept an eye toward the deer, which remained still. His second shot knocked the deer down, killing it outright. Upon examination, Swartzell remembered, his first shot "furrowed the left eyeball" and brought the animal to a halt. The second shot struck the deer as it tilted its head. But the writer remarked that the distance was "all of 300 yards" and was "corroborated by several persons."

On another occasion, Swartzell was trimming some trees when he saw a "half grown" bear standing on hind legs taking in the scenery. Without a weapon of any

Rabbit Season - early 1900s "Oh, Pop, you should've seen the one that got away!" Rabbit hunting has never quite been the same since this postcard image appeared in the early 1900s. A humorous example of the photographer's art in the days before digital cameras and computers, this image once appeared in Elk County, with its deer-sized cotton-tail. Similar novelty photos promoted hunting and fishing adventures around the state, usually illustrated with immense trout or mammoth pheasants, always dwarfing the humans, horses or automobiles in the picture. It is a unique novelty from a bygone era, prompting the quip, "You should've seen the one that got away!" - Kepler Studio Collection

kind he, "Very quietly made his way toward the brute until within close quarters. Then putting forth all his brawn, like a policeman, he nabbed the Bruin." A great struggle ensued, with shouting and growling, until Swartzell's brother heard the commotion and came running. The bear, estimated at 18 months, was brought back to the homestead. The writer recounted, "Years ago, Mr. Swartzell was noted far and wide for his collection of 'varmints.' He generally had a couple of bear on hand, a deer or two, and a fox, a coon or an owl, now and then a collection of snakes..."

THE JUNIATA HUNTRESS

Perhaps one of the most unusual hunting stories to emerge from county history revolves around Dorcas Elizabeth Holt Stackpole, of McVeytown, termed by Henry W. Shoemaker as "The Huntress of the Juniata."

George F. Stackpole, editor of the *Lewistown Gazette*, wrote about his ancestor, Dorcas Holt Stackpole, in 1912: "James Stackpole came to what is now McVeytown previous to 1789...He became enamored of Dorcas Holt and married her when she was eighteen years of age and they kept an hotel along the present old pike a short distance below McVeytown... Dorcas, his wife, was of a very vivacious nature, loved parties and believed in having a good time and stopped at nothing when there was fun ahead. She could fiddle like a man and could dance with the best, and with it all, including her hotel experience, which she

70

continued to run after the death of her husband, was a good Presbyterian."

In the days when she was running the hotel, she saw a deer crossing the Juniata River one day, chased there by some hunters. George Stackpole continues the story, "Dorcas ran to the water and caught the deer by the horns just as it emerged from the water, and, after a hard struggle, succeeded in drowning it. As the combat was going on the hunters reached the opposite shore of the Juniata and seeing what was going on they called to her, 'Go it, Dorkey,' and she did 'Go it' until she had the deer into venison..."

Stackpole concluded, "... which she probably could do, as she was a very large women and thought nothing of jumping into the pig-pen and killing a hog."

HUNTING TODAY

Mifflin County has a large number of permanent hunting camps throughout the townships and contains acres of state game land. Thousands of individuals, families and their friends enjoy these retreats at all times of the year, not just during hunting season.

Many of these stories just recounted are subject to the whims of time and memory, both of which have a way of increasing size and distance the farther one moves from the event. But that's not the point. From the earliest American Indian hunters, through the colonial period, and agricultural age, down to this new century, hunting in all its forms has a long established, local tradition, replete with stories and accounts. Regardless of one's opinion of the sport today, hunting is part of our Mifflin County heritage.

A Mifflin County Tradition - Deer Season, 1958
"Seven antlered deer by noon" was noted on the back of this photo showing the buck hunters of Short Drive Camp. Located on the east side of Long Mountain in Mifflin County's Armagh Township, the now disbanded hunting camp was formed by veterans and others shortly after WW II and functioned through the 1970s. (Hunters identified l to r - Row 1: Bobby Dean Keller, Warren Yetter, Charles "Shorty" Armstrong, Robert "Milky" Goss, Henry Fisher, John Glick, George Grove, John Davies, Bob Irwin; Row 2: Bobby Johnson, Bob Keller, Ray Kauffman, Sr., Kyle Fisher, Harry Taylor, Bob Schmitel, Harry Armstrong, Ross Fisher and Paul Armstrong.) - Photo Kepler Studio Collection

Mifflin County Trivia
"Is groundhog a poor substitute for mutton?"

1. According to the 1886 History of the Susquehanna and Juniata Valleys, all but one of these hunted wild animals have left skeletal remains within the borders of Mifflin County. Which one didn't?
a. elk   b. beaver   c. bison   d. lynx   e. red deer   f. wild turkey

2. In 1655, Dutch historian Van der Donk wrote about Indians trading with Dutch settlements along the Atlantic seaboard. He noted that such trading arrangements brought eighty thousand of one type of animal skin from the interior, seemingly our area of central Pennsylvania. What animal skin was being traded?
a. buffalo   b. beaver   c. bear   d. mink

3. The Moravian minister John Heckewelder, missionary to the Delaware Indians and a chronicler of the colonial period, noted that the Indian people living in the Juniata River area considered this territory prime hunting ground. What species did the Indians value in the area?
a. deer   b. beaver   c. bear   d. elk

4. In his letter to an English friend, Charles Hardy, who had just purchased a lot in Lewistown upon which to build, wrote in 1791 about the Mifflin County area.
　　"This is a fearful country for wild creatures..." he explained, telling his reader... "dears, bars, wolves and panters..."were plentiful." (Charles was no speller.)
　　Which of these comparisons did he make about the wild creatures hunted locally as substitutes for common table fare? (More than one)
a. bear meat made a good bacon substitute
b. venison was a nice replacement for beef
c. wild duck replaced domestic chicken
d. ground hog was a poor substitute for mutton

TRIVIA ANSWERS: 1. c   2. a   3. a,b and d   4. a and b

8 - County's First Drive-thru Window

Major's tavern,shown in this sketch, was located at the corner of North Main and East Third Streets in Lewistown, and appeared in The Lewistown Gazette over 100 years ago.

We live in an age of drive-thru windows. Somewhere in California is a drive-thru funeral home, where one can view the deceased from the comfort of the family mini van. And in Las Vegas is the drive-thru wedding chapel where the "I dos" are spoken from the front seat. So if you thought McDonald's, Wendy's, or even KFC had the county's first drive-thru window, better go back a couple centuries.

Mifflin County's first drive-thru window was located in Peacock Major's Tavern at Main and Third Streets, Lewistown as early as 1803. Once described as the town's most famous hostelry and traditionally termed The Wayside Inn, the establishment is also credited with the introduction of oysters to the local cuisine.

There was an opening in the log building on the Main Street side. A rider never had to dismount, as the barkeep passed the grog through the hole! Rumor has it that Mrs. Peacock had the hole boarded up.

Major was born in 1748, served in the American Revolution, was president of the Town Council in 1814 and died in 1829, the year the first canal boat arrived in Lewistown. He owned several properties on Third Street, according to the number of deeds recorded in his name.

The sketch above depicts Major's tavern, located at the corner of North Main and East Third Streets in Lewistown, and appeared in The Lewistown *Gazette* some 145 years ago. At that time the old log building was torn down to make way for a brick home. It shows an old locust tree that was cut down in 1881.

A social slogan in hotels in those early days was, "Claret for the flippant youth; port and sherry for the ladies; but a gentleman drank only his brandy and whiskey, and that straight."

Yet Peacock Major's inn provided for those not accustomed to strong spirits. Drawn from a deep covered well, those preferring Nature's beverage could rely on "the coolest water in town."

9 - Fort Granville's "Mysterious" French Letter

Model of Fort Granville located in the McCoy House Museum, Lewistown, PA.

This defensive fortification, built in 1755 along the Juniata River just southwest of what would become Lewistown, was the scene of a bitter struggle during the French and Indian War. The fort was named by Pennsylvania's Provincial Governor Robert Morris in honor of John Carteret, Earl of Granville. It was garrisoned by Provincial troops to protect the settlers of what was then Cumberland County, until its fall in late July, 1756. Little was found amid the fort's ruins in early August of that year, except a letter written in French, which was taken to the governmental authorities of the colony. The letter was described by Pennsylvania historian William A. Hunter in 1960 as "a puzzle in that day and a mystery in ours." The war was a clash of empires, brought to the Juniata Valley almost 250 years ago this summer, that historians argue eventually brought about the American Revolution itself.

How did Fort Granville come to be built and then burned so soon after its construction? And what is known about the "mysterious" French letter? Taken from the archives and research library of the Mifflin County Historical Society and other historical records, here is a brief account of Fort Granville and the "mysterious" French letter.

74

The *Pennsylvania Gazette* reported the destruction of Fort Granville in its August 19, 1756 edition. The paper distilled the essence of several letters it received plus the eyewitness account from an escaped soldier, taken prisoner when the fort surrendered. The *Gazette* noted that on July 30, a small force remained in the fort while Granville's commander, Capt. Ward and a larger group, had gone to guard harvesters.

"...under the command of Lieutenant Armstrong...the fort was attacked by about 100 French and Indians...the next morning the enemy...crept within 30 or 40 feet of the Fort... they carried a quantity of pine knots and other combustible matter, which they threw against the fort... to which they set fire... and a hole was made, through which the lieutenant and a soldier were shot and three wounded..."

"...the enemy called upon the besieged to surrender and told them that they should have quarter if they surrendered...one John Turner immediately opened the gates..." Those within were taken prisoner, including 22 soldiers, 3 women and a number of children. The *Gazette*, further noted that "they set off, after setting up French colours near the fort on which they left a shot pouch, with a written paper in it."

The fort was later burned. Only ashes and what became known as the Mysterious French Letter, remained. The smoldering debris that was Fort Granville sent local settlers fleeing for the security of Carlisle and points east. Pennsylvania's Colonial government was shocked by the attack.

In the Autumn of 1755, the frontier held thousands of settlers, but after Fort Granville's fall in 1756, scarcely one hundred remained. Pennsylvania's Colonial Governor Robert Hunter Morris delivered a message in August, 1756, to the Assembly, saying:

The people to the west of the Susquehanna, distressed by the frequent incursions of the enemy...are moving to the interior parts of the Province and I am fearful that the whole country will be evacuated...

A group of petitioners wrote in late August, 1756: It is therefore greatly to be doubted that (without a further protection) the inhabitants of this county will shortly endeavor to save themselves and their effects by flight...

After the fort's destruction, little remained. Col. John Armstrong, writing to Governor Morris on what Captains Ward and Armstrong discovered upon returning to the scene, reported: ...they found parts of eight of the enemy burnt in two different places, the joints of them being scarcely separated, and parts of their shirts found, through which were bullet holes... Burned, they believed, after the prisoners were marched out of sight, preventing any eyewitnesses of French causalities after the fight. Nothing of military value or otherwise remained when the ruins were inspected.

All, that is, except for the French letter. This curious document roused interest, and was sent by courier through the chain of command, all the way to the Governor and his council. Correspondence traced its journey, as noted in the Pennsylvania Colonial Archives. From Lt. Hoops to his superior, Capt. Hance Hamilton, "I have sent express to you with the French letter..."

From Hamilton to Lt. Col. Armstrong, "I have last night received a letter by

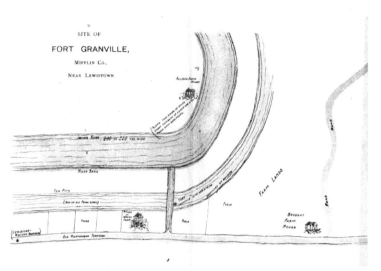

Map of Fort Granville - This represaentation of the Juniata River and canal near Lewistown indicates that the site of Fort Granville was obliterated by the construction of the Juniata Division of the Pennsylvania Canal. From *The Frontier Fort of Pennsylvania*, 1896 - MCHS archives

express from my Lieutenant which I have enclosed, with the original of the French letter, left at Fort Granville ."

Was it a warning from the French? Would it change the course of the conflict started, no less, then by a young George Washington in 1754?

HISTORICAL BACKGROUND

The destruction of Fort Granville in 1756 was a frontier incident in a global war. The struggle pitted the major powers of the age, eventually involving much of Europe, all the way to the Far East. Control of vast stretches of territory in North America were also in the balance.

The French held the St. Lawrence, Ohio and Mississippi River Valleys, while the British held the Atlantic Coast. British settlers greatly outnumbered the French, who were mostly traders, not intent on settlement or encroaching upon traditional American Indian territory. To offset this numerical British advantage, the French enlisted various Indian groups to their side, thus giving the war its name.

Known as the Seven Years War in Europe, the French and Indian War would be a vicious, bloody, hard fought conflict, marked by brutal atrocities perpetrated by both sides. The period would see, for example, Colonial Pennsylvania offering bounties for Indian scalps, with a sliding scale for men, women and children. It was an era of attack and reprisal, romanticized in James Fennamore Cooper's Last of the Mohicans, a classic tale of the French and Indian War.

The British - French conflict started in 1754 over the control of territory and lasted until the Treaty of Paris in early 1763. In North America, France relinquished Canada and all her lands east of the Mississippi River.

The bill for safeguarding and expanding her American colonies was considerable. Building forts, amassing troops and material cost Britain vast sums. The taxes levied to pay for the war would antagonize the same colonials who once cheered the Red Coats sent to defend them. Another war, the American Revolution, would eventually result in Britain losing her American colonies, except Canada, and see the rise of an unparalleled world rival. The French and Indian War opened the door for the independence of the American colonies.

FRENCH & INDIAN WAR STARTS IN PENNSYLVANIA

Over two years before Fort Granville fell, in wilderness claimed by both France and Britain, young George Washington and 150 Virginians headed for Fort Duquesne at the forks of the Ohio River, where Pittsburgh stands today, to expel the French from the area. At the same time, the French sent a small force led by Jumonville (Joseph) Coulon de Villiers to warn the British away from the same territory.

Along the way, Washington surprised the Jumonville party, killing and capturing all but one. The French at Fort Duquesne got word of the clash and dubbed Jumonville's death an "assassination."

The opening volley of the French and Indian War was fired at what today is Jumonville Glen, near US Rt 40, in western Pennsylvania's Fayette County. Washington moved south to Great Meadows and erected Fort Necessity. Surrounded by the pursuing French and their Indian allies, Washington eventually surrendered.

In 1755, after Fort Necessity's fall, General Edward Braddock led a large British force to drive the French from Fort Duquesne, but was routed southeast of their destination by a combined French and Indian force. After this debacle, the frontier erupted in turmoil, as emboldened invading war parties came ever eastward.

Yet, the events at Fort Granville were arguably a direct result of Washington's action at Jumonville Glen. The French officer at the gates of Mifflin County's frontier fort, demanding its surrender that summer in 1756, was Capt. Francois Coulon de Villiers, Jumonville's brother.

FRONTIER PROTECTION

Writing in his landmark book, *Forts on the Pennsylvania Frontier*, William A. Hunter considered that with a Quaker dominated Assembly, "Pennsylvania had in fact no military tradition and no machinery of defense." The area was totally unprotected.

The Pennsylvania Assembly eventually moved, approving money to fund the distribution of arms and ammunition to three counties: Lancaster, York and Cumberland. Mifflin County was then part of Cumberland County.

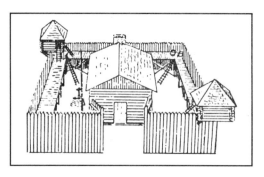

Fort Granville Model - In a letter signed by Benjamin Franklin and others, a description of the forts to be built stated, "...each one of them fifty feet square, with a block house on two of the corners and a barracks within, capable of lodging fifty men." - MCHS Image

In addition, a string of defensive forts was planned, including Fort Pomfret Castle (near Richfield), Fort Granville (Lewistown), Fort Shirley (Shirleysburg), Fort Lyttleton (Fort Littleton).

In a letter signed by Benjamin Franklin and others, a description of the forts to be built stated,

...each one of them fifty feet square, with a block house on two of the corners and a barracks within, capable of lodging fifty men.

Governor Morris had written a letter to General Edward Braddock stating,, "Enclosed I send a plan of the fort...which I shall make by setting logs of about ten foot long in the ground, so as to enclose the store houses. I think to place two swivel guns in two opposite Bastions, which will be sufficient to guard against any attack of small arms."

No contemporary sketch or drawing of the fort exists today. Whether or not its construction followed this design, Fort Granville was formally manned March 28, 1756. Unfortunately, the location had no source of water from within, only the nearby Juniata River.

That spring and early summer saw raids into the area. On July 22, a force challenged Capt. Ward to come out and fight. Considering the state of his supplies, he decided to stay behind the fort's protective walls.

Raiding parties ranged over the area. Some settlers were murdered and families taken captive. Then a lull in the attacks occurred, giving Ward the confidence to split his command. He took the majority of the troops to guard harvesters. The remaining 24 soldiers, plus settlers at the fort, were under Lt. Edward Armstrong.

SIEGE OF FORT GRANVILLE

The Pennsylvania *Gazette* reported that Fort Granville was undermanned when the siege began and it was assumed the enemy put this advantage to good use. Capt. Coulon de Villiers, his French regulars and a force of Delawares under their leader, Captain Jacobs, may not have known Granville's garrison was depleted at all.

The Mifflin County Historical Society's 1956 booklet, From These Ashes

There Shall Rise... Fort Granville - 1756, a bicentennial publication commemorating the fort, states, "Contrary to earlier assumptions de Villiers did not know that Capt. Ward had left with many from the garrison. Rather the Frenchman had intended to attack Fort Shirley, but his Delaware guide for some reason brought him to Fort Granville..."

Dr. Raymond Martin Bell, in an April 6, 1939 Lewistown *Sentinel* column titled "Sesqui Echoes" explained, *In June, 1756, he (Coulon de Villiers) set out to attack Fort Cumberland (Md.) but sickness forced him to return to Fort Duquesne. On July 13, 1756, he set out again planning to go to*

The people to the west of the Susquehanna, distressed by the frequent incursions of the enemy...are moving to the interior parts of the Province and I am fearful that the whole country will be evacuated... - Robert Hunter Morris, Pennsylvania's Governor, from *Pennsylvania Colonial Records*

Fort Shirley via Kittanning. He had 32 Indians (Loups-Delawares, Chouannons-Owls and Illinois) when he left Kittanning on July 17. On July 30 at noon he found himself before Fort Granville. His guide probably made the wrong turn at Mount Union.

ILL SUPPLIED GARRISON

Pennsylvania's Commissary General, Elisha Saltar, is quoted in the Pennsylvania Archives as being very concerned about the viability of Fort Granville. He wrote,

I am very sencilbe (sic) a great part of the soldiers have left their posts & come to the Inhabitants... (Fort Granville) is so badly stored with ammunition, not having three rounds per man...

In the spring of 1756, efforts to supply Fort Granville were hampered by high water. In a letter to Governor R. H. Morris, Capt. James Burd penned, *I intend to have marched this morning for Fort Granville, but the creeks are so high the carriers can't attempt to get their horses and loads over, but hopes to be able to go tomorrow morning...I am informed that they are entirely out of all manner of provisions...which is a bad situation, as the enemy are constantly visiting them...*

Pennsylvania Archives quotes a letter from Fort Augusta dated August 14, 1756 from Col. Clapham to Governor Morris, in which he wrote: *...this loss (of Fort Granville) was occasioned by want of ammunition, having received a letter two or three days ago from Col. John Armstrong, that they had in that fort only one pound of powder and fourteen pounds of lead...*

One or two swivel guns were probably part of the armament at Fort Granville, but with the supply of powder so low there effective use would be questionable. Interestingly, local tradition told of the fort's "brass cannon" being buried in the woods by the enemy after the surrender. No relics of the battle or siege has ever been found in later years.

Fort Granville fell much as the Pennsylvania *Gazette* reported it on August 19, 1756.

FRENCH LETTER REVEALED

The letter made its way to the colonial authorities. William A. Hunter in Forts described the letter as "a puzzle in that day, a mystery in ours." Hunter noted that an attempt at translation was made by Joseph Shippen, as recorded in his journal under August 18, now part of the Shippen Family Papers.

The French letter was archived for almost ninety years when it was made available to historian I. Daniel Rupp. He made a literal transcript from the original in December, 1844. The copied text appears in Rupp's 1847 *History and Topography of Northumberland, Huntingdon, Mifflin, Centre, Union, Columbia, Juniata and Clinton Counties.* Rupp characterized it as a "mere fragment of a letter, incoherent - has many omissions, which are not easily supplied, without knowing particular circumstances under which it was written."

Several transcripts in French appear in Rupp's history, pointing to the difficult nature of reading the original handwriting . Rupp printed a somewhat disjointed English translation. To compound the mystery, since Rupp's 1844 encounter with the document, the original French letter vanished. Hunter observed, "The 'French Letter,' which has since disappeared, was copied by I. D. Rupp...and has the best description of it in his History..."

In 1955, almost two hundred years after the letter was found amid the ruins of Fort Granville, and one hundred years since Rupp last saw it, Dr. Raymond M. Bell revisited the mystery. Bell acknowledged the disappearance of the original, but asked a fellow faculty member and language expert, Dr. A. Richard Oliver of Washington and Jefferson College, to analyze Rupp's French copy. Bell noted that the person who must have copied the letter for Rupp, evidently did not know French, due to inconsistent errors in the text.

After careful study, Dr. Oliver concluded that the letter had no military value and shows simply the presence of French officers among the attackers. The letter was written by a servant-girl who was attempting to escape the amorous pursuits of her master and who wrote this final letter to explain her reason for leaving. Here is Dr. Oliver's translation of the mysterious French Letter:

...because I never looked at you with an affectionate heart; and you never hope for any indulgence on my part after the annoyance you have caused me. So look elsewhere than to me. Do not be a fool any longer over an inconstant who thinks only of his (or her) pleasure. Believe me, search for your fortune elsewhere; as for me I think only that. There is nothing which can change my feelings. Good-bye.

It is not late. I am leaving tomorrow. You have always said to me, "It is not convenient for you to stay here." That did not suit you.

The more you take measures to change me, the more rude I should be. Do not think that I serve you in order that you would think badly of me. For if you do not wish to be bound, go away from me, for I shall not know how to resist.

> *Your Servant*
>
> *Josephine Clere*

The letter appears to be a simple declaration: "This romantic affair has ended."

How or why the French letter came to be among the burned fragments at Fort Granville remains a mystery to this day. William Hunter suggests two possibilities: the letter was accidentally left behind by the French lover or it was intentionally placed there, perhaps as a practical joke, by French soldiers.

Two other explanations are suggested by Dennis P. McIlnay in his book, *Juniata, River of Sorrows.* McIlnay notes that the letter may have been left by a French soldier as a sort of memorial, when his companion was killed during the fight or committed suicide over his spurned love. Or perhaps Coulon de Villiers, French commander of the attacking force at Fort Granville, may have ordered the letter posted as an admonition or warning to the British that "their" affair in Pennsylvania was over, that, plus avenging the death of Coulon de Villiers' brother in 1754, killed by British forces under a young George Washington, the act that started the war in the first place.

Perhaps the Provincial government missed a subtle French gesture, or soldiers left the letter as a joke. The truth will likely remain unknown. One fact remains: a simple letter written by a French servant girl, found at a battle site and its treatment after the fort's fall, points to the magnitude of the event. Under other circumstances, this humble artifact might have gone unnoticed. Instead, the "mysterious" French letter of Fort Granville is part of our local history and the French and Indian War.

Fort Granville Markers - Located on West Fourth Street, Lewistown, PA adjacent to the Pennsylvania Dept. of Transportation Building. The 1947 PHMC marker on left, 1916 marker on right.

"Was it a Spanish dollar?" - Fort Granville Trivia

Ft. Granville - This bronze plaque once graced an uncut stone monument in 1916, now rests on a concrete base at the PennDOT Building on W. 4th Street, Lewistown, PA.

The Frenchman who captured and burned Fort Granville in 1756, Francois Coulon de Villiers, survived the French and Indian War and lived in French New Orleans, until his death in 1794. He came from an illustrious family of military men. His brother, Louis, died of smallpox at Quebec in 1757. For what was brother Louis best known?

[a] inventing an early rifled cannon
[b] defeating Washington at Fort Necessity.
[c] designing the new French flag
[d] uncle to Napoleon Bonaparte

2. In September, 1756, Col. John Armstrong and a force of Provincial soldiers attacked the Indian village of Kittanning, located north of Ft. Duquesne, in response to the attack on Ft. Granville. This same Col. Armstrong has a connection to Joseph Yoder, Amishman from Lancaster County and ancestor of Big Valley's Joseph W. Yoder. The latter, a famous Mifflin County writer, authored a series of books on Amish culture, most notably, *Rosanna of the Amish*. What is the connection between Col. Armstrong and the elder Yoder?

[a] Armstrong was married to Yoder's sister
[b] Yoder and Armstrong once farmed together in Lancaster
[c] Yoder bought Armstrong's house
[d] both men once traveled with George Washington.

3. In 1965, what did Mifflin County's Jaycees plan to do as an historical tourist attraction?

[a] present an annual fair and play   about Fort Granville
[b] construct a full scale replica of Fort Granville off W. 4th St.
[c] create a museum to Fort Granville in the old Temple Theatre complex
[d] reenact the burning of Fort Granville every August on Dixon Field

4. The Pennsylvania Historical and Museum Commission dedicated a marker on March 24, 1947, to the memory of Fort Granville. It was not the first marker remembering the frontier fort, in fact, you might say there have been three over the years. Where are or were the other Ft. Granville markers?

[a] the first marker, 1916, was moved in a dispute and relocated, this one was later placed beside it
[b] all three markers stand together on West 4th Street

[c] the first plaque was stolen and was never replaced

[d] one plaque is in the new courthouse, one on W. 4th Street and one by the Juniata River

5. In 1928, Harry S. Hagan, was searching along the banks of the Juniata River for Indian artifacts. He was in the general vicinity of where Fort Granville was believed located. He found something that was connected to this early era. What relic of the French and Indian War period did he find just west of Lewistown?

[a] the rusted hammer and lock from a Pennsylvania rifle

[b] a brass button from a French army uniform circa 1755

[c] a monogrammed pewter spoon

[d] a Spanish dollar dated 1750, with holes near the edge, as if worn

TRIVIA ANSWERS:

1. b

2. c (According to Joseph W. Yoder, in his book, *Rosanna's Boys*, Yoder relates that his ancestor bought the house in Menno Township that was on the Armstrong tract, although he asserts Armstrong never actually lived in it.)

3. b (A number of articles in the Sentinel described the recurring idea of a full scale reconstructed Ft. Granville. The concept was tossed around in 1954 and then again in 1965, but never acted upon.

4. a (According to coverage in the local press, a dispute of ownership and access to the original location brought about its relocation. The Fort Granville monument was first placed on ground once occupied by a Jamesway Dept. Store and later Quality Farm Supply, formerly C. T. and Your Building Center.)

5. c (The *Sentinel* headline on this page tells the tale of a remarkable find, a pewter spoon.)

THE SENTINEL

SATURDAY, APRIL 21, 1928

SPOON IS FOUND NEAR SITE OF FT. GRANVILLE, 150 YEARS OLD

Pewter Spoon Bears Name of T. R. Holt, Son of Dorcas Holt, After Whom Dorcas Street W a s Named

PRESENTED TO
G. F. STACKPOLE

The Finder, Harry S. Hagan, Gives It to Descendant of Former Owner; Student of Indian Lore Has Extensive Collection

What is considered to be one of the most remarkable finds of ancient cutlery in Mifflin County in recent years was made three years ago along the banks of the Juniata Riv-

10 - The Journal of Philip Vickers Fithian

It was a fateful year, 1776. Thomas Paine's Common Sense was published that January. The spring and summer saw the Continental Congress meet in Philadelphia. The Declaration of Independence had been endorsed by the same body on July 2nd and by the 9th, all thirteen colonies voted their support. Meanwhile, British General Howe landed 10,000 men on Staten Island and by August, his forces numbered 32,000, including 9,000 mercenaries from Germany. An attempt at a peace conference failed and General Washington evacuated New York City to a position on upper Manhattan Island, Fort Washington, and fended off a British attack at Harlem Heights in September.

At the same time, a young Colonial, an army chaplain from a New Jersey militia regiment, lay upon his death bed in a camp near Fort Washington. It was a feeble excuse for a bed, though, a scant layer of straw covered by a couple blankets barely kept him a few inches from the cold floor. He shared a meager shelter with three other soldiers, two as sick as he.

The minister wasn't felled by a British musket ball, but one of the many Revolutionary War-era diseases so easily spread among young soldiers. The medical lexicon of the 18th century recounts many: Hospital Fever, Malignant Bilious Fever, Smallpox, Barbadoes Distemper or the Bloody Flux. Causes ranged from drinking stagnant water, eating tainted food, or from lice, mosquitoes, and an assortment of sinister pathogens.

The young chaplain suffered from dysentery, had a raging fever, and worse. A friend, Rev. William Hollingshead of Fairfield, N.J., visited him and tells of the encounter in his diary dated October 4, 1776: "He is reduced to the lowest state one could imagine possible for human nature to support, besides which, he has no physician to attend him but an unskillful quack of a surgeons' mate, and no nurse but an unknowing country lad. Alas! how unhappy a situation is this." Rev. Hollingshead returned over the next three days, only to find his friend fading, until on the morning of October 8, he, "closed his eyes upon the things of time and is gone to try a Spiritual World. His illness continued for only seventeen days..."

The young chaplain Hollingshead wrote about was Rev. Philip Vickers Fithian. Fithian kept a diary during his journey through the Kishacoquillas Valley in 1775 as a Presbyterian missionary. His account is a window on colonial life in what would become Mifflin County.

Philip Vickers Fithian was born on December 29, 1747 at Greenwich, New Jersey not far from Delaware Bay in the southwestern part of the state. His parents were Joseph and Hannah Vickers Fithian. His ancestors came from England, making a home on Long Island in 1640. He was tutored by two Presbyterian ministers and later attended Princeton College. His classmates there were the likes of James Madison, Aaron Burr and "Light Horse Harry" Lee. At the time, the college was known for preparing preachers and teachers. In the introduction to Fithian's 1775 - 1776 journal, edited by Robert G. Albion and Leonidas Dodson in 1934, the authors note that at the time of the Revolution, about half of the Presbyterian clergy were Princeton graduates.

Fithian took the advise of Princeton's President John Witherspoon, and spent a year (from October, 1773 to October, 1774) at Nomini Hall, Robert Carter III's Virginia plantation, to tutor the Carter children. The Presbytery of Philadelphia licensed him, but with vacant pulpits few and far between in the settlements, he was sent out on the missionary circuit on May 9, 1775. This first tour took him into Virginia from New Jersey. After a tour south then north again through the Shenandoah Valley, Philip journeyed from Winchester, Virginia, eventually crossing into Pennsylvania. He attended a meeting at Mercersburg, then, traversing the state from Fort Loudoun, crossed the Juniata River near

Andrew Boggs' Eagle's Nest, July 31, 1775 — "For all this Settlement I would not live here; for two such Settlements – not for five hundred a Year– nothing would persuade me ..."
- *The Journal of Philip Vickers*

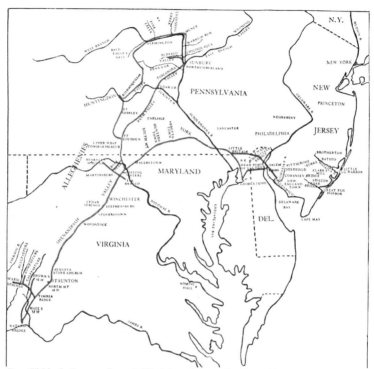

Rev. Fithian's Journey through Virginia and Pennsylvania - This map was drawn by Robert G. Albion, Associate Professor of History, Princeton University in 1933. It accompanied Dr. Albion's work, *Philip Vickers Fithian: Journal, 1775 - 1776*, published by Princeton University Press in 1934. A copy of this now rare book is in the collection of the Mifflin County Historical Society. - MCHS image

present-day Mifflintown and on to Northumberland (Sunbury).

Next, he traveled north to Muncy and followed the West Branch of the Susquehanna westward to Bald Eagle (Flemington), Bald Eagle's Nest (Milesburg), and Penn's Valley. Next it was over the Seven Mountains to East Kishacoquillas Valley (Reedsville), West Kishacoquillas Valley (Belleville) and eventually Huntingdon and Fort Shirley. By August 8, 1775, he was home in New Jersey. He maintained a diary throughout the trip, suggesting at one point that his words would be for posterity, two hundred years hence. Yet Fithian wasn't the first missionary into the area, nor the first to keep a journal recounting early Mifflin County.

The First Presbyterian Missionaries

In Theodore Roosevelt's 1889 *The Winning of the West*, the future president wrote about the lands west of the Susquehanna River, " The backwoodsmen were Americans by birth and parentage...but the dominant strain in their blood was that of Presbyterian Irish - the Scotch-Irish..."

"In the hard life of the frontier they lost much of their religion, and they had but scant chance to give their children the schooling in which they believed...the creed of the backwoodsman who had a creed at all was Presbyterianism..."

When Mifflin emerged as a county of its own in 1789, there were four established churches within its boundary, all Presbyterian. The earliest settlers petitioned the church for ministers to come and deliver the word of God. Just ten years from the destruction of Fort Granville and only three years after the signing of the treaty ending the French and Indian War in the colonies, settlers filtered back into the area. Pontiac's War in 1763-64 and other Indian actions kept the back country on edge. No murders were noted in Mifflin County at this time, but tradition tells that Indians killed Hugh Brown of Wayne Township in 1763.

As frontier turmoil between settlers and Indians subsided in 1765, J. Martin Stroup, in his *Genesis of Mifflin County* recounts that two missionaries were "to go together... and preach at least two months in those parts..." The first missionaries arrived in the region in August, 1766. The Rev. Charles Beatty and Rev. George Duffield were sent by the Philadelphia and New York Synod. The ministers separated near Port Royal, in present- day Juniata County, at Captain Patterson's, now Mexico. On August 25, 1766, Beatty pushed on through the Lewistown Narrows and then to points west with Joseph Rupie, an interpreter and Levi Hicks, who spent years as an Indian captive.

Rev. Beatty kept a journal during this time, which was published in London in 1768. In it he comments on his trip through the Narrows, "The roadway, bad, being on the bank of the river, a small path and a great many trees fallen across it." His first stop in Mifflin County was at the home of Thomas Holt, to feed the horses. Beatty noted, "Near Thomas Holt's house stood Fort Granville."

Traveling westward along the Juniata River, about 10 miles from Holt's to just east of McVeytown, the little band, engulfed in darkness, became lost in a storm. They found shelter at John McCartney's house and were "entertained in the best manner in the peoples' power."

The next day his journal records the first sermon delivered in Mifflin County. Beatty wrote, "There never was any sermon preached in this settlement before...it was the first... ever preached in these parts." The settlement was expansive, Beatty wrote, extending 25 miles up and down the river on both sides. The settlers hoped more would follow and the minister speculated on a neighboring settlement in the Great Valley, Kishacoquillas Valley, "...This valley is about 30 miles long and five or six

"...the creed of the backwoodsman who had a creed at all was Presbyterianism..." - Theodore Roosevelt, *The Winning of the West*, 1889

wide...mostly good land. At present there are but five or six families in it, but more expected next spring." Other missionaries are recorded to have ventured into the area during the late 1760s. By the mid-1770s, another missionary journey passed through what was to become Mifflin County, as the Rev. Philip Vickers Fithian began his first mission tour.

Excerpts from the Fithian Journal

Rev. Fithian was a dedicated diarist. Edward P. Alexander, Director of Interpretation at Colonial Williamsburg wrote in 1967, "Once in a great while historians find a firsthand account that provides striking insight into the past. Only rarely is such a document written with the perception and charm that make its readers feel as if they had participated in the incidents described...The journal...of Philip Fithian constitute this kind of source."

Fithian's words appear here extracted from a series of articles appearing in the Lewistown *Sentinel* written by newspaper editor and county historian J. Martin Stroup in the 1950s, from the 1957 book *Genesis of Mifflin County* by J. Martin Stroup and Raymond Bell, and from the 1934 edited transcription by Robert G. Albion of Princeton University and Leonidas Dodson of the University of Pennsylvania, with punctuation and grammatical usage as used by Fithian.

The missionary's 1773-1774 journal chronicles his time as tutor at Nomini plantation and life in the Old Dominion. His first missionary journey into the frontier began in 1775 and this journal recounts the events of daily life on the Pennsylvania-Virginia frontier and in the Continental Army around New York, ending in early October, 1776 with his death. Excepts here cover his trek through this part of Pennsylvania, late summer, 1775.

Rev. Fithian reported on his stay with Andrew Boggs, first settler in what is now Centre County, where their supper consisted of "...Fish, Suckers, Chups, & Venison..." He also commented on what proved to be a great fear, the area's Indian population. Fithian wrote:

Monday, July 31, 1775 - *Many Trees on this road are cut, by the Indians, in strange Figures; in Diamonds -- Deaths Heads --Crowned Heads -- Initial Letters -- Whole Numbers -- Dates of the Years -- Blazes.*

The conditions of the dwelling of his host caused the young Fithian great anxiety. The degree of cleanliness, or the lack of it, distressed him greatly! The night he spent at Boggs' Eagle's Nest revealed his most consuming fears and went like this:

Near present-day Milesburg, Centre County, July 31, 1775 - "Now, Laura, when I am at the farthest Frontiers of this Colony m & among the wild – natured Savages, I am in Fear— Indeed I am..." – *The Journal of Philip Vickers Fithian*

Soon after we had dined, two Indian Boys bolted in/they never knock or speak at the Door/with seven large Fish

-- One would weigh two Pounds! – In return Mr. Boggs gave them Bread, & a Piece of our Venison; down they sat in the Ashes before the Fire, stirred up the Coals, & laid on their Flesh – when it was a little roasted, they bit it off in great Mouthfuls, and devoured it with the greatest Rapacity...I sat me down on a three-legged Stool; raw Flesh & Blood in every Part— Mangled, wasting Flesh on every Shelf— Hounds licking up the Blood from the Floor — An open Landlady — Naked Indians & Children — Ten hundred thousand Flies — O! I fear there are as many Fleas. Seize me soon, kind Sleep; lock me in thy sweet Embrace before these Vermin hurt me — O! so soon as I lay me down, let me rest on thy Bosom & lose my Senses — Stop! O stop— Sleep to night is gone— ! Four Indians come driving in, each with a large Knife & Tom-Hawk — Bless me two other strapping Fellows! Indeed I am sick of my Station - All standing dumb before us...I am glad to keep bent at my writing...Six Large Indians!

Now, Laura, when I am at the farthest Frontiers of this Colonym & among the wild – natured Savages, I am in Fear— Indeed I am —

For all this Settlement I would not live here; for two such Settlements– not for five hundred a Year– nothing would persuade me– !

A few days before embarking on the Mifflin County leg of the journey, Rev. Fithian spent a few nights at the home of Captain Potter in Penn's Valley and offered some interesting observations.

Penn's Valley - Sunday August 6 - *I rise early, before any in the Family except a Negro Girl. Just at my Bed's Head is a Window under which stands a Table - here I had laid my clean Linnen finished last night by Mrs. Potter. The night was very stormy; when I waked this Morning I found a large Dog had jumped in through an open Light of the Window & had softly bedded himself, dripping with Water & Mud, among my clean, new-washed Clothes! At first I felt enraged; I bore it however with a Sabbath-Day's Moderation...*

Monday August 7 - *I must stay another Day in this valley. Tomorrow I am to have Company over the Mountain...I write these Lines, sitting on a Log, with my Paper on the back of my Pocket Book & upon my Knee, under a large Spruce-Tree, close upon the Bank of Penn's Creek...The creek roars foaming by me, enlarged with yesterday's great Flood...*

..."No, Madam, I must dry the Butter first" - Mrs. Potter's Girl was bringing a Plate of Butter yesterday Morning from the Spring-House. It rained & Butter will retain the Drops on its Surface - Innocent Miss, therefore, with great Care for Neatness, was holding the Butter close to a very large Fire- What are you at there says Mrs. Potter to Peggy? - "I am drying the Butter, Madam!"

Penns Valley, August 7, 1775 — "Mrs. Potter's Girl was bringing a Plate of Butter yesterday Morning from the Spring-House..." - *The Journal of Philip Vickers Fithian*

The Seven Mountains - The next day's entries detail Rev. Fithian's trek across what he described as a "tall, pine-covered mountain." Forewarned that the journey will be unpleasant, Captain Potter somewhat assuaged his fears with a payment of twenty-five shillings toward his mission.

Tuesday August 8 - *Mr. Thompson came, we breakfasted & set out - But the first mountain we had to climb by far exceeded all I have yet gone over. It is long Steep. The ascent however were trifling, for the Road lies along the Side of the Mountain & winds gradually upwards; but the Rocks-vast Stones of every Size & Shape, make it not only troublesome, but, in Fact, dangerous to go over...*

On the Top of this -- O Another! -- Another, & still Higher! -- One, who like me has been little used to go over such high Hills can have, by bare Description, no Conception, not even an idea, of the rough romantic Prospect...A long view, more than forty Miles, over the Tops of very Tall Trees are, apparently, two & three hundred Feet below us, & within Gunshot of us...

On we rode over the other Mountain; & the other; & the other -- Eighteen Miles & four Mountains! On the Summits of these Hills, is yet great Plenty of very sweet Huckleberries...

Kishacoquillas Valley - *At last we came in View, from a lofty airy Ridge, of our desired Kishacoquillas Valley; we stumbled down to it, ten miles, from the East End... to one Fleming's...*

We trotted gently along, I was busy viewing the broad level Country between two such huge Hills -- We met a Woman, says Thompson to her, "How are your Family, Marget?" -- "Thank you, Tom," says She, "they are all on their feet, thank God."

Wednesday August 9 - *To Day I visited 'Squire Brown; I should make his House my home, by Appointment of Presbytery, but where I am my Horse is well & carefully fed, I will not then leave it for a Hazard -- The 'Squire lives in a pleasant Spot. On a creek, & very near the Mountain. There is a Gap too through which, run the creek & the public road to Juniata. He has a Grist Mill, Saw-Mill, a large farm, & is carrying on an extensive business...*

Squire Brown's - August 9, 1775
— "The 'Squire lives in a pleasant Spot. On a creek, & very near the Mountain. There is a Gap too through which, run the creek & the public road to Juniata. He has a Grist Mill, Saw-Mill, a large farm, & is carrying on an extensive business..." - *Fithian Journal*

I have heard no News from below since I left...The 'Squire has some. He tells me that a ship has been brought into Philadelphia, loaded from Britain, with Powder & Arms, destined Southward, for the Negroes -- That nothing material since the Skirmish at Bunker's Hill, has taken place between the Armies at Boston...

In one of Mr. Fleming's Fields is a natural Curiosity worthy of Remark -- He took me to see it. In a field near the Mountain & near the middle of the Field, in a level spot, clear of Stones also, & a good distance from either Bush or a Stump, is a small Hole in the Earth, eight inches in Length, & five in Breadth, of an oval form; it looks like the Holes of Ground-Hogs, Pole-Cats & other such Earth-housed Animals. But its Depth is the curiosity. Take a small stone, the size of a man's fist, & let it drop into the hole, it will go clattering down, as tho' among Stones, & be near a full minute falling! ...the Stone strikes against the Sides of the hole often, yet it must, in my judgment, descend more than a hundred feet!

Squire William Brown was one of Fithian's many hosts during his stay in Kishacoquillas Valley and he was kept busy with visiting, sight-seeing and preaching. He did not want for conversation here. Even his mountain guide, Mr. Thompson, was a source of amusement for the young reverend.

Thursday August 10 - *Thompson who came over the Mountains with me is a Droll. Last night our Fire was almost out. "Peggy," quoth he, "bring in some Bark to save the Fire" - "Indeed Tom, answered the Girl. I am tired, pulling Flax all Day & cant"– "Well then," quo' Tom, "run out & call the Neighbors to see it die."*

Fithian perceived the area's universal plainness of speech. He couldn't quite believe, what he termed "Familiarity in Conversation" was so apparent.

"... Every Man, in all Companies, with almost no Exception, Calls his Wife, Brother, Neighbor, or Acquaintance, by their proper name of Sally, John, James, or Michael, without ever prefixing the customary Compliment of 'My Dear,' 'Sir,' 'Mr.' &c."

While exploring the valley, Rev. Fithian frequently comments upon the quality and quantity of the crops harvested and the methods employed by the local farmers.

Afternoon I walked over to Mr. Cuthbertson's, half a Mile. He has a large, well-improved Farm. This present Season he reap'd nine Hundred Dozen Sheaves of wheat & one Hundred Dozen of Rye.

Much to Fithian's surprise, one of Mr. Cutbertson's sons was a Princeton graduate, Fithian's own school, Class of 1768. They had quite a reverie of college memories.

The Lunar Eclipse - August 11, 1775 - In the early morning hours, while Rev. Fithian was staying on the John Fleming farm between Milroy and Reedsville, all the family arose between the hours of twelve and three a.m. to witness an eclipse of the moon. Fithian described it as a "considerable" eclipse and commented:

Eclipses of the Moon are so frequent [infrequent] that I suppose there are but a few, who, with me, agreed to Want their Rest, for the sight.

I am moved with Wonder when I view these periodical Intermotions of such vast bodies.

This event causes Fithian to think of home, friends, his future wife (Their marriage was but ten weeks away.) and his financial affairs. He pines for home and laments, "If this is what they call Homesick I pity the poor Irish."

Being of stout heart and a practical man, he shook off this melancholy feeling

Kishacoquillas Valley, August 11, 1775 — "I am moved with Wonder when I view these periodical Intermotions of such vast bodies." - *The Journal of Philip Vickers Fithian*

and headed for Mr. Cuthbertson's after dinner noting: *Took a Walk to the side of the Mountain with Miss Nancy & Fanny (Fleming) They are chatful enough, which is rare here with the lonely Virgins. I drank with them sociably a Dish of Coffee & returned to my Cabbin by Dark.*

Saturday, August 12, 1775 - *It is wonderful to take Notice, in this long Jaunt, how much real Fondness exists between me & my Horse.*

He, poor Brute, will follow me from the House to the Stable, & Field; around the Pasture, & from the Fields Home, submissive & obedient as a well taught Spaniel.

East Kishacoquillas Valley - Sunday, August 13, 1775 - *A fine day. I rose early. At 'Squire Browns we held Worship. Here is a large Society...We were in the forenoon in a large barn, it was too small, & we went out into a fine Meadow under a high western Hill - We had shade and were very comfortable.*

I think, by appearance, there are more People than I have seen at any place on the Susquehanna - Very many Women, of all Sizes, & drest in plain good Taste - And several men who in their Dress made as an important a Figure as I should wish to see in Town.

The Vulgar Custom - Monday, August 14, 1775 - Rev. Fithian compliments the grace and style of the locals and finds that in many ways their company is quite enjoyable, compared to his more cultured upbringing. On one particular evening, however, Fithian draws the line at what he terms, "a vulgar custom."

I was again at Mr. Cuthbertson's. The young ladies too are pleasant. After coffee in the Evening they bantered me on a Vulgar...Pardon me Ladies, I know you all believe it...I mean the telling Fortunes from the Leaves of Tea; or from the Grounds of Coffee...

Miss, however, after we had done our Coffee, with a shy designing Air, began the Charm - She took her Cup with very little of the Liquor, & all the Settlings from a full cup; She must look at no person, til' She turned it round many Times ...She then turns up her Cup in the Saucer...the Fortune... she turned about to me, prim as an unpolluted Vestal, without one wrong-indented Dimple in her face - She turned to unfold the Oracle.

"You, Sir, have been for a considerable Time fond of a middle sized, fair-Faced, grave young Woman."

And, my good Cassandra, where will this fondness end? But of this the Oracle said not...

Rev. Fithian goes on to chastise the ladies and gentlemen, at least in his journal, for wasting time on such nonsense, which he characterized as "Female, tea-

Table Scandal!"

Insect Enounter - On his way home from the fortune telling episode, Rev. Fithian captured an insect he termed quite large and of the "Grasshopper Kind." It "...sings upon Trees in the Evenings all the latter Part of Summer." His description continues,

It is a large, green, Oval-formed Grasshopper. The sound is made by the upper Part of its Back; This part of the Wings which make the Noise is very thin, glassy, springy & the Colour of Isinglass. The two Wings rub together, not unlike a Pair of Scissors, & under them is a hollow Drum, to form & emit Sound...I have long heard them...their notes were never pleasing to me, yet I never before could take one...Commonly called Katy Did.

The Vulgar Custom, August 13, 1775 — "You, Sir, have been for a considerable Time fond of a middle sized, fair-Faced, grave young Woman." - *The Journal of Philip Vickers Fithian*

Underground Wonders - Tuesday August 15, 1775 - Squire Brown took Rev. Fithian on a ride to see the natural "curiosities" of the valley. They traveled about three miles east to a cave, most likely on the site of the present-day Eastern Industries Quarry at Naginey, and entered a cavern, now long gone, that the astonished minister figured could hold two-hundred fifty people, without touching one another! In 1775, this geological feature presented itself, according to Fithian, "...towards the East End, & near the Middle of the Valley, in a large Wood, at a considerable distance from any house" as a "vast, & surprising Cavity in the Ground."

Yet during Fithian's visit, he describes the entrance as "ragged, craggy, &, in Appearance, very dangerous," with "large misshapen stones...loose & threatening every Moment to fall out!" Squire Brown and the excursion party needed some amount of persuasion to convince Rev. Fithian to enter, but enter he did and gave a good account of the wonder.

The Bottom of the Cave was, I think originally sandy, & smooth; now many Tons of Rocks are lying over more than half the Bottom which makes it both difficult & unpleasant to walk through the Whole.

In all its Parts within, it is very sonorous - If I had not been so very much afraid, I could have sung with great Ease & Grandieur in it - But it was with much Uneasiness that I could stay a Minute to measure its Dimensions.

I am told a violin sounds through it with exquisite Delicacy - I think also it would improve, in a height measure, the German Flute - But no Musick could, by Softness, or Force, have long detained me, where terrible Danger was visibly overhanging...

...I took its Dimensions in paces; with great Accuracy as the rough Bottom would permit.

93

The Entrance is an imperfect Arch, whose Base is 28 Paces, or 84 feet, & Height, in the highest Part, 10 feet. From the Middle, or Centre of the Entrance, to the farthest Part, thirty-five Paces - 105 feet. Length within, in the longest Part, forty five Paces - 135 Feet.

At the entrance, from the Top of the Arch , upwards to the Bottom of the Mound, or Earth, it is 45 feet; all which is solid Lime-Stone Rock. Upon the whole, it is the most curious & remarkable Work of Nature I have yet seen.

'Squire Brown & many others who live in this Neighborhood, tell me, that they have seen, handled, & brought out, Ice from this Cave, late in July - Some do say that after hard & long Winters the Ice does not all dissolve in the Course of the whole Summer!

...the Air is uncommonly , indeed I thought it dangerously cold, or rather damp & shivering; The Place is, in its Nature, gloomy...All was still, but the Noise of the Drops of Water, steeping & falling through the Rocks; this adds much to the Horror of the Place - The Drops of Water, in a strange Manner & Degree, do actually petrefy; harden into Stone!

This hardened Water stands in many Places through the Cave, in tall, slim, very white, some dun, marble-coloured, & Beautiful Columns, four, five, & six Feet high. I broke off a Part, & brought away with me, some in a most delicate Grain pure White...All indeed to me is Wonderful!

First View of Alexander Caverns - The next destination on Rev. Fithian's tour was a stop at another local natural wonder, the wet entrance to Alexander Caverns. Located about four miles northeast of Reedsville, it is the source of Honey Creek ,and was known later as Mammoth Spring. *Roadside Geology of Pennsylvania* cites the opening as the third largest spring in Pennsylvania, averaging 14,000 gallons per minute.

Rev. Fithian describes the visit as follows: *On our Return, we called & entered another which is a watry Cave. The Entrance into this small, not large enough to receive two Persons at the same Time, but opens at once into a vast dark Cavity; some rays of Light indeed enter at the narrow Entrance, & at the opening where the Water runs out of the Rock, enough to discover the hanging Collumns of petrified Water.*

...the Drops in the Water here is prodigiously grand, it drops always, plump-plump; & the Inside is very sonorous. Mr. Alexander's House stands over Water where a Boat of two Ton would <u>Float!</u>

West Kishacoquillas Valley - A Wedding - Wednesday August 16, 1775 - Rev. Fithian accompanied Squire Brown on horseback to West Kishacoquillas Valley. The Squire was off to marry a couple and the reverend was invited along. He gave quite a description of this pioneer wedding, never hiding his distain for his humble parishioners.

We rode up; it was a little Cabbin, they were dining; We entered but all continued eating - There were four Women, Four Men And Four Children. I view'd them all, but, from their appearance, could not single out to my satisfaction who

Alexander Caverns - This 1973 pen and ink drawing by Mifflin County artist Anne Kepler Fisher (1925 - 1977) was an illustration in Jack H. Speece's Alexander Caverns and depicted the traditional story of the local stream's name. According to the tale, a storm blew the bee hives of James "Honey Jim" Alexander into the waters of the stream that emanated from his cave and it's been known as "Honey Creek" ever since. Rev. Fithian looked upon the cave and house above and stated, *"Mr. Alexander's House stands over Water where a Boat of two Ton would Float!* - Journal of Philip Vickers Fithian, 1775.

---

was the Groom & Bride. After they rose from Dinner, one of the Men brought us a Dram in a Bottle of Whiskee. We drank & after some Time, the "Youthful Pair" singled out themselves - Expectation, now glut thy Wish - The Girl look'd asham'd, tho' lusty; She held down her Head; ...yet I saw, in her dancing Eyes...that they only accorded with her transported heart! She pronounced the Ceremony after the 'Squire feebly & apparently, with Reluctance - But oh! her Bosom burned!

But the Groom - In appearance, a scurvy, futile, unmeaning Drill - He seem'd highly pleased, but a vulgar looking, ragged, Weather-worn Peasant.

Sunday August 20, 1775 - *We held Sermon in a Barn of Mr. Brotherton's — But a few were present, compared with last Sunday's Assembly...Some however from that End are here, Mr. Fleming & Family, Mr. Cuthertson &c. — Miss Polley Laundrum, the Village Toast,a young Lady lately from Maryland...young, neat, exceedingly beautiful, was at Sermon, too...*

These August, feverish, Dog-Day Suns, after preaching two Sermons, I am always much troubled with a sore Head-Ach...

Monday August 21, 1775 - *Very hot. Mr. McDowel for my Supply gave me*

Plain Speaking Locals August 10, 1775 - "... Every Man, in all Companies, with almost no Exception, Calls his Wife, Brother, Neighbor, or Acquaintance, by their proper name of Sally, John, James, or Michael, without ever prefixing the customary Compliment of 'My Dear,' 'Sir,' 'Mr.' &c." - *The Journal of Philip Vickers Fithian*

twenty Shillings, 1 pound. Put not tour Trust

in Man was Solomons Advice – I find to Day that he was very right...I took my Leaveof this kind family & the whole Valley– I rode alone between the Mountains til' the Valley becomes very narrow, & vastly stoney, & through it I past to the Bank of roaring Juniata...

Fithian left the Kishacoquillas Valley. As his journal continues, he notes Jack's Mountain and "Standing-Stone" Mountain along the way to Huntingdon. Within months, his journey brings him home where he married, but unfortunately it was a short-lived union. Fithian became a chaplain in the Continental Army and died in October, 1776 of a camp-born illness.

The Fithian Journal's Place in History

The excerpts presented here are just tantalizing bits of an extensive, fascinating perspective of pre-Revolutionary central Pennsylvania. Although Philip Vickers Fithian never returned to what became Mifflin County, his writing remains one of the most illuminating descriptions of the area at this time. "The unique value of this journal lies in its intimate, objective picture of American back-country society in the opening months of the Revolution," commented editors Albion and Dodson in their 1934 edition of the Fithian journal. Their edition also contains extensive footnotes and appendices, plus the added journal excerpt of Rev. William Hollingshead, who recounts Fithian's last days.

Some Additional Reading on Rev. Fithian

Unfortunately, no recent reprint exists of the portion of Fithian's writings that recounts his Central Pennsylvania wanderings. The complete 1934 title is *Philip Vickers Fithian: Journal, 1775 - 1776 Written on the Virginia-Pennsylvania Frontier and in the Army Around New York* Edited By Robert G. Albion and Leonidas Dodson Princeton University Press 1934. The Mifflin County Historical Society has a copy of this edition in its Research Library, as do most research libraries. Occasionally, a copy of the 1934 edition can be found for sale on the Internet through rare book outlets. There are reprints of Fithian's other writings available, including : *Journal and Letters of Philip Vickers Fithian, A Plantation Tutor of the Old*

Dominion, 1773 - 1774 Edited by Hunter Dickinson Farish, University Press of Virginia, 1996. This is a good starting place for additional reading on this unique diarist from America's colonial history.

Mifflin County Trivia
"Does he dislike rattlesnakes?"

1. According to the July-August 2001 issue of *Weatherwise*, a meteorological journal, what weather term, still used today, is Philip Vickers Fithian credited with writing about in his Journal, apparently for the first time?

[a] "Dog Days" - hot, summer days
[b] "Nor' Easter" - Eastern coastal storm
[c] "Bermuda High" - Atlantic high pressure near the Bermuda Islands
[d] "a falling glass" - a Mercury barometer showing a drop in barometric pressure

2. The house in which Fithian was born and lived still stands in Greenwich New Jersey. Today, it's called the Fithian House, but also goes by another name, because of its specific use during the Revolution. What is that unusual name?

[a] Tea Burner House
[b] Gun Powder House
[c] The Patriot's Refuge
[d] Spy's Haven

3. Rev. Fithian commented in his diary on Wednesday, December 22, 1773, "The notes are clear and inexpressibly soft, they swell, and are inexpressibly grand; and either it is because the sounds are new, and therefore please me, or it is the most captivating instrument I have ever heard." The instrument he heard that day was played at a family concert in Robert Carter 's manor house in Virginia, where Fithian served as tutor. What was the instrument he heard for the first time?

[a] banjo
[b] French horn
[c] glass armonica
[d] harpsichord

4. During his 1775 journey through the wilderness of this area, of what or whom is Rev. Fithian seemingly most concerned about encountering?

[a] serpents, ie. rattlesnakes
[b] savages, any American Indian

[c] beasts, ie. black bear

[d] intoxicated robbers

5. On July 29, 1775, Rev. Fithian was staying with a Mr. Read, a few days prior to his trip over the Seven Mountains into the Kishacoquillas Valley. He frequently comments in his journal about the type and quality of food served. On this particular occasion, in addition to locally picked huckleberries, Fithian enjoyed something else there he hadn't had for awhile. What was it?

[a] a glass of port wine

[b] a dish of clear coffee

[c] roasted beef

[d] wild rose honey

6. On August 10, while staying with Squire Brown in Kish Valley, Rev. Fithian disparaged what a local man, Mr. Cuthbertson, and his mother were about to undertake and she "...a women more than fifty!" What were the Cuthbertsons going to do?

[a] the pair planned to take in orphaned Indian children

[b] mother and son were going to raft down the Susquehanna River

[c] ride horseback to Albany, New York

[d] walk to Philadelphia

TRIVIA ANSWERS:

1. [b] "Nor' Easter" - Eastern coastal storm [The Oxford English Dictionary credits Fithian's journal with the first recorded use of the term.]

2. [a] Tea Burner House (Fithian was born in the house and later joined a group of Greenwich, N.J. patriots, according to the town's history, known as the "Tea Burners" who stole a shipment of tea and burned in the town square. A monument, near the spot of the historical event. Greenwich is a seaport town along the Cohansey River, within 5 miles of the Delaware Bay.]

3. [c] glass harmonica

4. [b] savages, any American Indian [Fithian recounts that his guide took a fresh deer kill hanging near an Indian camp along the trail and was fearful the owner would appear and demand compensation, or worse.]

5. [b] a dish of clear coffee

6. [c] ride horseback to Albany, New York

11 - The Riot

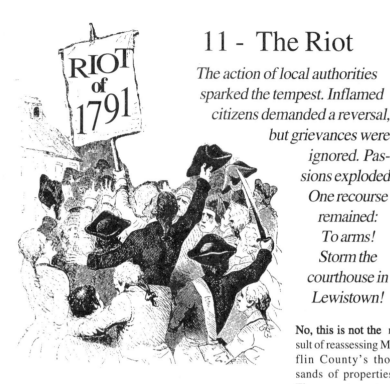

The action of local authorities sparked the tempest. Inflamed citizens demanded a reversal, but grievances were ignored. Passions exploded! One recourse remained: To arms! Storm the courthouse in Lewistown!

No, this is not the result of reassessing Mifflin County's thousands of properties. The current county officials should have no fear. This citizen action took place over two hundred years ago. Today, that disturbance is known as the Riot of 1791. It marks one of Mifflin County's most exciting moments, with a bitterness, some might argue, that lingers to this day. The appointment of a judge sparked the controversy and revealed the growing pains of the newborn county. Mifflin County was almost two years old, carved from Cumberland County and a bit of Northumberland County in 1789, and included what would become Juniata County. Residents there lived "below the Long Narrows," while the rest of the county's citizens lived "above the Long Narrows." Today, this six mile gap is referred to as the Lewistown Narrows, Shade Mountain on the west with its nose at Lewistown, and Blue Mountain on the east with its nose at Macedonia, north of Mifflintown.

From the beginning, there was antagonism about the placement of the county seat, with the Narrows being the geographical dividing line. Those below the Narrows favored a more centrally located site over Lewistown's northern location. Early records and news articles indicate that those below the Narrows had one true desire - a county of their own. Petitions to the Pennsylvania Legislature for a separate Juniata County were submitted almost annually for four decades.

Mifflin County's divided condition, although not the cause of the riot, was

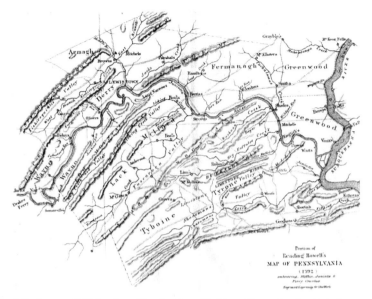

Mifflin County - 1792: Portion of Reading Howell's Map of Pennsylvania which shows the larger Mifflin County prior to its division into Juniata and Mifflin in 1831- *History of the Susquehanna and Juniata Valleys,* 1886 - MCHS image

the backdrop in front of which these momentous events played out.

JUNIATA WANTED A SEPARATE COUNTY

The strong passion for separation was reflected in a petition to the Pennsylvania Legislature. In 1801, those below the Narrows sought to remove the county seat to Mifflintown. One point in their petition read: "That numbers of your petitioners who live below the Long Narrows (and have to pass through to get to Lewistown) live at a distance of 37 miles from thence; and those who live above the Narrows (except a few persons in the West end of Wayne township, who are petitioning to be annexed to Huntingdon County) do not exceed eighteen miles from the seat of justice."

This petition also asserted that, in 1788, a more centrally located county seat was selected by a neutral commission. Its opinion: the logical place for the county seat should be at the plantation of John Harris, later to be Mifflintown, and not Lewistown. The petitioner's stance was that Lewistown was selected by "artful conduct" and that the legislature was "ultimately deceived." Accusations of "intrigue, spurious petitions, privity and connivance" were set forth in the nine points of the 1801 petition. This petition was denied by the Legislature and those below the Narrows languished, but submitted numerous requests for establishing a new county over the subsequent decades.

THE FIRST COURT HOUSE, 1790

The act establishing Mifflin County, empowered the commissioners to "build and erect a Court House and prison, suitable and convenient for the public." The language of the act implies two separate structures, but in all probability, economic reasons dictated a dual-purpose structure. This building was erected in 1790 on the site of the present jail. It was made of logs cut from the nearby forest, then standing close by.

It was two stories high with an outside staircase leading to the court room above, so as not to leave the prison rooms below exposed to the public. It was in this upper room where court was held that September, 1791, when the rioters came up from below the Long Narrows to prevent Samuel Bryson from taking his seat on the bench. - MCHS image

Taken from the petition of 1818, an excerpt states: "The old townships of Milford and Fermanagh alone in our proposed new county are now nearly as numerous and much more wealthy, and will sell for more money than all of Mifflin would have at the time of its erection, in 1789."

In 1831, Juniata gained county status. The efforts of John Cummins, Legislator from Mifflin County and resident from below the Narrows, finally turned the tide in Juniata's favor. With this background in mind, it was a citizen from below the Narrows, one Samuel Bryson, who was at the core of the 1791 disturbance.

SAMUEL BRYSON WAS RIOT'S CENTRAL FIGURE

In most historical events, nothing happens in a vacuum and in this case the spark that lit the riot's fuse was an earlier action by newly appointed associate justice Samuel Bryson. He was a store keeper from Franklin County, involved in the War of Independence and was elected a lieutenant in 1777 who served in the Second Regiment, Pennsylvania Line. Bryson married Ann Harris, the daughter of John Harris, who laid out a town upon his own land in lower Mifflin County and named it Mifflintown, in honor of Pennsylvania's first governor, Thomas Mifflin. Bryson opened a store one mile above Harris's plantation and also owned a farm and distillery on Lost Creek.

Bryson was later appointed a county lieutenant, with the right to confirm commissions. As was the custom of the day, regiments elected their own officers, who served by the popular support of the men in the ranks.

For whatever reason, the records are silent on this point, Bryson refused to commission two colonels elected by their respective regiments. This was a slap in the face, an affront to the institution, an act that would be remembered! So when Bryson, along with three other local men, received the appointment of associate justice of Mifflin County, the members of those regiments and their friends were so incensed and outraged at Bryson's elevation, they pledged that he would never serve in that capacity.

CLARKE RECOUNTS RIOT

Perhaps the most reliable eye witness account of the riot comes from deputy state's attorney John Clarke, on hand for the opening of the new court. His recollection appears in the report he submitted after the riot. Clarke took an active role in quelling the disturbance and was himself placed in mortal danger during those pivotal hours when tempers were most volatile.

That session of court was scheduled to open Monday, the 12th of September, 1791 in Mifflin County's first court house. This two story, log structure was located at the corner of Wayne and Market Streets, where the present Mifflin County Jail was built. The newly appointed associate justices, Thomas Beale, William Brown, Samuel Bryson and James Armstrong were to gather on that day. They met before noon to open the court, but Justice Beale was late, and proceedings didn't commence until three that afternoon.

When Beale did arrive in town, he was requested to accompany the other justices and the officers of the court to the court house, but he declined to go. This was to prove a sign of his fidelity and it wasn't with Bryson. The procession moved to the court house without him, where the judges' commissions were read, the court opened, and the officers and the attorneys of the court were sworn in. At this point, an adjournment was called until ten o'clock next morning.

THE MOB ARRIVES

That night, the taverns and hearth fires below the Narrows must have been witness to many an oath and invective aimed against Samuel Bryson. His rather injudicious act of not confirming those militia colonels was coming back to haunt him At nine o'clock the next morning, word arrived in Lewistown, that a large body of armed men had assembled at Jordan's Tavern on the Juniata. They were armed with guns, swords and pistols vowing

I told them they might kill me, but Judge Bryson they could not ... the words "Fire away!" were shouted through the mob. - STATE'S ATTORNEY JOHN

to proceed to the court house and remove Bryson.

State's attorney Clarke, with the concurrence of Brown, Bryson and Armstrong, agreed to dispatch Prothonotary Samuel Edmiston, Justice Beale, Sheriff George Wilson and two attorneys to proceed and meet the rioters. The court's decree to Sheriff Wilson: tell the rioters the court was alarmed at their proceedings, order the mob to disperse and restore order. Having dispatched this delegation, the principals returned business.

Court opened and prepared to get down to work with the grand jury, already impaneled and waiting. At eleven o'clock the sound of a fife echoed up the dirt streets of the county seat, heralding the approaching mob. Smoke filled the air as muskets were discharged. The angry band appeared in front of the court house! Three men on horseback were in the lead. The delegation sent to quell them walked behind, under guard. Upon their arrival, all those held were freed, except Sheriff Wilson, who was detained by four of the rioters.

The excited justices looked to Clarke. He, after all, was the representative of the Commonwealth, the state authority! They ordered him out to address the rioters. He went out and lectured the gathering, warning them of the danger of their acts. Clarke remonstrated the crowd, declaring serious consequences would result if they persisted. The unwavering mob pressed forward shouting to their leaders, "March on! March on! Draw your sword on him! Draw your sword on him! Ride over him!"

Clarke remembered:

"I seized the reins of the bridle that the principal commander held, William Wilson, brother of the Sheriff. He was well mounted and well dressed, with a sword, and, I think, two pistols belted round him, a cocked hat, and one or two feathers in it. He said he would not desist, but at all events proceed and and take Judge Bryson off the bench, and march him down the Narrows to the Judge's farm and make him sign a written paper that he would never sit as Judge again."

At this point, Wilson drew his sword, telling Clarke he would injure him unless he let go of the reins. The crowd surged forward, almost pushing Clarke to the ground. One of the mob stepped up, a nephew of Judge Beale, and pressed a cocked pistol to Clarke's chest, fully intending to shoot.

Clarke dropped the reins and kept one step ahead of the mob until he arrived at the foot of the court house steps. He met Judge Armstrong there and the two of them ascended the steps determined to defend the stairs and were quickly joined by other members of the local bar, effectively blocking the stairway to the court room.

Referring to Bryson, the mob was screaming, "March on, damn you, proceed and take him!"

Armstrong replied, "You damn'd rascals come on! We will defend the Court ourselves! And before you shall take Judge Bryson, you shall kill me and many others, which seems to be your intention and which you may do!"

One of the rioters now grabbed Armstrong's arm, hoping to pull him down the stairs, but Armstrong struggled free. A point was reached where violence seemed imminent, as the metallic swish of unsheathing swords and the clicks of

The War of Independence was a recent memory for many on both sides during the Riot of 1791. The central figure, Samuel Bryson, was elected a lieutentant in 1777 and served in the Second Regiment, Pennsylvania Line. - *Genesis of Mifflin County*

pistols being cocked could be heard amid the shouting.

Wilson threatened Clarke at sword-point and the younger Beale aimed his pistol at Clarke for a second time. "I told them they might kill me, but Judge Bryson they could not, nor should they take him. The words, 'Fire away!' were shouted through the mob. I put my hand on Wilson's shoulder and begged him to consider where he was, who I was and reflect for but one moment.

I told him to withdraw and appoint any two or three of his most respectable men to meet with me in half an hour and try to settle the dispute." With great difficulty, Wilson moved the mob away from the court house. A temporary truce followed while the principals met at Alexander's Tavern to parlay, but the meeting broke up without resolution. Outside, Clarke again talked with Wilson and others, finally reaching an agreement he felt would assuage the rioters.

Wilson agreed that if Bryson would leave the bench and not sit during this court, the mob would disperse and offer Bryson no injury or insult. The men gave their mutual pledge of honor making the agreement binding. The reality of the situation, however, was that the momentum of the mob had yet to subside. Shortly, they returned to the court house with Wilson in the lead, but a fore-warned Judge Bryson had already departed the premises.

Clarke met Wilson and the mob at the foot of the stairs and wanted to know why they had returned, in violation of their agreement. Many of the group would have none of the agreement and were bent on Bryson's harm. Clarke told them the judge was gone. While Clarke was contending with an insistent Wilson, the

younger Beale cocked and presented his pistol to Clarke's breast, for a third time. Clarke's own passion now swelled, as he wrote, "The Younger Beale...insisted that Wilson and all...should go up (to the court room) but upon my offering to decide the matter by combat with him, he declined it and by this means they went off swearing and said they were out-generaled."

The crisis began to ease.

A round 10 o'clock that night, express riders were sent down the Narrows to collect men to rescue Sheriff Wilson.

— LEWISTOWN RIOT 1791

THE RIOT NEARLY REKINDLES

Court opened the next morning without incident, but tensions still ran high. A regiment, commanded by Col. McFarland, arrived in town to defend the court, if necessary. McFarland addressed the court. The justices thanked him, but felt his services were not needed.

At this point, Bryson was still on the bench. He read a statement, recounting the ill treatment he suffered, firmly declaring that no threat of harm would prevent him from taking and keeping his seat. He entertained the agreement, however, only because of an arrangement entered into on his behalf by some of his friends, an arrangement to prevent strife in the court.

The afternoon session was to reconvene at 2 o'clock, and was commencing to do so, when the sheriff and Judge Bryson apparently got into a scuffle. Sheriff Wilson struck at Bryson and also kicked at him, at which point Judge Armstrong forcibly restrained the sheriff and demanded order in the court.

Sheriff Wilson was immediately replaced by the Coroner and brought before the bench. A brief stay in jail was suggested and ordered. Sheriff Wilson went without incident. When word of the sheriff's detention reached beyond the walls of the court house, it didn't take long for some seventy men to gather. Shouting "Liberty or Death!" they attempted a rescue of the sheriff. Perhaps he saw the error of his action or the danger it provoked, for Wilson refused to be released by this mob.

Around 10 o'clock that night, express riders were sent down the Narrows to collect men to rescue Sheriff Wilson. This conjures an image of a Paul Revere-like ride, with galloping horses pounding through a moonless night, calling the faithful to arms! These were militia veterans, who saw service defending the frontier during the War of Independence. They knew for what they fought and the sheriff would be released!

Next morning, Clarke was informed that nearly three hundred men were assembled below the Narrows, ready for action. That number might be questioned, but not wishing to reprise the previous day's events, another delegation was sent down the Narrows. Several gentleman, according to Clarke, went to assure this gathering that Sheriff Wilson was released and they need take no further action. Happily for all concerned, this mob broke up without incident. The Riot of 1791 was over.

EPILOGUE

Judge Samuel Bryson outlasted the mob. Despite the riot, he was not forced to retire from the bench. In fact, he was appointed, along with Brown, Armstrong and Beale, to serve in the newly created Fourth Judicial District, which held its first session in December, 1791 at the very scene of the fracas, the court house in Lewistown. He died eight years later at age forty-eight.

Sheriff Wilson was released from jail and apologized to the court for his rash actions against Bryson. He served as sheriff of Mifflin County until his commission expired in 1792. William Wilson became the new sheriff on November 6 of that year.

Deputy State's Attorney John Clarke filed his report with Thomas Smith, President Judge of the Fourth Judicial District. In it he stated Judge Beale refused to sit with Bryson during the time of the riot and said so from the bench. Beale likely knew of the mob's plan, based upon his lateness that morning and refusal to walk with the other justices on their way to court. He also seemed to condone the actions of the rioters.

John Clarke made one final observation in the matter of the Riot of 1791. He noted in his report to Judge Smith, "I must now close the narrative with saying that, owing to the firmness of Judge Armstrong and the whole of the bar, I was enabled to avert the dreadful blow aimed at Judge Bryson...but unless the most vigorous measures are exerted soon, it will be impossible ever to support the laws of the State in that country or to punish those who transgress."

A lawless country or the growing pains of the new county and nation?

The War of Independence was a recent memory for many on both sides of the riot. George Washington was in his first term in 1791. Earlier that same year, he had personally selected the site for the proposed federal district on the Potomac River. Construction of the White House would begin the next year and the United States Capitol in two.

Congress enacted the Whiskey Act in 1791, setting an excise tax on distilled liquors and stills. Mifflin County's riot would be but a footnote in U.S. history, compared to the chapter on the Whiskey Rebellion of Western Pennsylvania in 1794 resulting from that tax. It tested the very concept of national unity. The workings of government were just being broken in. After all, Mifflin County had to wait seven more years for its first post office. Yet in the struggle to establish the new nation, the Riot of 1791 mirrored the country's growing pains. It remains a stirring illustration of Mifflin County's unique heritage.

Mifflin County Trivia

"When Mifflin and Juniata were one County"

The Western Star.

N° X.   VOLUME V.

LEWISTOWN, (*Pennsylv.*) PRINTED BY *EDWARD COLE*, where SUBSCRIPTIONS, ADVERTISEMENTS, ESSAYS, ARTICLES OF INTELLIGENCE, &c. Are received ; and Printing executed with CARE and DISPATCH.

PRICE—SINGLE, SIX CENTS]   MONDAY, May 13, 1805.   [TEN DOLLARS per ANNUM,

These questions on local history are from one of the county's early newspapers, *The Western Star*. It was established in 1800 and continued until 1807, at a time when Juniata and Mifflin were still one, with an office in Lewistown, Edward Cole editor/ publisher. The Mifflin County Historical Society has about 70 copies on microfilm. Twenty original copies of the newspaper were presented to the historical society by Dr. S. M. R. Reynolds of Chicago prior to 1964. His ancestor, Robert Means, was the subscriber whose name appears on the front page.

1. *The Western Star* of February 19, 1801 announced the arrangements for a grand celebration, suitable to the importance of the occasion, to be held in Lewistown. Tickets could be purchased for the March 4 event and donations to defray expenses were solicited. What was the special event?
[a] Celebration in honor of the victory of Thomas Jefferson and Aaron Burr in the 1800 election.
[b] Anniversary banquet honoring the county's men who saw service in the Revolutionary War.
[c] Community gathering to witness the drawing of the winners of the Susquehanna and Juniata Lottery, with profits used for waterway improvement.
[d] Welcoming Pennsylvania Governor Thomas McKean.

2. In 1800, Juniata County was still part of Mifflin County. Mifflintown manufacturer Samuel Jackson advertised in *The Western Star* in 1801 seeking a product for which he was willing to pay 18 cents a pound. He stated that if local people could provide it, he wouldn't have to purchase the product from Russia, thus keeping money in the local economy. What was Jackson trying to by locally?
[a] Lambs wool for blanket making.   [b] Hog bristles for brush making.
[c] Fish bones for fertilizer.   [d] Silica sand for enamel ware.

3. In 1802, *The Western Star* reported on action the Pennsylvania General Assembly was taking regarding the county's namesake, Thomas Mifflin. An inquiry was initiated, according to the newspaper, that would investigate something concerning Mifflin. What was being investigated?

[a] The proposition of moving Thomas Mifflin's remains to a burial plot in Mifflin County.

[b] Granting a request to deed a tract of land in Mifflin County back to the former governor's heirs.

[c] To find out if the documents naming the county after Thomas Mifflin were correctly executed in 1789.

[d] Determining the condition of Thomas Mifflin's grave and establish perpetual care, if necessary.

4. Also in 1802, *The Western Star* noted that horse races would be held in Lewistown, run in two purses. This was held at the fairground of its day, a place in town commonly referred to at that time as the Bullet Ground. (This was an area eastward from Valley Street above Marble Street, including what is now a portion of the Logan Street and Shaw Avenue area.) How did the Bullet Ground get its name?

[a] An early lead smelting factory was located in that part of town.

[b] A corruption of a sign that read "Bull to Let" at an earlier established cattle breeding pen situated there.

[c] A training ground where local militia shot mark and regularly drilled.

[d] An early owner of the ground once proclaimed, "That ground's like plowing bullets!" The term stuck.

5. In the May 13, 1805 issue of *The Western Star*, Mifflin County's third newspaper, a specialized school was opened by Blondel de St. Hilasse in Lewistown. Was his school for...

[a] French cooking   [b] European team fencing   [c] oil painting   [d] dancing

TRIVIA ANSWERS: 1. a   2. b   3. d   4. c   5. d

12 - Remember the Alamo! Mifflin County's Contribution to Texas Independence

*B*y 6:30 a.m. March 6, 1836, the last of the firing was over. The Alamo had fallen. It had been besieged for 13 days by a Mexican force numbering over 4,000 men, including infantry, artillery and cavalry. This army was led by General Antonio Lopez de Santa Anna and gave no quarter to the defenders. All 189 were overwhelmed and put to the sword.

The names of the defeated are legendary - William Barret Travis, James Bowie,

Davy Crockett. Travis was commander of the Alamo and was killed early in the fighting of March 6. Bowie was co-commander and was killed in his sick bed. Crockett was 50 years old when he died. The officers numbered 28. Volunteers made up the remainder of the compliment - 30 from South Carolina, 15 from Tennessee, 32 from the Gonzales area of Texas and 81 from different countries and other states. The volunteers from Gonzales are known in Texas history as the Immortal Thirty-two, the only fighters to respond to a plea for help during the thirteen day siege.

Yet among those killed that day over one hundred sixty-two years ago, ten were from Pennsylvania. Mifflin County claims three of those who died at the Alamo - David Porter Cummings, Jr., William McDowell and John Purdy Reynolds. Why did these young men make their way to such a place of destiny?

Start with Horace Greeley's words - "If any young man is about to commence in the world, with little to his circumstances to prepossess him in favor of one section or another, we say to him publicly and privately, Go to the West; there your capacities are sure to be appreciated and your industry and energy rewarded."

This advice, often paraphrased as, "Go West, young man!" was put forward by Greely, editor of the New York Tribune in the 1850s. His counsel came years too late for Mifflin County's Alamo defenders. Yet the sentiment imparted by his words - young men longing for adventure, seeking their fortune and leaving home for a new life - were likely the enticements that lured Cummings, Reynolds and McDowell on their fatefully westward journey ending at San Antonio.

The gold-seeking 49ers were drawn to California to "See the elephant," strike it rich and return home wealthy men. Hardships, described during the Gold Rush era as "Seeing the tail of the elephant," adversity so harsh as to send the faint-hearted scurrying home, were found in Texas, as well. California held gold, but Texas held an equally irresistible lure decades before the Gold Rush. Texas offered the tangible promise of land and something intangible, a new country.

In the years 1835 and 1836, Mifflin County newspapers were filled with news from Texas and stories of the struggle for independence from Mexico. There was a great flow of emigration from northern states into Texas. Two of the Mifflin County men, David P. Cummings, Jr., and John Purdy Reynolds were drawn there and with their departure westward, local interest in the events in Texas were greatly heightened. William McDowell is believed to have made his way to Tennessee and then to Texas.

DAVID PORTER CUMMINGS, JR.

Cummings is perhaps the most written about of the Mifflin County Alamo threesome, both locally and in Texas. A chance meeting in the 1960s with local historical society members and a Cummings relative, added to the body of information.

Col. and Mrs. Donald G. Lambert of Southport, Maine, visited with Mr. and Mrs. J. Martin Stroup of the Mifflin County Historical Society in 1964. Mrs. Lambert was a descendent of the Cummings family, and greatly enlarged the society's file of facts on this Alamo hero.

David's father, Major David Cummings, was a local supporter of the Texas cause. Although his home was in Connellsville, he spent much time in Lewistown in the 1830s during construction of the canal. He had served in the

David Porter Cummings
Marker at Hill Grove Cemetery, Connellsville, PA. His father, two brothers and three sisters are also buried at Hill Grove. - MCHS photo

War of 1812 and was taken captive at the Battle of Beaver Dam in Canada. Maj. Cummings was sent to England where along with other prisoners of war he was held in the old prison of Dartmoor. He was paroled after six months in a prisoner exchange.

After the war he found his way to Fayette County as a mail contractor, finally settling in Connellsville. Maj. Cummings represented Fayette County in the Legislature and is said to have supported the concept of establishing a public school system. Alas, this was a very controversial issue and he was defeated for re-election.

When the Juniata Canal was planned, Cummings moved to Lewistown and built the section between Lewistown and Huntingdon in 1830. He married a Cecil County, Maryland girl, Elizabeth Cathers in 1801. They had twelve children, six sons and six daughters. The Major died in Lewistown in 1848 and is buried in Connellsville.

David, Jr. lived locally with his sister, Mrs. Thomas McKee, and grew up with his friend, John Purdy Reynolds. It's not known if Reynolds and Cummings journeyed together, but their mutual interest in the west, love of adventure, the draw of a new country to be won and settled compelled them to leave home for Texas.

David, Sr. bought a case of rifles from the State Arsenal in Harrisburg and sent it with his son to the Texas cause. The young Cummings learned the surveyor's trade, which he would later put to use. He traveled to Gonzales and then Bexar where he joined the Alamo garrison in January or February, 1836. While surveying land on the Cibolo Creek, he was met by the Gonzales Ranger force and entered the Alamo with them.

The Daughters of the Republic of Texas honor Cummings as a member of the Immortal Thirty-two, men distinguished by the fact that they were the only Texans to respond to the appeal of Col. Travis for help while surrounded by Santa Anna's forces. The 32 men actually penetrated Mexican lines to join the doomed fighters in the Alamo. It is believed Cummings went to Texas by boat from New Orleans in December, 1835 and by foot to San Felipe where he sold a rifle for $30.

Insight into Cummings view of the situation in Texas, prior to the Alamo defeat, are included in his letters to his father - January from Gonzales and February from San Antonio and were reprinted in local newspapers during the time period. His two letters, which follow, appeared in the Lewistown *Republican* in 1836.

Gonzales Texas Jany 20th 1836
Dear Father
The scarcity of paper together with other difficulties I have had to labor under has

---

LEWISTOWN REPUBLICAN
APRIL 12, 1836

It is more than probable that our late fellow townsman, David Cummings, Jr. whose letter we published in our last number, fell at the massacre, in the Alamo of San Antonio. He was a young man, twenty-one years of age, and his untimely fate is sincerely lamented by his relations, and numerous friends in this place.

At the request of several persons we have inserted the notice below.

TO THE RESCUE.

A meeting of the citizens of Lewistown, and Mifflin county, favourable to the adoption of measures to aid and assist our brethren in Texas, will be held at the court house, on SATURDAY EVENING next.

[Gazette please copy.]

TO THE RESCUE: Mifflin County newspapers like the *Lewistown Republican*, reported on events in Texas.

112

prevented me from writing before this and indeed it is a matter of Claim whether this letter will ever reach the United States. I arrived at the mouth of the Brazos about a month ago in a vessel from New Orleans and have traveled on foot by San Felipe to this place leaving my trunk with books, and two rifles with Mr. White at Columbia 10 miles above Brasoria having sold my best rifle for $30 at San Felipe. I saw Genl. Houston and Presented him your letter. He advised me to get a horse & proceed to Goliad where he would see me in a short time again. I have accordingly come on thus far with that intention as to connect myself with a Company of Rangers on the Frontiers to keep off the Indians, But it is most probable I will go on to San Antonio de Bexar and there remain until I can suitably connect myself with the Army or until an occasion may require my services. Every man in this country at this time has to go upon his own footing as the Government at present is unable to make any provisions for the Army. However a change for the better is expected soon and affairs is expected to be in a better condition. Provisions are very scarce here and traveling or living is attended with considerable expense--- All owing to the great number of Volunteers from the U. States besides the Emigration of Families into the upper Colonies is unprecedented for the past five months. Though under rather indifferent circumstances myself at this time, I have no reason to complain of my coming to this country as I find nothing but what might have been expected. On the contrary I have the satisfaction of beholding one of the finest countries in the world and have fully determined to locate myself in Texas I hope to be better situated to write you more about this country, and as I have not much time Can say very little at present, More than inform you what I am about &c &c. A Gentleman is going East to day by whom I intend Sending my letter. Letters have been intercepted to the Mexican citizens of Bexar informing them of the arrival of 2,000 troops on the Rio Grande, and now coming on to retake that place in consequence of which, Many of the Mexicans have secretly left the place, and prepar- ations are now making to fortify the town. All our Troops have been ordered to Copano to proceed against Matamoras.
I remain yours Affectionately
D.P. Cummings

San Antonio de Bexar   February 14th 1836
Dear Father
I wrote you from Gonzales and soon after left ther for this place, yet under different views from what I stated in as a sudden attack was expected on our garrison here and were called on for assistance. It is however fully ascertained that we have nothing of the kind to apprehend before a month or six weeks as the Enemy have not yet crossed the Rio Grande 180 mi. distant from this place nor are they expected to make any movement this way until the weather becomes warm or until the grass is sufficiently up to support their horses we conceive it however important to be prepared as a heavy attack is expected from Sant Ana himself in the Spring as no doubt the despot will use every possible means and strain every nerve to conquer and exterminate us from the land---in this we have no fear and are

113

confident that Texas cannot only sustain what she now holds but take Mexico itself did She think on conquest. The northern Indians have joined to our assistance and the volunteers from the United States are every day flocking to our ranks which from the liberal promises of the Government and desirable resources of the Country seem determined to sustain themselves or sinke in the attempt, Many it is true have left the country and returned home to their friends and pleasures but of such Texas has no use for and her agents in the U.States should be careful whom they send us for assistance we want men of determined spirits, that can undergo hardships and deprivation Otherwise they are only a pest and expense to their fellow Soldiers-to the first class (tho I would be the last to advise in any case), I say come on, there is a fine field open to you all no matter how you are situated or what may be your circumstances. At least come and see the country, as a farmer, mechanic or a Soldier you will do well-I believe no country offers such strong inducements to Emigration, affording all the conviences of life that man can devise-what I write is from my own observation and from what I hear from those who have resided for years in the Country. I am to leave this to return to the Cibilo Creek in company with 10 others to take up, our lands we get as citizens which is more then 1100 acres for single men, men of family 4428 acres our volunteer pay is 20$ per month & 640 acres at close of war. Any communication to San Felipe de Austin you may make with postage paid to the Boundary line I will get or send to Stiles Duncan Natchitoches, he could mail it to San Felipe as I would be very glad to hear from you all. It might be that I might be of some benefit to you here provided any of you could have a mind to come out and indeed to speak sincearly this would be the Country for us all, nothing could induce me from my determination of settling here, tho my disposition may not be like most others. I should like you could once see it.-a visit by Jonathan would improve his health I have been very healthy since I have been here and am improving.

Yours affectionately,
D. P. Cummings

P.S. There is one thing might be proper for me to add members have been elected to a convention of all Texas to meet on Ist March, which will make an immediate declaration of independence--upon the faith of this event great speculation is going on in Lands, tho the office for the disposal of the public lands is not yet opened but is expected will be in a Short time. The price of Land has risen greatly since the commencement of the war, and a declaration of Independence will bring them to vie with those of the U. States tho---they can be purchased from 50 cts to 5$ per acre by the League depending as their improvement. Or convenience to settlements---not Country is now settling faster---As I will most likely be engaged in surveying of public lands I might be of service to some of our friends in procuring disirable or choice locations.
D. P. Cummings

JOHN PURDY REYNOLDS

Born on March 14, 1808, John Purdy Reynolds was the son of David and Polly Reynolds. David Reynolds was a prominent citizen of Lewistown. He helped build the Juniata section of the Pennsylvania Canal. Later he was a general dealer in merchandise, using the canal to ship goods to eastern markets. In 1809, David Reynolds was appointed by Governor Snyder as county register of wills, clerk of the orphan's court and recorder of deeds. He also served as county judge from 1823 until his death in 1839.

John Purdy Reynolds completed his undergraduate studies, by some sources, at Franklin College in Lancaster County, and studied medicine in Philadelphia.

Local historian J. Martin Stroup of the Mifflin County Historical Society, conducted

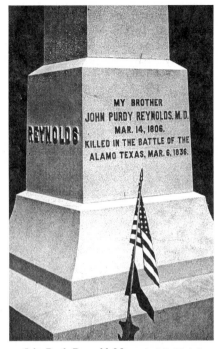

John Purdy Reynolds Monument, St. Marks' Cemetery, Lewistown, PA. Believed to be the only monument memorializing the Alamo battle outside of Texas.

extensive research in the 1960s into this area of Reynold's life. He found authentic sources that indicate he practiced medicine prior to leaving for Texas. It was common at this time to associate oneself with an established physician to practice and train to become a doctor, but the exact location could not be found for Reynold's training.

His family believed him to be a doctor, as well. The Reynold's family erected a marker at St. Mark's Cemetery in Lewistown which bears this inscription:

"My Brother, John Purdy Reynolds, M.D., March 14, 1806, killed in the Battle of the Alamo, Texas, March 6, 1836."

How did Reynolds reach Texas? Contemporary accounts in the local newspapers say that he went to Texas for the express purpose of aiding the Texans in their fight to win freedom from Mexico. It is entirely possible he did, as some accounts suggest, travel to Texas via Tennessee with the legendary Davy Crockett and his volunteers. In fact, some sources call him the medical officer or senior medical officer, yet records from San Antonio don't list him as such.

Reynolds was certainly acquainted with David P. Cummings, growing up together in Lewistown. In addition, both boys were cousins of Stephen Cummings, who founded, with John W. Shugart, *The Lewistown Republican and Working Man's Advocate.* It is perhaps this relationship that caused Wallace L. McKeehan in his *Sons of DeWitt Colony Texas* to assert that "cousins" Reynolds and Cummings came to Texas together.

Yet a tantalizing letter suggests Reynolds made the journey with another Mifflin Countian, William M. McDowell.

WILLIAM M. MCDOWELL

For over a century after the siege of the Alamo, the roster of the dead listed William M. McDowell as a volunteer from Tennessee. This changed when a spirited correspondence began between Walter Lord, author of the Alamo history, *A Time to Stand,* and J. Martin Stroup of the Mifflin County Historical Society.

In a letter to Stroup, dated November 23, 1960, Lord states:

"From time to time you have thoughtfully forwarded me information on David Cummings and John Purdy Reynolds....and now I would like to show my appreciation in a far better way than mere words: I have found a third man from Mifflin County in the Alamo! This third man is William McDowell....I do believe Mifflin County must lead all other areas in the East in supplying Alamo defenders!

An exhilarated Stroup wrote just three days later, "Your letter about William McDowell and the Alamo gave us quite a thrill."

Documents, found by Lord in the University of Texas Archives in Austin, revealed McDowell moved from Mifflin County to Henderson County, Tennessee. He left for Texas from there with Reynolds, according to a letter from McDowell's brother, George McDowell, to the Vice President of Texas dated Oct. 9, 1837.

George was writing from Lycoming County, Pa., trying to find out if his brother had been killed in another Texas battle. He wrote:

" I will proceed to inform you that my brother, William McDowell a resident for several years of Henderson, Co., Tennessee, but a native of Mifflin County Pennsylvania...left Tennessee with his friend John Purdy Reynolds (M.D.) also a native of Mifflin County..." On the historian's research scale of one to ten, a discovery like this rates an eleven!

With McDowell now counted among the Mifflin County heroes, the stage was set for a local ceremony to honor their memory.

LOCAL CEREMONY HONORS THREE

A "Remember the Alamo" ceremony was held on March 7, 1959, sponsored by the Mifflin County Historical Society. This event occurred, although not always on a March date, for several years when the observance was interrupted. After a lapse of almost thirty years, the ceremony of remembrance was reestablished in 1990.

The event began anew, due to the joint efforts of Paul Bryan of Mifflin County and Jim Dearing of Centre County. Held annually at St. Mark's Cemetery in

Lewistown, the ceremony recognizes and remembers these local heroes. It is scheduled for the Saturday that falls closest to March 6.

The governor's office of Texas sent a Texas State Flag to the ceremony organizers. It is displayed at the Reynolds monument during the proceedings each year. Bryan noted in his remarks at the 1990 ceremony, "It was a long time coming. It's only fitting that we should honor brave men like these who fought and died for the freedom we take for granted."

So, Remember the Alamo! It's part of our Mifflin County heritage.

FLINTLOCK ENSHRINED AT THE ALAMO MAY HAVE MIFFLIN COUNTY LINK

How did a Pennsylvania rifle, now displayed in Texas, find its way to the Alamo? Was it brought to that historic battle by John Purdy Reynolds, or one of Mifflin County's other Alamo heroes, William McDowell or David Cummings? It seems that the answers will forever remain a mystery, but circumstantial evidence may point to some possibilities.

Stock details of a Dickert
Pennsylvania Rifle -
Early American Gunsmiths
by H. J. Kauffman, 1952

One gun - proclaimed, by the April 27, 1924 edition of the *San Antonio Light*, as "the only weapon from the actual fighting" - was put on display in Texas earlier this century. Found in 1874 during an excavation of the Alamo's surface floor, it was kept in private hands until its presentation to the Alamo for public view in 1924. That gun was attributed to the Frenchman - and historically elusive - Louis Moses Rose, who claimed to have fought in Napoleon's army. It was proclaimed at the time, by U. S. Army and other experts, to be of French origin, Napoleonic of type and age, possessing higher qualities than the average weapon of 1836. But Rose fled the Alamo prior to the final assault, was illiterate, and made many unsubstantiated claims after the battle. This gun remains a dubious relic, at best.

But what of the flintlock, the only rifle on display at the Shrine of Texas Liberty at the Alamo in San Antonio, Texas, can it be traced to Pennsylvania?

The rifle was found, according to Steve Beck, assistant curator, Library of the Daughters of the Republic of Texas, by a Mexican peon after the battle. He concealed it under debris. The peon was assisting in the gruesome job of carrying the dead to the funeral pyre. That grim task completed, the peasant concealed the rifle and later turned it over to Col. Frederick W. Johnson of the Texas Army. In 1839, Col. Johnson presented the rifle to the first mayor of St. Louis, William Carr Lane. From Lane, it passed to his successor, William L. Ewing, and later to Mayor Henry Kock. Colonel Walter T. Siegmund of East Alton, Ill., purchased it from Kock's family and returned it to the Alamo. Today it is enshrined with a ring worn by Alamo commander William B. Travis and an original mission bell.

The 60-inch, .58 caliber rifle of Pennsylvania design bears the the maker's name on the barrel, "J. Dickert." Believed to be Jacob Dickert, an eminent gunsmith from Lancaster County, famous for his finely crafted guns. Dickert was born in Maintz, Germany and came to America in 1748 with his parents. He established his gun shop in 1762. Moravian Church records show he died in 1822, age 82.

Unfortunately, Dickert kept no written records of his rifle sales. John Purdy Reynolds was believed to have been an undergraduate at Franklin College at Lancaster. Did he buy a Dickert rifle then and take it with him to Texas? No records, letters, or other documents have turned up to clarify this point.

It is known Reynolds moved to Tennessee and eventually left there with McDowell for the Texas territories. Sources point to Reynolds leaving Tennessee with Davy Crockett's group, although some Crockett biographies never mention Reynolds as one of his "boys."

The Tennessee volunteers did carry rifles of the Pennsylvania variety and at the time of its presentation to the Alamo in 1947, it was thought this rifle might have been Crockett's famous "Betsey." Careful research dimmed that hope, however, revealing that the excitement was generated by a chance remark. One of Crockett's great-grandsons thought it "looked like" the rifle seen in sketches of their celebrated ancestor.

Time honored stories tell of the deadly effect these rifles had in holding the Mexican onslaught at bay during the Alamo siege. By most accounts, the Tennessee "boys" did give an accounting of themselves, but the defenders could never have traded shot for shot with the overwhelming numbers in the assaulting army at the Alamo.

The actual owner, most likely, will never be known. It is tantalizing to imagine, however, that this Pennsylvania long rifle may have traveled the long journey from Lancaster to Lewistown to the Alamo!

From the Pages of...

The Lewistown Gazette
February 7, 1877

"Don Pedro Club Celebrates Ground Hog Day"

 Those carefree, amusement-loving, jolly, fond-of-anything-that's-good-to-eat junior bachelor businessmen of the town are making merry. Specializing in their usual mix of feasting and song, the Don Pedro Club held a banquet, which seems to be the first time in the annals of Lewistown, that celebrated the virtues of the ground hog. This club had we don't know how many men out for we don't know how many days prior to the dinner scouring the countryside for the elusive woodchuck, intent on making a meal of his wild flesh. But alas, for the insatiate members the game would not bite! So they were compelled to eat common hog and called him "Proxy."

13 - William Henry Harrison's Log Cabin

N *o matter how far and wide you roam, there often seems to be a Mifflin County connection in some very unexpected places. Take for example a bus tour in the late 1990s made by members of the Mifflin County Historical Society.*

William Henry Harrison
(1773 - 1841)
Image from *The True Republican*, 1847 - MCHS

While visiting the stately homes of Virginia, the hardy band of Mifflin County historians came to Berkeley Plantation, on the James River, the ancestral home of two U.S. Presidents, William Henry Harrison (1773 - 1841) and his grandson, Benjamin Harrison (1833 - 1901). During the walk through Berkeley, Dan McClenahen, tour member and the society's resident specialist on all things Mifflin County, revealed the county connection to the first President Harrison.

The Whig Party's symbol during the election of 1840 was the log cabin and it was a local boy, Richard S. Elliott, who created the Whig emblem so popular at the time. It was the election that also coined the slogan, "Tippecanoe and Tyler, too." William Henry Harrison and John Tyler against the incumbent president, Martin Van Buren and vice-president Richard Johnson. The latter ran in 1837 on the slogan "Rumpsey-dumpsey, rumpsey-dumpsey, Colonel Johnson killed Tecumseh!"

During the heat of the campaign, a Democratic newspaper editorialized that all Harrison wanted in life was a two thousand dollar pension, plenty of hard cider, and a log cabin. His supporters pounced upon the idea and claimed their man had indeed been **born** in a log cabin, though Berekley Plantation could hardly qualify as such a humble abode, his campaign overlooked that detail.

The Whigs assembled parades that included log cabin floats and barrels of hard cider. The log cabin appeared on badges and supporters composed log cabin songs, with lines like these:

Let Van from his coolers of silver drink wine
And lounge on his cushioned settee.
Our man on his buckeye bench can recline;
Content with hard cider is he.

Harrison beat Van Buren that November, but spoke for two hours in a cold March rain during his inauguration, contracted a cold that developed into pneumonia and was dead by April 4, 1841, serving only thirty-one days. The excerpt below is from the *Historic Souvenir of Lewistown, Penna.*, published by The Sentinel Company in 1925, which details the Harrison - Mifflin County connection.

DID YOU KNOW? - That it was a native Lewistown printer boy, Richard Smith Elliott, a son of Maj. William P. Elliott, who when just out of his teens made the first drawing of the Log Cabin adopted and exclusively used as a party emblem in the exciting campaign of 1840, when General William Henry Harrrison was the Whig candidate for President of the United States?

Young Elliott took his cue from a Baltimore paper supporting Van Buren for reelection, who in an editorial had referred to general Harrison sitting in a log cabin with a barrel of cider as his companion and after a conversation

 with Mr. Thomas Elder, in the old stone mansion built by John Harris at Harrisburg, it was arranged that Elliott should produce a model of the cabin. - *Historic Souvenir of Lewistown, Penna.* 1925.

Harrison's Log Cabin - An American icon created by Mifflin Countian, Richard S. Elliott for Harrison's 1840 campaign. This image is from the masthead of Horace Greeley's paper *The Log Cabin*. The paper sold some 80,000 copies each week, and the *New York Times* called it "the most effective campaign paper ever printed." This image appeared in the April 10, 1841 edition that announced Harrison's untimely death. - Author's collection

14 - Fifty Years in Chains
A slave narrative first published in Mifflin County

*U*ncle Tom's Cabin, the novel by Harriet Beecher Stowe, was conceived out of her scorching abolitionist convictions. The tale was written in 1851, and appeared in stage adaptations for over twenty-five years. An 1852 stage production gave us our modern impressions of characters like Little Eva racing across the ice floe just steps ahead of the seething bloodhounds or the foul villainy of Simon Legree. Such impressions stirred audiences to swoon, for many, Uncle Tom's Cabin was their first theatre experience.*

"**Uncle Tom's Cabin** has become almost world-wide in its currency and fame. Songs founded on its more affecting incidents are beginning to be sung at nearly every house." -- *New York Daily Tribune*, September 19, 1853 - *Author's Collection*

The **melodrama** had an overpowering effect against slavery in much of the United States, Europe and even the Orient, gaining for Uncle Tom a place as the most celebrated fictional character of the era. "Uncle Tom" and "Simon Legree" even became part of the language. Some argue Uncle Tom helped bring on the Civil War. Abraham Lincoln is said to have commented when meeting Mrs. Stowe, "So you're the little woman who made the book that made this great war."

Two decades earlier, a small book written in Mifflin County swept many parts of the country with as much abolitionist fervor as Uncle Tom's Cabin. It wasn't a fictional Uncle Tom, but the firsthand account of Charles Ball, slave and runaway. In graphic detail, this narrative was recounted to a Lewistown attorney and published by a Mifflin County printer in 1836, but the title became obscured with time. The volume rests with the other rare books in the historical society's vault. It's appears very ordinary, with a well worn, dark brown leather cover, but covers can be deceiving.

1836 local newspaper advertisement for *The Life nand Adventures of Charles Ball, a Black Man* - MCHS Archives

This rare book is titled *The Life and Adventures of Charles Ball, a Black Man* and is the life story of an escaped slave, Charles Ball, who lived in Mifflin County in the 1830s. Ball's life story chronicles his birth in Maryland to a slave mother, of being sold into slavery and sent to the deep South to work on cotton plantations in the Carolinas and Georgia. He escaped twice, but was captured and returned to his owners. Ball spent one year's service in the U.S. Navy under Commodore Barney during the War of 1812.

He stowed away on a cotton boat bound for Philadelphia on a third and successful attempt to escape. Ball was helped by Quakers to move further north and eventually settled in Lewistown. It was at that time Charles Ball dictated his life story, eventually to become a sensation twenty years before Harriet Beecher Stowe's famous *Uncle Tom's Cabin.*

The title *Fifty Years in Chains* came later, originally it was written as *Slavery in America - The Life and Adventures of Charles Ball* by Mifflin County attorney Isaac Fisher and published by John W. Shugert of Lewistown in 1836. This was the first edition of Ball's narrative, with a second and third editions being published by John S. Taylor of New York in 1837. In the late 1960s, Dover Publications and Kraus Reprints, reprinted the narrative, but not before the true origins of the book were revealed.

LOCAL HISTORIAN CONTACTED BY NEW YORK PUBLISHERS

The late J. Martin Stroup, Mifflin County Historical Society past president and Lewistown Sentinel editor, was contacted by Dover Publications in 1969. Dover wanted to reprint Charles Ball's narrative, but found some clouded history concerning the initial publication of the book. Stroup was also contacted by Philip S. Foner, Professor of History at Lincoln University of Pennsylvania, editor of the reprint for Dover Publications.

Foner and Dover wanted to know more about the author, attorney Isaac Fisher. Ball retold his story verbally to Fisher, who wrote down the accounts over some period of time. Ball told him about his punishments for trying to escape, the slave auctions, daily chores of a slave, and the treatment meted out to slaves in that part of the South for even minor offenses. The publisher wanted to know something of the voracity of Isaac Fisher, who is credited in the Taylor editions of 1837 with being an honest author in a most unusual way - through a letter.

PROMINENT MEN ATTEST TO FISHER'S AUTHENTICITY

In the introduction to the 1837 editions from New York, two prominent Lewistown men gave testimonials affirming the facts stated in the book. A letter from David W. Hulings, local attorney and founder of an early county newspaper *The Mifflin Eagle* and W. P. Elliott, justice of the peace and one of the founders of the *Lewistown Gazette,* is included in this introduction. It is dated July 18, 1836 and states, in part: *...we know the black man whose narrative is given in this book....that we have heard him relate the principal matters contained in the book concerning himself, long before the book was published.*

Who was the author of Ball's story? A puzzling fact is that Fisher's name doesn't appear in area histories of members of the Mifflin County Bar.

J. Martin Stroup finally came across information about Fisher in a 1945 article in the *Daily News* of Huntingdon, Pa., written by Albert M. Rung under the title, "Notables Now Forgotten."

THE AUTHOR REVEALED

Much of what Rung learned of Fisher came from the memoirs of Richard S. Elliott, son of W. P. Elliott. This memoir, a copy of which is in the society's research library, credits Isaac Fisher with authoring the narrative of Charles Ball.

Fisher was born in Delaware in the late 1700s or early 1800s and studied the law in that state at an early age. Ultimately he became a member of the Delaware Bar. He later toured various parts of the country, including the South. The memoir reveals that Fisher's uncompromising stand against slavery can be traced to that time in his life.

Eventually he returned to Pennsylvania, settling in York and then Lewistown, where he resided for over twenty years. Fisher was admitted to the Huntingdon County Bar, but no reason can be found to explain why he never joined the Mifflin County Bar.

During his 1835 tour of Pennsylvania by canal packet, Senator Henry Clay stopped in Lewistown for a visit. No less a person then Isaac Fisher was chosen to make the welcoming speech for Senator Clay. Unfortunately, history never noted all of Fisher's words of welcome. One of the local newspapers did record Fisher's concluding sentence of Clay: "Sir, your fame is as broad and deathless as the winds of Heaven." Also recorded was that "Clay's countenance indicated he never heard the like before."

Fisher moved to Huntingdon in 1843 and lived there until his death in 1858. A lifelong bachelor, Isaac Fisher is buried in Huntingdon County.

THE LIFE OF
CHARLES BALL
The tragedy of Charles Ball's life
and most slaves born at this time, is one of chance. When he was

A man who is master of only four or five slaves is generally the most ready of all to apprehend a run-away, whom he happen to catch straying from his plantation; and generally whips him the most unmercifully for his offense.

The law gives him the same right to arrest the person of a slave seen traveling without his pass that it vests in the owner of five-hundred Negroes...petty tyrants are the most oppressive... - Charles Ball

born in the late 1780s, slavery was all but dead in the North and dying in the South. Slavery existed all across colonial America. In Mifflin County for example, the 1790 census reveals that 17 families owned a total of thirty-one slaves.

Quaker Pennsylvania passed the first emancipation act in 1780 progressively freeing slaves over time, while thoughtful Southerners like Jefferson and Washington felt that slavery would eventually end. A French visitor to the South noted "they are constantly talking about abolishing slavery and of contriving other means of cultivating their estates."

The old plantation system was built on tobacco, rice and indigo. Few growers planted sea-island cotton, then mostly along the Carolina coast. Separating the cotton seeds from the lint was a costly proposition, so from a purely economic view, slavery just didn't pay as the 1700s waned.

Enter Eli Whitney and his Cotton Engine or "gin." Suddenly, an economical method of removing seeds from the lint was at hand and at the same time the world's textile mills discovered cotton. When the importation of slaves was prohibited by acts of Congress, those slaves already in the United States suddenly became more valuable.

It was during this transition to a one crop cotton economy in the South that Charles Ball found himself. He described that his own worth as a slave was dependent on how fast he could pick cotton. Whether he was a prime field hand commanding top dollar or a lower ranked worker hinged on this ability.

Excerpts from Charles Ball's *Fifty Years in Chains*:

Working on Sunday...

While in the Cotton South, Georgia or South Carolina, Ball was able to work for others on Sunday and keep what he earned. He explained,

I often hired myself to work on Sunday, and have been employed in this way by more than twenty different persons, not one of whom insulted or maltreated me in any way...The practice of working on Sunday is so universal amongst the slaves on the cotton plantations, that the immorality of the matter is never spoken of.

Ball related that Sunday was no different than any other day on the plantation. No special set of clean clothing on Sunday. In fact, clean clothes were reserved for Monday, since Sunday was wash day on their cotton plantations.

Types of slave owners...

A man who is master of only four or five slaves is generally the most ready of all to apprehend a runaway, whom he happen to catch straying from his plantation; and generally whips him the most unmercifully for his offense.

The law gives him the same right to arrest the person of a slave seen traveling without his pass that it vests in the owner of five-hundred Negroes...petty tyrants are the most oppressive...

On poor whites...

The white man who has no property no possessions and no education is in Carolina, in a condition no better than a slave, except he is the master of his own person...whilst the slave is bound...to the plantation...

Many live in wretched cabins, not half so good as the houses which planters provide for their slaves. Some of these cabins...are made of mere sticks...Some fix their residence in the pine woods... gathering turpentine.

In the South these white cottagers never work on the plantations for wages...the slave owner would never permit it...The slaves generally believe that however miserable they may be...it is preferred to these poor white people. This sentiment is cherished by the slaves and cultivated by their masters, who fancy that they subserve their own interest...

While on the run...

Charles Ball described his escape from Georgia around the time of the War of 1812. Following the North Star at night and hiding by day, it was an arduous, harrowing escape, taking six months to make his way back to Maryland. Always the chance of capture, he spent the first night in a Georgia swamp.

There must have been in the troop, at least twenty horsemen; and the number of dogs was greater than I could count,,...as they ran through the woods...I knew all of these men and dogs were in search of me...I should be hunted down like a wild beast.

After gaining the Carolina shore, I took an observation of the rising moon and of such stars as I was acquainted...When daylight appeared I could see that the

country around me was well inhabited and the forest in which I lay was surrounded by plantations.

Charles traveled by night and found hiding places by day, until he recognized the place where he was sold, in Columbia, South Carolina. He followed this same pattern of traveling until he reached North Carolina. During this escape, Charles was on the run for almost six months and found himself in central Virginia, where he was captured and jailed.

I knew I was not far from Maryland and I fell into great indiscretion and forgot the wariness and caution that had enabled me to overcome so many obstacles...Anxious to get forward I neglected to conceal myself before day...I ran by a house near the road and a man opened the door and called to me to stop.

When I didn't, he set his dog on me...The dog was quickly vanquished by me stick...but a party of patrollers eventually surrounded me...They ordered me to cross my hands, which order not being immediately obeyed, they beat me with sticks and stones until I was almost senseless and entirely unable to make resistance. They bound me with cords and dragged me by the feet and threw me into the man's kitchen like a dead dog.

Run-a-way - *There must have been in the troop, at least twenty horsemen; and the number of dogs was greater than I could count, as they ran through the woods...I knew all of these men and dogs were in search of me.* - Charles Ball, 1836

Unable to produce the necessary papers according to the law, Charles was placed in jail until his identity could be established. After thirty-nine days in this jail, Charles found a weakness in one of the cell door timbers and escaped one night, crossing the Potomac River returning to his Maryland home.

About one o'clock in the morning, I came to the door of my wife's cabin and stood there, I believe about five minutes before I could summon sufficient fortitude to knock. I at length rapped lightly on the door and was immediately asked in the well known voice of my wife, "Who is there?"- I replied, "Charles."

She then came to the door and opened it slowly and said, "Who is this that speaks so much like my husband?" I then rushed in and made myself known to my wife, but it was some time before I could convince her that I was really her husband, returned from Georgia. The children were then called up, but they had forgotten me...

My wife, who at first was overcome by astonishment at seeing me again in her cabin...seemed to awaken from this dream and gathered all the children in her arms and thrust them into my lap, as I sat in the corner, clapped her hands, laughed

SLAVE AUCTION - *My grandfather was brought from Africa and sold as a slave in Calvert county, in Maryland. I never understood the name of the ship in which he was imported, nor the name of the planter who bought him on his arrival, but at the time I knew him he was a slave in a family called Maud, who resided near Leonardtown. My father was a slave in a family named Hauty, living near the same place. My mother was the slave of a tobacco planter, who died when I was about four years old.* - Charles Ball, *50 Years in Chains,* 1836 - Image from *Gone are the Days* illustrated history of the Old South by Harnett T. Kane, 1955

and cried in turns...and in her ecstasy forgot to give me any supper, until at length I told her I was hungry.   Before I entered the house I felt I could eat anything in any shape of food, but now that I attempted to eat, my appetite fled, and I sat up all night with my wife and children....

With my heart thrilling with joy, when I looked at my wife and children who had not hoped ever to behold me again; yet I feared the coming daylight, which must expose me to be arrested as a fugitive slave, I passed the night between happiness in the present and dread of the future.

During the War of 1812...

Charles Ball recounts how during the War of 1812, black slaves "deserted" their masters and fled to the British fleet. Since the British did not recognize slavery as legal, British naval officers treated the escapees as free men.

The slaves of a Mrs. Wilson effected their escape in the following manner. Two or three of the men ...ran away and got to the fleet...they stole a canoe and went off to the nearest ship that lay by the shore. When on board, they informed the officer of the ship that their mistress owned more than a hundred slaves, whom they left behind...They were advised to return home and remain there until the next night...bring all the remaining slaves with them...the officer promised he would send a detachment of boats to the shore to bring them off.

On the next night, having communicated their plans to some to their fellow slaves...they rose at midnight and partly by persuasion and partly by compulsion, carried off all the slaves of the plantation....they kindled a fire on the beach...and the boats of the fleet came and removed the whole party on board. In the morning, when the overseer of Mrs. Wilson arose and went to call his hands to the field, he found only empty cabins...

Ball served in the US Army during the War of 1812 and was discharged in 1814. His wife died in 1816 and he moved to near Baltimore. By 1820 he had remarried and accumulated about $350 through hard work and thrift and bought twelve acres there which he farmed.

Returned to slavery...

In June, 1830, the unthinkable happened - Ball was kidnapped by slave hunters while he was working his fields near Baltimore. He was thrown into jail, to be returned to Georgia. He thought at this time how different his life would have been if he had deserted to the British during the war.

In time, he convinced one of his captors to allow him to escape and Charles made his way to Philadelphia. He continues...

After remaining in Philadelphia a few weeks, I resolved to return to my little farm in Maryland...sell my property for as much as it would produce and bring my family to Pennsylvania.

Upon arriving in Baltimore, I went to a tavern keeper, whom I formerly supplied vegetables from my garden. The man appeared greatly surprised to see me...he showed me a hand-bill ...offering one-hundred and fifty dollars for my apprehension. I fled Baltimore that very night and went to my former residence, I found a strange white man there...who told me the woman and children who were here were carried away as escaped slaves and sold in Baltimore for the south...

Eventually, Charles would learn the worst of all news from a local black woman who had information - his family was taken by his former masters from which he escaped in Georgia.

This intelligence almost deprived me of life..it was clear that some slave dealers had come in my absence and seized my wife and children as slaves and sold them to such men as I had served in the south. They now passed into hopeless bondage...I was advertised as a fugitive slave...liable for arrest at any moment and to be dragged back to Georgia. I rushed away in despair and returned to Pennsylvania.

Charles Ball would live out his life in Pennsylvania, but even there not quite safe from slave catchers.

For the last few years, I have resided about fifty miles from Philadelphia, where I expected to pass the evening of my life...without the least hope of ever seeing my wife and children...fearful to let my place of residence be known, lest even yet...as an article of property, I am of sufficient value to be worth pursuing in my old age.

The life story of Charles Ball was recorded in Mifflin County by Isaac Fisher in 1836. His was a compelling story that helped influence the feelings of pre-Civil War America.

15 - Mifflin County Reacts to Slavery

INCLUDING...

THE THRILLING ESCAPE OF FUGITIVE SLAVE RICHARD BARNES & LEWISTOWN SUED BY SLAVE CATCHERS

In 1774, the tax lists of what would become Mifflin County included the assessment of sixteen slaves as taxable property. Seven were held by settlers south of Jack's Mountain, while the remaining nine lived in Kishacoquillas Valley. Many prominent local settlers owned slaves, and were active in their churches. In an earlier assessment, dated 1767, made when our area was part of Fermanagh Township, Cumberland County, three slaves were listed as valuable possessions. By the Census of 1790, the number of locally held slaves stood at thirty-three among seventeen families.

On March 1, 1780 the General Assembly passed the Pennsylvania Gradual Abolition Act, the first emancipation statute in the United States. Section 3 reads in part: *Be it enacted...by the representatives of the freeman of the commonwealth of Pennsylvania...that all persons, as well Negroes and Mulattos...who shall be born within this state...shall not be deemed and considered as servants for life, or slaves; and that all servitude for life, or slavery of children, in consequence of the slavery of their mothers, in the case of all children born within this state...shall be, and hereby is utterly taken away, extinguished and for ever abolished.*

In 1793, Congress approved the Fugitive Slave Act, which laid out the rights of slave owners to recover a runaway slave. Rewards were offered in local newspapers, accompanied with woodcut illustrations like the one above from the 1820s. But rewards led to excess. Any African-American, freeborn or runaway, were potentially subject to seizure and many were kidnapped by slave catchers to be returned to plantations below the Mason-Dixon Line. This is what happened to Charles Ball, as told in his narrative, *50 Years in Chains*.

PENNSYLVANIA AND MIFFLIN COUNTY REACTS TO SLAVERY

As viewed today, it seems obvious that the "peculiar institution" is diametrically opposed to all moral and ethical principles we hold dear. Yet in the 18th and 19th centuries, this was not universally held. James Clyde Sellman noted in his work *Abolitionism in the United States* that:

Although it is hard to imagine, white society did not see slavery as a moral or philosophical problem until a small number of outspoken individuals made it a problem. Beginning in the 1750s members of the Society of Friends, or Quakers, took the lead in challenging the institution. The most important Quaker antislavery activists were New Jersey Friend John Woolman, the author of the pamphlet Some Considerations on the Keeping of Negroes (1754), and Philadelphia Friend Anthony Benezet. During the mid-18th century Woolman traveled widely in British North America, appealing to Friends to free their slaves.

In 1775 Benezet and Woolman played a leading role in founding the first American antislavery organization, the Pennsylvania Society for the Abolition of Slavery. ...the Society of Friends reached consensus on the issue and became the first institution in the United States to condemn slavery as a moral wrong.

An event in the City of Brotherly Love would touch Mifflin County in a profound way. The convention of the American Anti-Slavery Society was held at Philadelphia, December 4, 1833. Those assembled ratified a constitution that states, in part: ...it [the American Anti-Slavery Society] shall aim to convince all our fellow-citizens, by arguments addressed to their understandings and consciences, that Slave holding is a heinous crime in the sight of God...

FERVENT LOCAL ABOLITIONIST
REV. JAMES NOURSE OF PERRYVILLE

Much of what we know today about the county's reaction to slavery came from George R. Frysinger, local historian and founder of the Mifflin County Historical Society. J. Martin Stroup's series of articles on this topic appeared in the Lewistown *Sentinel* in 1966, and relied heavily on Frysinger's collection and files.

Stroup concludes that when the clarion-call for the abolition of slavery came from Philadelphia in 1833, it was taken up here in 1834 by, among others, local Presbyterian pastor Rev. James Nourse, who during his career translated the New Testament into English from the original Greek. The pastor was born in Washington, D.C. and served at a couple Pennsylvania churches before being called to the East Kishacoquillas Presbyterian Church in Reedsville.

His stay in Reedsville lasted a few short years,

Rev. James Nourse
Milroy Presbyterian Church
(1834 to 1849)

Maclay House by William S. Peightel, 1988

The Maclay House - Milroy, Pa. - This drawing by local artist William S. Peightel shows the house of Dr. Samuel Maclay. Built in 1825 and listed on the Pennsylvania Register of Historic Sites, the Maclay House is located in Mifflin County's Armagh Township in the village of Milroy. Maclay was active in the local abolitionist movement, along with Presbyterian pastor, Rev. James Nourse. - *Historic Homes and Buildings in Milroy and Armagh Township*, by Raymond E. Harmon, Reedsville, PA 1988.

when he left for Williamsport in 1833. Gibson's *History of the Huntingdon Presbytery*, tells why he resigned:...owing to the trouble arising from the agitation of the temperance and antislavery causes, both of which he was a zealous advocate, he resigned that charge and moved to Williamsport.

A committee was formed at the direction of the Presbytery to reconcile the factions at the Reedsville church. It became evident that this was not possible and a new church was organized out of the Reedsville congregation in 1834. The recommendation came down that the new church not be established closer then three miles to Reedsville, so the Armagh Township village of Perryville, later known as Milroy, was selected. The newly formed church called out to its former pastor, Dr. Nourse, to return to them, becoming the Milroy Presbyterian Church's first minister. Shortly, a number of local abolitionists began to organize in the village.

Dr. Nourse, Dr. Samuel Maclay, John Taylor and Samuel Thompson gathered to work for the antislavery cause. Frysinger commented on the group, "...[they] united in safely conducting a number of runaway slaves over the Seven Mountains from Milroy to Centre County."

This abolitionist sentiment wasn't universally held throughout Mifflin County, however. Frysinger observed,

In those days...the term abolitionist was contemptuously used by many, while others contended themselves neutral or indifferent, looking upon it as a southern affair.

One incident that occurred on Saturday, August 29, 1835, according to

Frysinger, involved a young man with abolitionist leanings who arrived in Lewistown. He spread the word around town that he would lecture that evening. The topic - abolition.

Frysinger continued:

The news spread like wildfire, and before night he [the young abolitionist] was followed through the streets by a number of men and boys, who occasionally threw rotten eggs, apples, etc. crying, Lynch, lynch! and every indication of a riot was manifested. Observing the state of feelings, the gentleman prudently retired to Perryville, nine miles away, where he received a better reception.

Stroup noted in his series that no Mifflin County newspapers of that time are available to check the account.

MILROY'S 1825 MACLAY HOUSE

Dr. Samuel Maclay was a prominent local citizen,and active abolitionist. He was the son of William P. Maclay and the grandson of another Samuel Maclay, a United States Senator from Pennsylvania. The doctor's uncle, William Maclay is credited with being Pennsylvania's first United States Senator. Maclay's South Main Street home is located several doors from the Milroy Presbyterian Church.

The 1825 structure, today the private residence of David and Sandy Goss, is on the Pennsylvania Historical and Museum Commission's Register of Historic Sites. Over the years, the Maclay House, which is not a public museum, has been occasionally open for small group tours.

The following partial description is from commentary distributed during those limited tours: *It was in the Maclay House, under a window of the front bedroom in a space between the porch roof and porch ceiling that slaves were hidden. There is evidence of a tunnel leading from the basement under the highway to the bank of Dry Creek just across the road.*

Runaway slaves were able to escape from the house into the brush along the banks of the stream, and continue over the Seven Mountains and on to freedom in Canada. In recent years, the tunnel has been filled in and walled up.

A THRILLING ESCAPE FROM SLAVE CATCHERS

"The punishment of kidnapping is not proportioned to the offense and requires to be increased."

These are the words of Pennsylvania Governor William Findlay in an address to the Legislature in 1819. The governor referred to the taking of would-be escaped slaves by slave catchers. He found the practice of seizing any black assumed to be a runaway abhorrent and further noted: I have observed that it is usual to take colored persons in numbers, in chains together, through our state without any inquiry being made into the cause...

Pennsylvania soon gave a degree of protection to freedmen, by passing a law that required slave catchers to appear before a state court and show proof of ownership before any "kidnapping" could occur. The thrilling escape of Richard Barnes occurred in 1834, when a group of southern planters came through Lewistown.

SLAVE CATCHERS ENTER TOWN - *...a group of southern planters came through Lewistown. Their arrival was unannounced, on horses the locals considered "splendid mounts." They were searching for runaway slaves....* -Lewistown *Sentinel* series by J. Martin Stroup, 1966

Their arrival was unannounced, on horses the locals considered "splendid mounts." They were searching for runaway slaves. While here, they had a local man, Richard Barnes, arrested on being a suspected runaway slave. He was placed in the county jail.

One of the planters identified him as a slave from his plantation, which Barnes vehemently denied. The whole town became interested in the case. Barnes was locally known and liked, respected for his hard work around the town. It was generally believed he was a fugitive slave who reached Lewistown by way of Fulton County, through Shirleysburg and Mt. Union, then down the Juniata River to Lewistown. Fugitive or not, Richard had earned a place in the community and in the hearts of many citizens, runaway or not.

Pursuant to Pennsylvania law, a trial to determine ownership was quickly held in Mifflin County Court. Unfortunately, Richard was judged to be the planter's property before a packed court room. The sympathetic sheriff, purposely careless, allowed Richard Barnes to slip away on his return to jail.

With the enthralled crowd from the court house in pursuit, Richard ran up Main Street to Third Street, then east to near Dorcas Street, where he climbed down an open well. The swell of people encompassed the mouth of the well, jockeying for a glimpse of the forlorn runaway. The degree of his desperation was so great and his determination to never return to slavery so intense, Richard Barnes swore he would drop himself into the dark waters below and drown himself.

The slave catchers were among the members of the gathering, and quickly realized the mood of the assembled townspeople - they sided with the hapless Barnes, who now believed his cause was hopeless. A man well known to Barnes, Urie Jacobs, his present employer, assured him of his safety if he would only come up. It was only by this guarantee that he reluctantly climbed from the well, unsure of what awaited him. To the astonished runaway AND the equally flabbergasted slave catchers, the gathered citizens raised $250 on the spot and purchased Barnes from his would-be masters.

J. Martin Stroup noted in his 1966 Lewistown *Sentinel* series that he had personal recollections from his mother of Barnes and his family. Stroup stated: *Barnes lived in Lewistown on West Third Street for the rest of his life. The writer*

Milroy Presbyterian Church, shown in this drawing by William S. Peightel, 1988

Abolitionist Convictions Guided Milroy Presbyterian Pastor - The Milroy Presbyterian Church, shown in this drawing by local artist William S. Peightel, was formed when its congregation split with Reedsville's East Kishacoquillas Presbyterians in 1834 over temperance - especially the local manufacture and use of intoxicating liquor. The new church's pastor (1834 to 1849) was Rev. James Nourse. Rev. Nourse was a staunch abolitionist and espoused fervent views against the use of alcohol. He died in Iowa in 1854, but his remains were brought back by the Milroy Presbyterians and interred in the church's cemetery. - *Historic Homes and Buildings in Milroy and Armagh Township,* by Raymond E. Harmon, Reedsville, PA 1988.

remembers his mother [Stroup's mother], who was born in 1855, tell of Richard Barnes' wife, known in the Martin family of Vira as Auntie Barnes...being brought out from town to help during harvest and at other times such as butchering...Stroup's mother also remembered seeing old Richard Barnes, then blind, in the Barnes home on West Third Street.

Stroup also detailed an interesting anecdote from Barnes' later life. The local historian continued: *He lived to be over 100. In 1869, the Lewistown Gazette announced plans for the "Old Stagers" of Lewistown to hold a picnic. The paper printed a list of 27 white men, all over 70 years, also three colored citizens. These were Richard Barnes, Frank Snowden, and Samuel Hill. The "grand picnic" of the old timers was to be in charge of the oldest resident as president. The Gazette said it was difficult to determine the oldest, but that Richard Barnes apparently held seniority, claiming to be 104 years old.*

Unfortunately, the Old Stagers never got together, the picnic was never held.

BALL AND BARNES - WERE THEY THE SAME PERSON?

Considering the effects of the Fugitive Slave Acts, an escaped slave wasn't safe or free from capture, even in Pennsylvania in the 1830s, when Charles Ball and Richard Barnes were living in the area. A slave might change his name to prevent capture while a fugitive, but always remained vigilant if he or she wanted to elude capture.

The after dinner speaker at the Mifflin County Historical Society's September, 2000 banquet, Dr. Anadolu-Okur, made a most interesting point during her lecture on the Underground Railroad. Charles Ball and Richard Barnes, local men who were once slaves, but escaped bondage, *were really the same person*. Local historian J. Martin Stroup wrote of them as two individuals. However, Dr. Anadolu-Okur cited as her source, a book by author Charles L. Blockson, who states that "Barnes" was really Ball's alias.

"Perhaps the most famous of the escaped slaves to have lived in Mifflin County was Charles Ball, who escaped to Lewistown. Ball, Maryland slave, was the subject of an important book, *A Narrative of the Life and Adventures of Charles Ball, A Black Man*, published in 1836 and reprinted in a new edition with the title *Fifty Years in Chains, or the Life of an American Slave*.

In his narrative, Ball traces his life as a slave in South Carolina, Georgia, Maryland and as a fugitive escaping on the Underground Railroad to Lewistown, using his adopted name, Richard Barnes. Ball died in Lewistown at the age of 104." - *Hippocrene Guide to The Underground Railroad* by Charles L. Blockson NY Hippocrene Books, 1994.

LEWISTOWN SUED OVER RUNAWAY SLAVE FREED BY CROWD

In March, 1966, another article dealing with Mifflin County and slavery appeared in the *Sentinel*. J. Martin Stroup had found a journal kept by an uncle, which contained several personal recollections of another episode of a runaway slave being released by a local crowd, this time by force. The manuscript from which Stroup quoted was written by James M. Martin in 1892. He recorded stories told to him by his father, J. McGinnis Martin, plus his own personal memories.

This slave-hunting saga occurred about 1820 in Lewistown, and was told to James Martin by his father, J. McGinnis Martin, who lived at the time with

THE SENTINEL

FRIDAY, MARCH 11, 1966   SECOND SECTION   PAGE THIRTEEN

Underground Railroad Postscript:

Boro Sued 146 Years Ago For Slave Freed by Crowd

By J. MARTIN STROUP

Recently The Sentinel published a series of three articles by the writer having to do with slave colored man haundcuffed and shackled, resisting to the extent of his ability, while two broad-brimmed slouch-hatted southern

James Martin's story of the fugitive slave who was sheltered at the Vira farm follows: "The owner of Pine Cottage

We boys climbed lamp posts and dry goods boxes and looked on. My UncleJoseph Martin, with a dry goods box for a rostrum was exhorting the slave drivers to repent, amend their ways, perhaps to meet an avenging God... J. McGinnis Martin, 1820 - Lewistown Sentinel article, 1966

his father, Samuel Martin of Vira, Derry Township. There was an "excitement" in the Diamond, the Public Square, McGinnis Martin recalled. He and the other boys his age (about 10 years) ran to the scene.

A slave gang in Washington, DC - Such sights in the nation's capital, even in pre-Civil War years, raised questions about the "pecular institution." The convention of the American Anti-Slavery Society was held at Philadelphia, December 4, 1833. Those assembled ratified a constitution that states, in part: ...it [the American Anti-Slavery Society] shall aim to convince all our fellow-citizens, by arguments addressed to their understandings and consciences, that Slave holding is a heinous crime in the sight of God... - *Anti-Slavery Society Convention, 1833*

McGinnis remembered: *I found a Dearborn wagon in which there was a large colored man handcuffed and shackled, resisting to the extent of his ability, while two broad brimmed, slouch-hatted southern drivers sat upon and held him in the wagon which they were ordering be driven to the river. But the gathering crowd had blocked the way. The wagon was stopped. The chained Negro squirmed, struggled and finally threw himself from under the swearing drivers into the mud where he wallowed and tried to regain his feet, while the drivers jumped upon him, swore and cussed, and flung him again into the wagon. One of them seized him and sat upon him.*

The crowd was growing larger, a large number of free Negroes were crowding around. They were very much excited and ready to spring to the rescue if encouraged. We boys climbed lamp posts and dry goods boxes and looked on. My Uncle Joseph Martin, with a dry goods box for a rostrum was exhorting the slave drivers to repent, amend their ways, perhaps to meet an avenging God at judgment.

Again the poor manacled Negro, with groans threw himself into the mud. The air was full of cursing. Uncle Joseph's patiences was exhausted. His exhortation was having no effect. The cruelty of the drivers was too much.

Stroup recounts that at this point, McGinnis' Uncle Joseph gave the word and the local freemen surged in and lifted their mud-stained brother from the mire, carrying him to the nearest blacksmith shop to remove his shackles and handcuffs.

McGinnis finishes: *After swearing awhile, the slave drivers took the advice [of the gathered crowd] to leave and prevent trouble. But in the years after, they sued the town under the Fugitive Slave law and received pay...but the Negro was a free man.*

137

16 - 1861 Migration to Haiti

*M*embers of Mifflin County's black population emi-grated to the Caribbean island nation of Haiti in 1861. Based upon articles which appeared in the Lewistown Sentinel forty years ago, these brief accounts reflect information originally written by late county historian and newspaper editor, J. Martin Stroup.

The outbreak of war in 1861 immersed Mifflin County with events of the impending conflict. Talk of war and the eventual departure of the Logan Guards that spring occupied much of the local press. Just weeks before the tempest of the Civil War broke over the nation, a local newspaper reported on an event that would create great interest in the county's black community - a proposed migration to the island nation of Haiti. The February 28, 1861 edition of the Lewistown *Gazette* reported on the proposed migration: *A large meeting of our colored population was held Monday last, John L. Griffith in the chair, to take into consideration the propriety of adopting measures to move to Hayti (Haiti). We have no doubt that country offers strong inducements to emigrants, both in climate and production, and that once there, and their houses in order, few would wish themselves back in the United States.*

The hopes of the colored man must be in himself and although respected here...his position must always be an inferior one, instead of favoring his advancement, is actually retarding it.

A month later, March 28, 1861, the *Gazette* printed this information under the headline, "Emigration":

A large meeting of our colored citizens was held in the colored public school house. Prayer was by Rev. William Grimes who chaired the meeting. The Right Rev. Bishop Paine...stated briefly that the time had arrived when the colored man has become a subject of legislation...and his condition can be bettered in no place so well as in Hayti...

Members of the black community planned to investigate the possibilities of this monumental undertaking.

MIGRATION TO HAITI THE PROMISED LAND?
Those gathered at this meeting elected officers and created an association to further the cause. The plan to move to a promised land was not without controversy. In the Lewistown *Gazette* of March 28, 1861, an item appeared that denied any truth to a rumor going around the community. A letter was allegedly circulated

asking the "white brethren" of town to donate funds for the journey. The association sent no such request, although one of its members did.

The group planned to send an agent on ahead to Haiti to check out the possibilities for the move. In the fall of 1861, the *Gazette* informed the community that:

The colored population has been fluctuating in opinion...of remaining here or going to Hayti (1860 spelling). All was excitement as 70 persons left for the West Indies.

The newspaper listed the names of fourteen families and nine individuals which came to seventy, a sizable departure for a community that numbered in the hundreds of that era.

THE MOVE IS PLANNED

In December of 1861, the local newspaper began reporting on numerous letters sent by the emigrants to relatives back in Mifflin County. The group had left town weeks earlier and reached St. Mare, Haiti on November 2, after "a pleasant voyage of eleven days." The editor of the *Gazette* noted, "They speak favorably of their reception and of the country."

Around the middle of December, 1861, John L. Griffith, who volunteered to go on ahead to Haiti as the group's agent, reported on the progress of the Lewistown colony. Griffith said that the fare for transporting 82 Negroes from Lewistown to New York had been $80. Each traveler had been given a $32 outfit and each had $40 that was personally raised. He noted:

They seemed to be contented with their new home...they think they have found the promised land. Forty Negroes from Bellefonte and thirty more from Lewistown would be leaving for Hayti in the spring.

The exact source of the funds was never stated in the newspaper, although a statement appeared in a seemingly related item: "Will not some kind person head a subscription for them with $10 as Mr. T. J. Hoffman did the first."

WAS HAITI A PARADISE?

By the spring of 1862, disenchantment set in for some in Haiti's Lewistown colony. Two men returned to town with a discouraging report, but a letter printed in the *Gazette* from emigrant Archie Saunders told of "the only place on Earth for the colored man."

For many of the Lewistown emigrants, the French-speaking black island nation would indeed seem like a promised land politically, compared to the United States of the mid-1800s.

By February, 1864, the *Gazette* printed a letter from S. J. Baptist, former Lewistown resident, stating that those who moved to Haiti two years earlier are doing well. The cotton crop was selling, he reported, at a high price and their initial hard times are over. Baptist, one of the organizers of the migration from Lewistown also noted, "White people are held in great respect in Hayti."

HAITIAN RELATIVES

Mention of the Haitian migration was absent from the *Gazette* as years passed. Locally, there seemed to be mixed feelings about the success or failure of the movement. In fact, the paper never printed an explanation for the movement or if other groups actually moved to Haiti as was reported in Baptist's letter.

Although the *Gazette* of the 1860s never mentioned the reason for the migration, it seems obvious today - freedom - plus better living conditions and employment opportunities were hoped for in Haiti.

The Mifflin County Historical Society's 1999 video, *A Walk Through Lewistown's History* notes as a result of the 1861 migration, Haitians living on that island today, have ancestral roots traced to Mifflin County.

Comments from the readers of *Notes from Monument Square* are always welcome. As editor, I received correspondence on the Haitian migration article from Ms. Jeannette L. Molson, a direct descendent of a Mifflin Countian who traveled to Haiti in 1860 and later returned. Because of the unique information Ms. Molson was seeking. I felt our readers would appreciate reading the entire letter.

If any of our members or friends might have additional information to share on this topic, please contact the writer directly, Jeannette L. Molson, P.O. Box 1406, Davis, CA 95617 or e-mail: JLMolson@aol.com or this newsletter.

Dear Editor:

I read your article in the November 2000 issue of Notes from Monument Square. I am a direct descendant of one of those who emigrated to Haiti and returned. I am Samuel D. Molson's great great granddaughter. I have had the pleasure of visiting my great great grandfather's birthplace twice, once in 1985, and again in 1992 with my father.

Now for the reason for my letter. I have, for over the last 20+ years, been researching the Molson's of Lewistown. I have copies of information that has been provided to me by researchers in your county. The late Dr. Charles Eater sent me copies of clippings on my great great grandfather's involvement in the emigration to Haiti. There was mention of a ship "The Flight" that sailed for Haiti. I have been trying to learn who actually sailed on that ship but to no avail. Your article mentions that there were 'names of fourteen families and nine individuals' listed. Is it possible for someone to provide me with the names of those individuals? I have attempted to locate this information through the NY Journal of Commerce and other sources but have come up blank. Evidently passports were not required at that time.

This was not the only member of my family who emigrated to another country. Many African Americans left the U. S. prior to the Civil War to go to Africa. There are descendants, living today in the U. S., who are direct dependents of Mary Ann Molson Deputie, sister to George, Samuel D., John, and William Molson, all of Lewistown.

A response, in the newsletter, would be sufficient or someone could e-mail me.

The Molsons of Lewistown in the words of Jeannette L. Molson
THE GENEALOGY BUG BITES

I caught the 'bug' in 1979. Since I knew so little about my father's family, I decided to see what I could find on the MOLSON family. I made a trip to Lewistown, as well as some other places, in 1985, trying to gather as much information as I could.

One thing led to another and here I am 20+ years later still digging away. I have a penchant to learn the truth, whatever that may be, and a determined doggedness, to see a project to its conclusion.

Learning about my ancestors helps me to know a little bit more about myself. I was born and raised in California. I've been employed by the State of California, a local school district where I tutored special needs students and lastly with the University of California at Davis, until a disability forced me into retirement five years ago. Now, I am free to research for as long as I am able. Two years ago, I started a family newsletter as a way of keeping the family up-to-date on current events as well as what happened in the past.

RESEARCH YIELD RESULTS

I have written, over the years, several letters to the Mifflin County Historical Society. I have gathered information on the sons of Mary Ann (MOLSON) DEPUTIE who were missionaries in Africa. Three of her sons, all born in the U.S., served as Presbyterian and Methodist Missionaries from 1869 to as late as 1903. Two of her sons, and a son-in-law, returned to the U.S. on one occasion trying to get monetary support for their missions. There are many letters, written by the Deputies, that were sent through the auspices of the American Colonization Society. An article, on Mrs. Deputie, was written in Frederick Douglass' newspaper, 30 Mar 1855, indicating her displeasure with Africa.

Edward Banks Molson, Sr.
(1840 - 1896) and family

The photo above was sent to the MCHS and appears here courtesy of Jeannette Molson. Edward Banks Molson, Sr., the son of Samuel D. Molson, is the gentleman seated with a young child (Jeannette's grandfather, Edward Banks Molson, Jr.) on his lap.

John MOLSON (1816 - 1896) had a son who fought in the 107th NY Infantry, Company F, which is the same regiment that 'marched to the sea' with General Sherman. Unfortunately, James S. MOLSON, died on 26 May 1864, after having served in campaigns at Gettysburg, Chancellorsville, Antietam, and New Hope Church, in Dallas Gap, GA, where he died of his wounds.

James was only 22 years old.

David W. MOLSON served with the 48th regiment, PA Infantry, Company B, until he was discharged, by General Burnside, for being a mulatto. All of this information is documented in military records, pension records and in the case of James S. MOLSON, in the History of Steuben County, NY under Military History.

Hannibal C. MOLSON (1837 - 1899) has an extensive biography written about him in the *Cleveland Gazette* 27 Dec 1884.

Mifflin County Trivia
"Does a tree grow in Burnham?"

1. A cedar tree grows by a house in Burnham, once the residence and office of Dr., & Mrs. McNabb, the Logan House gift shop is there today. The tree has an interesting history associated with it. What is the significance of that cedar tree?
[a] It came from Dwight Eisenhower's Gettysburg farm as a gift to Dr. McNabb.
[b] It was developed at the Penn State botany department's greenhouse as a totally new species named Juniperus pennsylvaniana.
[c] The seed from which the Burnham tree grew came from a 2000 year old Cedar of Lebanon in the Holy Land. [d] Dr. McNabb transplanted the cedar himself from the trolley right-of-way prior to clearing near the future Kishacoquillas Park.

2. Something happened to 125 miles of the township roads in Mifflin County by order of the Commonwealth of Pennsylvania. It was part of a promise made by Gov. Gifford Pinchot and took effect in January, 1931. What happened?
[a] The roads were taken over by the Commonwealth.
[b] These rural roads were now to be patrolled by state police.
[c] Weight limits were placed on roads with bridges, due to many bridge collapses in the county.
[d] The state placed fences along these rural roads to contain farm animals.

3. A painting hangs in the McCoy House museum by artist George Hetzel. Born in France in 1829, he came to America at age 2. Hetzel painted in a style described today as the Hudson River School, which celebrates the beauty and splendor of the American landscape. His name is counted among many famous American painters of the 19th century. He died in Homewood, Pa. in 1899. Which of the following is not true about this painting?

[a] It won a prize at the 1876 Centennial Exposition in Chicago.

[b] The painting depicts a scene in the Seven Mountains.

[c] According to a 1945 publication, it once hung in a men's club in Pittsburgh.

[d] The unfinished painting was completed by Hetzel's son in 1900.

4. What is the connection between current Mifflin County Historical Society Past President Joseph E. Deihl and Pennsylvania's first governor Thomas Mifflin?

[a] Joe Deihl's maternal great, great, great grandmother was a cousin twice removed from Gov. Thomas Mifflin's wife, Sarah.

[b] After his discharge from the service following the Korean War, Joe disembarked at Philadelphia and stayed the night and had breakfast at the Governor Thomas Mifflin Inn, located in Ardmore, Pa.

[c] Landscaping bricks Joe used on his property to construct a brick border originally came from Governor Mifflin Alley, near the site where Mifflin is buried in Lancaster, Pa.

[d] Joe Deihl's Williamsburg house, which he built in Burnham, Pa., came from an 18th century design. Through his research, Joe found out that Thomas Mifflin's architect drew up the original plans for the house when it was constructed in Williamsburg in the 1700s.

TRIVIA ANSWERS:

1. c From All-Saints Parish newsletter, The Trumpet, Vol.2 #1

2. a Gov. Pinchot promised to "get the farmer out of the mud." Rural road paving and other improvements were instituted on these township right-of-ways. *Souvenir Booklet of Ltn. , p. 29*

3. d News item from *The Sentinel* dated November 10, 1922, discusses the painting that was then recently donated to the Mifflin County Historical Society by Louise Siegrist Hetzel, widow of Pittsburgh artist George Hetzel. The Hetzel painting shows a scene of Laurel Run, near Milroy and was painted circa 1870.

The Directory of Southwestern Pennsylvania Painters 1800 - 1945 DOES NOT list this painting by George Hetzel, and it is likely an unknown work to that publication. Special thanks to Mifflin County Historical Society Research Librarian Jean Suloff for sharing this information on the Hetzel painting.

4. c

17 - R. B. Hoover and the Lincoln Stone

*T*his Mifflin County na-
tive served in the mili-
tary during wartime. He
worked in print communi-
cations before and during
the war, but started polish-
ing his technological skills
at an early age.

Robert Burns Hoover
MCHS image

He mastered one advanced technology
of its time, only to champion a newer, more
progressive form later in life, one that remains an essential of 21st Century life. Following army service, he worked for an as-
tonishing forty-eight years in communications, counting the rich and famous in
industry, the military and government as his friends and acquaintances.

After the war, he moved from the county to the Pittsburgh area, then Ohio
and Illinois, eventually retiring in California. He was never to live here again
and made only infrequent visits. Still the fond memories of his local upbringing
remained strong and he kept up a lifelong correspondence with a hometown friend
until his death at age 79.

It wasn't his distinguished career we remember here in Mifflin County. In
fact, his name is generally unknown, except to a few local historians and perhaps
to a select number of area school children. No, this former Mifflin Countian
remains fairly obscure, yet his guiding spirit and support helped establish one of
Mifflin County's most distinguishing features - Monument Square. He brought
to that project an artifact of such historical significance, no other like it exists
anywhere else in the world.

His name was Robert Burns Hoover. He brought to Mifflin County the only
stone to be removed from the tomb of Abraham Lincoln, now the corner stone of
the Soldiers' and Sailors' Monument on the Square.

"What hath God wrought!" This was the first message sent by wire, tapped
out by Samuel F. B. Morse on May 24, 1844 from the U.S. Supreme Court room
in Washington, D.C. to the offices of the Baltimore and Ohio Railroad in Baltimore, Maryland. Morse's partner, Alfred Lewis Vail received the message and

144

retransmitted the same message back to Morse. This became the fastest means of communication for over four decades.

Two months later, Margaret Jane Hoover gave birth to a healthy baby boy at the Hoover's Lewistown residence. She and husband Christian named their second child Robert Burns Hoover. Little did they dream that their new child was destined to become a prime mover to honor the living inventor of the telegraph and be acquainted with the rich and famous of 19th Century America.

To understand R.B. Hoover's early fascination with the telegraph, one must understand how three families became intertwined during Robert's formative years - his own family, the Hoovers, the Cogley family of Lewistown and an orphan named Spottswood. This colorful mix of relationships led Robert to the telegraph and eventually to bring the Lincoln Stone to Mifflin County.

THE HOOVER FAMILY

Robert was one of five Hoover children born in Lewistown. His father, Christian, came to Mifflin County from Huntingdon County, Pa. in 1836 and married Margaret Jane Shull here in 1842. Margaret was from Perry County, and moved to the area in 1837 at age fifteen. The Hoovers had five children, but three died in infancy, leaving Robert and his sister, Prudence Anna Hoover who survived to adulthood.

Prudence married J. Lowry Himes and they had a home on Valley Street, where she died in 1897 at age 50. She and husband Lowry had one son, William Hoover Himes.

Shortly after his marriage to Margaret, Christian opened a cabinet making business that he was forced to close in 1848 due to poor health. Christian ran for Justice of the Peace in what was Lewistown's West Ward, won four times, eventually serving almost 17 years. An advertisement in the *True Democrat* dated Feb. 15, 1855 under Notice of Advertisements reads: *C. Hoover, Esq., will deal out justice, according to law, to all who are brought before him. Sinners, please take notice.*

He served as Justice of the Peace until his death at age 46 in 1865. A local

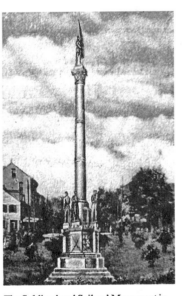

The Soldiers' and Sailors' Monument in 1906 - A monument to honor the memory of those who fought and died in the Civil War was the dream of Robert B. Hoover and other Mifflin County civic leaders, as early as the end of the war itself. It took decades to raise the necessary funds. This image was made by Lewistown photographer, Nolte. - MCHS image

145

newspaper termed his cause of death as "hemorrhage of the lungs." Christian Hoover was also Mifflin County Coroner, elected in 1839. He was a Mason and served as assistant superintendent and secretary of the primary department of the Lutheran Sunday School. He was buried in the Methodist Cemetery, Lewistown, Pennsylvania.

Mrs. Hoover remarried after Christian's death. Her second husband died in 1871 and she stayed for various periods of time with either Robert or Prudence. She lived in Lewistown at the time of Prudence's final illness. After that, she lived with son Robert until her death in 1898. Margaret contracted peritonitis as the result of eye surgery in Springfield, Ohio and died at age 76. Her burial was beside husband Christian in the Methodist Cemetery, Lewistown.

THE COGLEY FAMILY

Joseph M. Cogley and his second wife Sarah Fridley married in the early 1830s. Their oldest child was Elizabeth, followed by Jacob, Elias and Mary. The family lived on North Main Street, Lewistown, next to where the McCoy House Museum is today at 17 N. Main Street. All four worked in the local telegraph office at various times. Both Elizabeth Cogley and Elias Cogley were highly competent telegraphers, well recognized by their peers.

Elizabeth was born in 1833 and never married. She was a telegrapher from 1856 until her retirement in 1907, working her way from messenger to operator. At the start of the Civil War, Elizabeth received the telegram from Pennsylvania Governor Andrew G. Curtin asking for volunteers, resulting in Mifflin County's Logan Guards being among the First Defenders to arrive in Washington, D.C. At the end of an exceptional career, she was pensioned by the Pennsylvania Railroad and lived until 1922.

Local historian George R. Frysinger wrote in his unpublished 1924 history of the Cogley Family that Elizabeth, known as Miss Lib, "...was the instructor of three other members of the Cogley family..."- Jacob, Elias and Mary.

Jacob and Mary each worked as messenger, then operator at the Lewistown telegraph office. Jacob died at the young age of 23 in 1863. When sister Elizabeth was promoted to the Harrisburg office in 1863, Mary succeeded her as operator at the Lewistown railroad station until her marriage in the early 1870s to Wilson W. Hamaker. The pair operated the Coleman House in Lewistown. Mary died in 1921.

Elias was as accomplished as sister Elizabeth, according to Frysinger, who wrote, "He was a master of his profession, having worked his way from messenger boy to expert operator." His career took him around the United States and Canada, spending his last nineteen years at the Lewistown office of Western Union.

Elias retired in 1922, with a stunning sixty-six years of continuous telegraphic service with Western Union and the Associated Press! He was married to Henrietta Pitat of Ohio, but the couple had no children. She died in 1895. Elias died of injuries sustained in an auto accident near Parkesburg, Pa. in 1928.

CHARLES C. SPOTTSWOOD

In 1850, when telegraph poles were being erected and a line strung from Lewistown Junction to an office on the Square, Robert B. Hoover was seven years old.

Charles C. Spottswood was an orphan, born around 1823. He was brought to town as an orphan at age two from Gettysburg, Pa. and lived with the Joseph and Sarah Cogley family. The Cogleys raised the young Spottswood as one of their own. He married Nancy Jane Lilley in 1850. Later that year, Charles heard a series of lectures in town on a new technology - telegraphy. Samuel F. B. Morse spoke at the local Apprentices' Literary Society on the principle of sending messages over a wire via electrical current from a battery. Was this the spark for a career as a telegrapher? The allure of this most rapid means of communication engrossed him. His interest would become his profession when Charles became the first telegraph operator in the area, appointed agent at Mifflin County's first railroad station at Lewistown Junction. During this time he trained his foster sister, Elizabeth Cogley, in the art and science of telegraphy.

Apprentices' Literary Society Building on Third Street, Lewistown - Built in 1852, the society was founded in 1842 and sponsored lectures and speeches on literary and scientific topics. Spottswood was a founding member and heard the lecture on sending messages over a wire via electrical current from a battery.
- Image from *Historic Sounenir of Lewistown, Penna.*, 1925. MCHS Archives

Charles and Lilley remained in Lewistown until 1856, when they moved to Lake City, Minnesota. He died at his daughter's home in Minot, North Dakota in 1910. When he left the area, Elizabeth Cogley succeeded him at the Lewistown telegraph office and launched the Cogleys' lifelong association with the telegraph. Robert Hoover knew the Cogleys quite well during his childhood. Elias Cogley and Robert became brothers-in-law, each marrying sisters from Ohio. Later the pair would be business partners advocating a proposed fire alarm system for Lewistown.

Yet in Robert's early days, communications was in his blood. The US census of 1860 lists the 15 year old twice, once with his family and again with the Frysinger family, owners of the *Lewistown Gazette*, as a printer's apprentice. The lifelong friendship between R.B. Hoover and George Frysinger developed through this association.

YEARS OF NATIONAL CONFLICT

As the Civil War approached, local military activities touched Robert's life. His mother's brother, Chauncey M. Shull, joined the newly-forming Logan Guards

Lincoln's call for troops answered by the Logan Guards - A rememberance from 1913, recalled the event. "The military display was the most imposing ever gathered in the capital city (Harrisburg) up to that time...among them our own Logan Guards...and the Mifflin County Cavalry, afterwards know as the First Pa. Cavalry..." - George R. Frysinger

in 1858. Young Hoover became a drummer boy for the unit, but at only age 16, wasn't permitted to accompany the Guards when war came. One memorable event the youthful drummer would never forget happened on Washington's Birthday, 1861. A great celebration occurred in Harrisburg, as President-elect Lincoln passed through Pennsylvania on his way to Washington. Robert, as drummer boy for the Logan Guards, was present on that February 22, 1861. George Frysinger recalled the incident in 1913. Concern for the new president's safety was a theme running through the account. Frysinger wrote, in part:

"On that day a large U.S. flag was raised to the dome of the capitol building, run up...by soldiers of the War of 1812..."

"The military display was the most imposing ever gathered in the capital city up to that time...among them our own Logan Guards...and the Mifflin County Cavalry, afterwards know as the First Pa. Cavalry..."

"Thousands of citizens were present...literally packing the streets. Cannons boomed salutes...but the main feature of the day was yet to come. The vast multitudes took up a line of march to the Pennsylvania Railroad depot into which the train carrying the presidential party slowly rolled at 1:30 p.m.... announced by a salute of 21 guns. The president elect, with two chosen friends, alighted and were at once escorted to a barouche drawn by six white horses, the entire procession following to the Jones House, where on the portico he appeared in company with Governor Curtin and was greeted with prolonged cheers..."

"While all this was going on railroad officials, detectives, telegraph operators and others were busy trying to discover any signs of suspicion and at the same time planning for the President's secret exit from the city."

"...R. B. Hoover, then a drummer boy for the Logan Guards...saw Lincoln partly disguised, hastily making his way through the courtyard in the rear of the hotel to take a cab for a point on the tracks of the...railroad..."

148

Robert Hoover wrote to Frysinger in 1909, confirming that he spied Lincoln's exit, saying, "I was at Harrisburg with the Logan Guards at the time referred to. Lincoln was disguised in a long cloak and scotch cap and smuggled out of the rear door of the hotel, while 5,000 people stood in front hoping he would appear and make another speech..."

In June, 1863, Hoover joined a group of volunteers, including George R. Frysinger, who rushed to repel Confederate raiders on a foray into Pennsylvania. The Lewistown *Gazette* printed an account, again remembered by George Frysinger, in the July 18, 1929 edition: "...at 1 o'clock in the morning of June 15, 1863, people were roused from slumber by the clanging of the bell in the Courthouse steeple, and soon a crowd of several hundred answered the summons...The interior of the temple of justice was ablaze with light from every gas jet...when explanations by speakers...that word was received from State officials ...Confederate cavalry raiders heading to Mt. Union... volunteers to proceed at once to defend property..."

Volunteers arrived at Mt. Union station and were dispatched to Orbisonia and Shade Gap to barricade the mountain pass with trees and rocks. The action lasted only twelve days and no Confederate soldiers appeared. Robert Hoover and George Frysinger put out a newspaper using a press and type found in the village. The first editorial asserted that the paper was published by The Typos of Company A, First Regiment, Penna. Militia . The publication was testimony to precocious young men with too much time on their hands. The paper listed all the officers and men in the company, plus stories thanking the local ladies for their kindnesses and some farcical news items.

In late June, 1863, a more serious event led Robert Hoover to enlist and find himself at Gettysburg . By 1864 he was involved in telegraphic work for the Army and eventual employment with Western Union after the war.

THE CIVIL WAR YEARS

Hoover had joined a militia company on June 15, 1863, hastily put together to protect the Shade Gap area from anticipated Rebel forces. Encountering no Confederate raiders, "The Shade Gap Militia" returned home June 23.

R. B. Hoover enlisted with a group recruited by Capt. Henry A. Eisenbise in response to Governor Curtain's second call for emergency troops. On the 28th of June, the group left for Harrisburg, attached to the 36th Regiment, Pennsylvania Volunteer Militia, Company A. Hoover was mustered into service on July 4, 1863 for ninety days. His unit was sent to Gettysburg, to help clear the battlefield and bury the dead after the bloody days of July 1 through 3, but heavy rain and swollen streams hampered travel. Hoover's unit didn't arrive at Gettysburg until July 9th.

He was discharged on August 11, 1863 and returned to Lewistown on August 12. According to local newspapers Hoover "was later transferred to the U.S. military telegraph corps, and served with Grant and Sherman... until the close of the war." In the April 19, 1865 edition of *The True Democrat*, under the

Communities honored the fallen - Civil War monuments and memorials sprang up across the country, often sponsored by organizations like the GAR. The Grand Army of the Republic was a political force of the era and R. B. Hoover was its local commander in Springfield, Ill. in 1894. It didn't hurt in his drive to aquire the Lincoln Stone for his old home town.

heading Our Soldiers it was noted: "R.B.Hoover, of this place, who has been in Tennessee for a year or more in some civil capacity connected with army operations, is again home on a visit."

A TELEGRAPH CAREER

Communications was in Hoover's blood, from his early work in the newspaper business with George Frysinger, to telegraphy undoubtedly learned from the Cogley family, and later, through military communications. It seems natural that a job in the ever-expanding technology of that day would come to Robert Hoover.

Hoover began working in 1866 for a communications company not yet ten years old. Started in 1851 as the New York and Mississippi Valley Printing Telegraph Company, by 1856, it combined with other companies to form the Western Union Telegraph Company. It would become the largest privately owned and operated system in the world by the end of the 19th century.

Robert Hoover would work for Western Union for sixteen years. First in Allegheny City, Pa. and later in Marietta, Ohio. He managed the Allegheny City office until 1872. That year he was also hired as the Superintendent of Telegraph and Train Dispatcher for the Marietta-Cleveland Railroad. The man who hired Hoover was General A. J. Warner, president of the railroad and a former principal of the Lewistown Academy. In 1874, while Gen. Warner was in Europe, Hoover was placed in charge of the railroad.

Telegraphy, a new and growing technology in the mid-1800s, would be surpassed by a new form of communications - the telephone. In 1882, Hoover was lured from Western Union and began service with the Central Union Telephone Company at Springfield, Ohio, shortly transferring to the company's office in Springfield, Illinois. Central Union would eventually become part of the Bell system.

The *Lewistown Gazette* reported in its November 1, 1882 issue:

R.B. Hoover, who has been living in Ohio for several years past, has gone to Illinois to reside for the future. He has accepted a position as Assistant Superintendent of the Central Telephone Co. - the largest in the west. His headquarters will be at Springfield, Ill., the home and tomb of Lincoln.

Eventually, Hoover would be the company's general manager until his mandatory retirement in 1914.

CIVIC PRIDE INSPIRES IMPROVEMENT

During these years, R.B. Hoover was an advocate of community improvement.

150

His community spirit came early, as in 1863 when Hoover served on a committee of three, including friend George R. Frysinger, to draft a constitution and bylaws for Mifflin County's first YMCA. Annual dues was set at fifty cents. Hoover would be elected the YMCA's first vice-president.

In 1871, the telegraph operators of America unveiled a bronze statue in New York's Central Park honoring Samuel F. B. Morse. Hoover organized and saw this project to completion while the inventor was still living. Hoover promoted downtown improvements to enhance a community's appeal to developers and wrote back to his home town and his friend Frysinger on the topic, an idea that George was trying to advance in Lewistown.

A letter from Hoover appeared in the *Gazette* on Feb. 12, 1890. He wrote, in part, *I was pleased to see in a late issue of your paper an article on the future of Lewistown, from the pen of my old friend and schoolmate, Geo. R. Frysinger. Although it is not likely I shall ever live there again, my heart often goes out to that lovely little city on the banks of the blue Juniata, and I wish I could do or say something to enthuse the people of Lewistown into what we term in the west a business boom...*

Almost every western city has a public square, and yet in all my travels I know of none that could be made so beautiful and attractive as the one at Lewistown...What a fine place the center of your square would be for a soldiers' monument...a reflection on your enterprise and patriotism that the one town in this great nation which furnished the first company to report to Washington in defense of the Union has not yet honored the memory of those who did not return.

Frysinger had for some time, editorialized in the *Gazette* about the need for an improved downtown and a Civil War monument. Interest in the project was hard to generate, but when the 1895 Lewistown Centennial was being organized, Frysinger spearheaded another push for this cause. He wrote in the Gazette:

At the beginning of the Borough's second century let us organize a movement at once for a soldiers' monument. We have talked about it long enough. The entire county should be interested. It is a shame that the town and county that sent the first volunteers to the war in '61 is tardy in the erection of a suitable and even costly monument to her boys in blue. The time seems auspicious, everybody is ready for it, and let us call a county mass meeting on

The Lincoln Stone is inscribed with these words: "THIS STONE FROM LINCOLN'S TOMB IN SPRINGFIELD. ILL."

Saturday afternoon to inaugurate the movement.

The project began to take off. A committee formed and shares were sold for $1 each. Quarter shares were offered for a quarter. Eventually, a tax of $.84 per year for five years was assessed. In 1900, the effort received a tremendous boost.

HOOVER ACQUIRES THE LINCOLN STONE

Robert B. Hoover was elected commander of the Springfield, Illinois G.A.R. post in 1894, a position that gave him considerable purchase in the political world. The G.A.R., Grand Army of the Republic, was a national organization of Union veterans of the Civil War. In modern terms, the G.A.R. was an advocacy group that exercised tremendous political clout in the 19th

Erecting the Soldiers' and Sailors' Monument - A committee began to raise money for a monument by selling shares at $1 each. A quarter share could be bought for $0.25. Taxes were also raised to help pay for the memorial. Each taxpayer was assessed $0.84 every year for five years, but finally the $15,000 needed was raised, often a nickel at a time. Citizens of Mifflin County completed the project in memory of the Soldiers and Sailors in the War of 1861 - 1865 - photo MCHS Archives

and early 20th centuries. Hoover was a prominent Springfield citizen, who knew the rich and famous of his day, from Samuel F. B. Morse to Andrew Carnegie. He served on the Lincoln Memorial Association, too.

It's interesting to note, that controversy surrounded Lincoln's burial almost from the beginning. Mrs. Lincoln objected to a plan to bury her murdered husband in a downtown lot in Springfield. She insisted on having him interred at the park like Oak Ridge Cemetery. In 1876, a group conspired to steal Lincoln's body and stash it in an Indiana sand dune. The plan was to return the remains in exchange for the release of their leader, jailed on charges of counterfeiting!

Springfield eventually put a plan into motion to reconstruct Lincoln's tomb

Work completed June, 1906 -Workmen from Lewistown contractor D. R. Stratford and men from the Moore Brothers and Brault Company, Granite Manufacturers from Barre, Vermont, take a much deserved break after setting the finishing touches on the Soldiers' & Sailors' Monument. At the base of the monument, is a special stone which came from the tomb of Abraham Lincoln. It can be seen as a white rectangle in the base directly behind the boy standing in front. The monument weighs 125 tons and is sixty-four feet, six inches tall. It is made of Vermont marble. On the four sides of the monument are statues representing the four branches of the military at the time - Navy, Infantry, Cavalry and Artillery.
- photo MCHS Archives

in a larger, more secure form. In 1900, Robert Hoover acquired a granite block for his old home town. He wrote again to his friend, George Frysinger.

You will recall the last conversation we had on this subject (a soldiers' monument), wherein I promised you that if the people of Mifflin County would take the necessary interest in this movement I would get for them a corner stone for your monument from the tomb of Abraham Lincoln. I now stand ready to make good on the promise. In fact the stone is now in your town.

Lincoln's Tomb is being rebuilt, and the custodian, who is a friend of mine, has given me this stone, the only one which can or will be spared as it is their intention to use in rebuilding all the old granite stones, which have been for years in the Monument at Springfield, Illinois.

I told them what I wanted the stone for, and they recognized our claim, while rejecting all others. Being the first place to respond to the President's call for troops, it was deemed fitting to allow one stone to be used for the purpose named.

Hoover's complete letter was printed in the Lewistown *Gazette.* He sent the stone to Lewistown by rail from Springfield, on condition that a monument be built in the town square. A few weeks later, the stone was placed in a street window of the Mifflin County National Bank on Market Street to aide the fund raising effort. Some individuals offered matching fund to spur interest, children got into the act saving pennies. By 1906, the funds were raised for a total cost of fifteen thousand dollars. Construction would begin.

THE MONUMENT

George Frysinger, plus W. S. Settle and Ben Ruble of the Monument Committee announced the design for the

These rare snapshots show the crowd gathering in front of the Mifflin County Courthouse for the June 21, 1906 for the dedication of the Soldiers' and Sailors' Monument to Civil War veterans.- photo MCHS Archives

Lewistown decorated for the June 21, 1906 dedication of the Monument on the Square. Two children celebrated by placing coins on the trolley tracks at left at corner of Brown and Market.at the Mifflin County National Bank.- photo MCHS Archives

monument in the spring of 1906. By May, the Lincoln Stone was dressed and lettered by D. R. Stratford, ready to be placed in the base. Construction was expected to take about three weeks.

On May 7, 1906, a ceremony was held to place articles in a cavity behind the Lincoln Stone. A heavy glass jar was used to hold a list of soldiers from Mifflin County in the Civil War, a button and

The Square was awash in bunting and American flags during the dedication ceremony. The celebration and dedication ceremony was held June 21, 1906. Newspaper reports indicate 25,000 to 30,000 people came to witness the unveiling. The plan was for a rope to be pulled and drop the veil at the time of the dedication, but strong winds prior to the program tore the covering and offered a sneak peek. Tiny American flags were released from a balloon attached on a high wire from the courthouse cupola - photo MCHS Archives

badge from the G. A. R., other military records from the Civil War, United States coins for the five years of the war 1861 - 1865, plus an 1895 Lewistown Centennial medal.

The *Lewistown Gazette* noted that the jar was made airtight by, "three thicknesses of adhesive strips contributed for the purpose by Druggist J. A, Muthersbaugh. The wrappings were made fast by county seals kindly given for the purpose by the county commissioners."

A car load of granite figures destined to adorn the monument, arrived at the Lewistown depot on the same day. The completed monument tipped the scales at 125 tons. Height - 64 feet, 6 inches high. Material - Vermont granite. The four sides of the monument display designs of the branches of the military at the time - Navy, Infantry, Artillery and Calvary.

A celebration and dedication ceremony was held June 21, 1906. Newspaper reports indicate 25,000 to 30,000 people came to witness the unveiling. The plan was for a rope to be pulled and drop the veil at the time of the dedication, but strong winds prior to the program tore the covering and offered a sneak peek.

Monument Square just prior to the 1906 dedication ceremony
Vintage photo MCHS Archives

Tiny American flags were released from a balloon attached on a high wire from the courthouse cupola..

HOOVER RETIRES

For all his efforts on behalf of the Soldiers' and Sailors' Monument project, it's not clear if Robert Hoover attended the dedication ceremony in 1906. No reference to him is mentioned in the local papers. Hoover visited the area for the last time just prior to his retirement, when he attended the 50th anniversary of the Battle of Gettysburg in 1913.

As he reached his 70th birthday, rules at Bell Telephone dictated his mandatory retirement. After thirty-two years of service, he and second wife Margaret retired to Los Angeles, California. He kept up a steady correspondence with George Frysinger. In one letter, he invited George to come to California and live, noting his light bill was $1 per month, water 75 cents per month and gas for cooking and heating $1.50 per month. George didn't come.

In a letter to George R. Frysinger's brother, Maslin, dated September 30, 1922, Hoover reminisced about how he became a drummer boy in the Logan Guards and how his work at the *Lewistown Gazette* ended.

"You know I was a drummer boy in the Logan Guards, and when the Co. was called I spoke to George of the way your father canceled my apprenticeship - Capt. Selheimer came to the office and said, 'Come on, Bob, Uncle Sam is calling us. Get out your drum and come to the Court House.' I went to your father and said, 'Can I go, Mr. Frysinger?' He arose from his desk and exclaimed, 'Yes, and every boy in the office can go if needed to uphold the old flag.'"

George Frysinger received word that Robert Hoover died unexpectedly in Los Angeles May 12, 1924. He was 79. In addition to his wife, Margaret, he left five children, three daughters and two sons. He returned to Mifflin County only rarely after he left Lewistown in the late 1860s. Yet Robert B. Hoover's spirit of commitment to the community of his youth speaks to us today. The next time you drive past Monument Square, remember George Frysinger's old friend, Rob Hoover, the man who brought the Lincoln Stone to Mifflin County.

MIFFLIN COUNTY'S UNIQUE GIFT

A new technology - the telephone - enticed Robert Hoover from the telegraph. But it was community improvement that brought him back to his hometown. The Lincoln Stone, an incentive to the area to complete what he called a "labor of love" would be his gift to Mifflin County.

You may have had the opportunity to stand on the Square in Lewistown while watching a parade, military ceremony or other special event. You may have noticed the stone at the base of the monument, on the south side facing the Embassy Theatre. These words are inscribed on its face: "This Stone from Lincoln's Tomb, Springfield, Ill." Much of what we know today about R.B. Hoover and the Lincoln Stone comes from his correspondence with his lifelong friend George R. Frysinger, editor of the Lewistown *Gazette* for almost forty years and Mifflin County's 'original' historian. He kept prolific files of historical local events that survive today, including letters and clipping from and about his old friend "Rob" Hoover, Mifflin County's benefactor for a piece of American history.

Mifflin County Trivia
"Did lightning strike the bank, twice?"

1. The first parking meters came to Lewistown in 1938, but there were parking restrictions imposed on the downtown area prior to that. The borough imposed this new restriction in the form of an ordinance in 1932. What was the first parking restriction in Lewistown's history?

[a] Parking in front of stores was limited to customers only. Employees had to park off the main streets.

[b] Trucks were restricted to deliveries at specified rear entrances.

[c] Cars could not back into parking spaces, that kept the license plates from view by motor police.

[d] Parking on central streets was limited to two-hours

2. When the school year closed in 1958, something ended in the history of Mifflin County education. It was reported in the *Sunday Patriot News*, dateline Burnham, in what was then the Chief Logan Joint School District. What happened that was called "the end of an era?"

[a] The last of the one room schools closed in Mifflin County.

[b] Students could no longer go home at noon, with the last county district introducing a closed lunch period.

[c] Chief Logan district was the last to end the prohibition of married women being hired as teachers.

[d] The last horse drawn school bus ceased operation in the Maitland area.

3. It would occur two times in two years, at the Milroy Banking Company, located on the village square in Milroy, Armagh Township. The first time it happened was in 1935, then again in 1937. What occurred twice at the Milroy Bank?

[a] Two different cashiers accidentally lock themselves in the bank vault overnight.

[b] Lighting strikes the bank, causing extensive fire damage to the roof.

[c] The bank is robbed by masked bandits, who get away with thousands.

[d] Stone trucks from nearby Naginey Quarry lose control and crash into the building.

4. In 1957, retired Lewistown meat-cutter, Fred D. Henry and his friend and former co-worker Frank Dalby of Reedsville, prepared a "New Taste Treat" from a wild animal for the members of the City Hook and Ladder Fire Company. Henry noted, "Why in fifteen minutes even the crumbs were polished off..." The pair concocted 55 pounds of the exotic dish. What was this taste treat?

[a] Grilled beaver tails.

[b] Salted raccoon jerky.

[c] Sugar cured groundhog.

[d] Batter dipped, deep-fried opossum patties.

TRIVIA ANSWERS:

1.d Two hour parking restriction ordinance enacted June 13, 1932. *Souvenir Booklet of Ltn.*, *pg. 29*

2.a The *Patriot* reporter wrote in June, 1958: *An end of an era is reported here with the closing of school this Tuesday when the last one-room school house closes. The last four one-roomers to bow to progress: Hoopes School, Kline, Maitland and Vira. Pupils from those schools would be bussed to town schools in the Fall. The Vira school was believed to be the oldest of the four. Its teacher was Mrs. Dorothy T. Diess, who had thirty students in the first and second grades. She noted, "This would be the perfect set up if we had all the modern conveniences. There is a close teacher-pupil bond." Seven of the thirty who live nearby walked home for lunch. The pupils traveling by bus, carry their lunches in bags or lunch boxes. Drinking water is carried in a bucket from a nearby home of Clair Corbin and poured into a stone water cooler equipped with a spigot, from which children filled their cups. The two modern conveniences are the electric lights and a telephone. Until 1930, in the county, eight grades were taught in these buildings. Since 1911, 70 one-room schools closed across Mifflin County. Wayne Twp. had the most, with 14, the largest number receiving reimbursement.*

3.c In April, 1935, four masked bandits tie up cashier D. G. Meek and escape with $3,000. Then in December, 1937, a trio of masked men truss up assistant cashier Charles Ehrenfeld, bank director Taylor Reed and Wilson Civitts, 16, who just stopped in for some change. *Souvenir Booklet of Ltn.*

4. c The two found the best results in preparing the sugar cured groundhog: parboiling it then frying, then processing it like country cured ham. There are two schools of thought on the delicacy. There are no middle-of-the-fense nibblers. You either smack your lips or flatly turn away from the tangy taste of the wild meat. *Patriot News 9/14/57*

18 - County Medal of Honor Recipients

*A*uthorized by the United States Congress on July 12, 1862, the Congressional Medal of Honor was established during the Civil War. Those first medals were presented to enlisted men involved in a daring raid on Rebel railroad facilities in Georgia. By the end of that war, over 1500 medals had been awarded, most to enlisted men in the Army, although of that total, 307 went to the Navy and 17 to the Marines. Valor, bravery and gallantry are terms associated with recipients of the Medal of Honor and reasons for bestowing that award.

Four Mifflin County veterans, John Andrew Davidsizer, James Parker Landis, John Lilley, and William H. Rankin, all of whom saw service in the Civil War, were awarded the Medal of Honor for just such reasons. Davidsizer, Landis and Lilley received medals for Civil War service, while Rankin's medal

Mifflin County remembered local Medal of Honor Recipients John Lilley, John A. Davidsizer, James P. Landis and William H. Rankin at Rec Park Saturday, September 27, 1997. 2nd Pennsylvania Cavalry members shown here.

came during action against hostile Indians in 1872. The Mifflin County Veterans Association, in conjunction with several other groups, including the Mifflin County Historical Society, hosted a ceremony honoring Medal of Honor recipients of Mifflin County at Lewistown's Rec Park Saturday, September 27, 1997.

BRIEF BIOGRAPHIES OF COUNTY RECIPIENTS

John Andrew Davidsizer

Davidsizer was born in Lewistown, Pennsylvania April 26, 1834. He enlisted in Company C, 1st Pennsylvania Volunteer Cavalry May 19, 1861. He was wounded June 21, 1864 at Milford Station, Virginia. Davidsizer won the Medal of Honor for capture of a Confederate battle flag at Paine's Crossroads, Virginia April 5, 1865. He was discharged a Sergeant in Company A on June 16, 1865 at Clouds Mills, Virginia. Davidsizer died October 19, 1913 in Lewistown and was buried in the First Methodist Cemetery, Lewistown.

James Parker Landis

Landis was born July 20, 1843 in Yeagertown, Pennsylvania. He enlisted August 1, 1861 in Company C, 1st Pennsylvania Volunteer Cavalry and served as Chief Bugler on the regimental headquarters staff.

Landis won the Medal of Honor for capture of Confederate battle flag and "distinguished gallantry in action" at Paine's Crossing, Virginia April 5, 1865. He was discharged as Chief Bugler on June 20, 1865 at Clouds Mills, Virginia. Landis died December 1, 1924 in Yeagertown and was buried in Holy Communion Lutheran Cemetery, Yeagertown, Pennsylvania.

Medal of Honor recipient William Rankin portrayed by R. B. Wessell at Lewistown's Rec Park Saturday, September 27, 1997.

John Lilley

Lilley was born in 1827, although the exact date and location is unknown. He enlisted in Company F, 205th Pennsylvania Volunteer Infantry September 1, 1864. Lilley received the Medal of Honor for the capture of a Confederate battle flag and three prisoners in an assault on the works in front of Petersburg, Virginia, April 2, 1865. He was discharged as Private June 21, 1865, at Alexandria, Virginia. Lilley died May 12, 1902 in Lewistown and was buried in First Methodist Cemetery, Lewistown.

William H. Rankin

Rankin was born in 1836, believed to be February, in Lewistown, Pennsylvania. He enlisted in Company F, First United States Cavalry (Regular Army) at Harrisburg, Pennsylvania Septem-

ber 14, 1855. The unit was redesignated as the 4th United States Cavalry in August, 1861. Rankin served as First Sergeant of Company F during part of his third (1864-67) and fourth (1867-1872) enlistments. Thereafter served as Private and, later, a farrier (ranked as Private but paid as a Corporal). Farriers were responsible for shoeing and caring for the feet of all horses assigned to their company, between sixty to one hundred horses. This, in addition to his duties as a combat soldier.

Rankin won the Medal of Honor for "great gallantry in action against hostile Indians" on the north fork of the Red River in Texas Panhandle September 29, 1872. He was wounded in this action and initially left for dead, but survived and resumed active service shortly thereafter. Rankin's medal was awarded at Fort Griffin, Texas at evening parade on December 27, 1872.

William Rankin's old stone at the McCoy House, 17 N. Main Street, Lewistown, PA. The new stone is located at St. Marks' Cemetery.

Rankin retired April 11, 1890 at Fort Huachuca, Arizona. He died February 2, 1916 in Lewistown, Pennsylvania and was buried in St. Marks Community Cemetery, Lewistown.

The original grave marker was recently donated to the Mifflin County Historical Society, shown at right, and was placed in the yard adjacent to the alley at the McCoy House.

From the Pages of...

The Lewistown Gazette
November 4, 1858

"No Treats, but Halloween Tricks!"

 Hollow Eve. like the first of April, has always been considered a suitable occasion for playing practical jokes. Coming on Sunday evening of this year, our mischief loving boys would have been deprived of their usual amusement had they not taken time by the forelock and perpetrated their tricks on Saturday evening, and then followed up again on Monday evening. Some cabbage was stolen, as usual, but girls and boys pretty generally confined their annoyance to throwing corn at windows and doors. Some that were engaged in this "sport," might want the corn before the winter is over.

- Notes -
Mifflin County Sources, Selected Readings and/or Related Websites

Author's note concerning Internet sites: *Every effort was made to give complete, accurate Internet addresses. Listed addresses were active and accessible at the time written, however, as we all know, things do change on the Internet. I cannot be responsible for changes on Web sites. I make no claims for the sites beyond suggesting what each may offer as an example of type, content or possible usefullness as a resource. Thanks.*

1- Our county's namesake - Thomas Mifflin

There are no official biographies of Thomas Mifflin, but a thorough work that details Mifflin's political life and times was written in 1952 by Kenneth R. Rossman and was a valuable source for background and Mifflin's politics during the Revolution - Rossman, Kenneth R. *Thomas Mifflin and the Politics of the American Revolution* . Chapel Hill: University of North Carolina Press, 1952.

General Mifflin was inducted into the Quartermaster Hall of Fame in 1987. The web site for the hall of fame notes: "Mifflin Hall, the Headquarters Building for the Quartermaster School, Fort Lee, VA, historic Fort Mifflin in Philadelphia and Mifflin County, PA are named in honor of General Mifflin." Contacts: U.S. Army Quartermaster Center and School, 1201 22nd Street Fort Lee, VA 23801 or these web pages. www.quartermaster.lee.army.mil/ or www.qmfound.com/MG_Thomas_Mifflin.htm

* Also worth investigating: Marshall, James V.. *The United States Manual of Biography and History* . Philadelphia: James B. Smith & Co., 1856. Basic biographical data found on pages 177-178; plus a Web site called Colonial Hall. This Internet resource has the biographies of 103 founding fathers and 30 biographies of their wives located at www.colonialhall.com/mifflin/mifflin.php

2 - Artifacts Hint at County's Past

Raymond Harmon's *Mifflin County Revisited 1730 - 1990* describes the artifact collections of Sam Detweiler of Allensville and Jonas Yoder of McVeytown.

There are scores of published materials on artifacts at book stores and on the Internet. Ethical considerations and points about legality of collecting on public and private lands are important for every amateur collector to know and follow. One Web site listing titled "The Neverending Bibliography" enumerates a multitude of archeological materials. Here are just three:

* Custer, Jay F. *A Guide to Prehistoric Arrowheads and Spear Points of Eastern Pennsylvania and the Central Middle Atlantic.* Center For Archaeological Research, Department of Anthropology, University of Delaware, Newark. 2001 - Classification guide

* Fogelman, Gary L. *A Projectile Point Typology for Pennsylvania and the Northeast.* Fogelman Publishing Company, Turboville. 1988 - A method of dating projectile points

* C. G. Yeager, C. G. & Frison, George C. *Arrowheads & Stone Artifacts: A Practical Guide for the Amateur Archaeologist* Pruett Publishing Co., Boulder Colorado. 2000 - Ethical considerations discussed.

* Home of The Society for Pennsylvania Archaeology, Inc. can be found at www.pennsylvania archaeology.com/ or the Pennsylvania State Museum in Harrisburg at www.statemuseumpa.org/home.html. These are just two sites on the topic, but both have links to many related sites and Web pages.

3 - The Grasshopper War

From time to time, questions about the Grasshopper War are fielded at the Mifflin County Historical Society. Thanks to Patrick M. Reynolds *Pennsylvania Profiles* Volume VIII, page 373, (Red Rose Studio, Willow Street, PA 17584, 1984), for recounting the War of the Grasshopper. Mr. Reynolds cited the *Port Royal Sesqui - Centennial* (1812 - 1962) anniversary publication, Chapter 1 entitled "Indians" as one of his sources for the 1984 profile. *Mifflin County Yesterday & Today,* 1993, also retells the story.

The *Port Royal Times,* Thursday, July 20, 1876 - Historical Sketch of Juniata County by Rev H. C. Shindle also recalls the story:

Many traditions of fierce battles between the various tribes give point to this unpleasant truth—notably among them the bloody contest that has remained in history as the "Grasshopper War." The legend is, that squaws of several different tribes had collected together for friendly and social intercourse, and whilst thus engaged the children amused themselves in trying to catch fish. Bait being scarce, one of the children, succeeding in catching a grasshopper, succeeded also in arousing the envy of his less fortunate companions. A squabble ensued for the possession of the unoffending insect, which in time waxed so warm that the squaws took part in the contest. "The combat deepened," and soon the warriors became involved, and a bloody and disastrous war was the final result.

The traditions all agree as to the cause and the sanguinary character of this fierce contest, but they do not so well agree as to the locality of the conflict. We are inclined to think that the ground occupied by Messrs. Wetzler, Strouse and Turbett was the scene of this bloody fray.

* Complete text of Shindle's essay available at http:// freepages.genealogy.rootsweb.com/~milliken/jottings/shindle.html

4 - Legend of Bird Rock

Ben and Hattie Meyers' 1973 book, *Birds and Friends of Central Pennsylvania Mifflin County* recounts the legend of Bird Rock on pages 3 - 5, quoting Ben's Lewistown *Sentinel* column, "We Notice That" dated January 3, 1969. Although Ben Meyers died in 1971, Hattie gleaned information for the publication from his files of some 39 years, ten as Sentinel editor. Orb Rowden published the book in Lewistown at Mifflin County Printing located then in the old Sentinel Building on Dorcas Street.

Page 52 of *Historical Souvenir of Lewistown, Penna* Lewistown, PA: The Sentinel Company and Old Home Week Celebration Committee, 1925 has a photo and caption of Bird Rock.

Iva Anne Kepler Fisher (1925 - 1977) - Reedsville artist Anne Fisher created the Bird

Rock pen and ink for the book cover by Hattie Meyers mentioned in this article. Fisher painted her first oil painting in 1950 - an interior scene in Alexander Caverns. She is best known for her sketches and paintings of the old-order Amish of Big Valley, Mifflin County. Over the ensuring years, Anne Fisher created hundreds of paintings, sketches and decorated items. During the 1950s, Anne Fisher tried her hand at decorating iron ware. Skillet clocks were a speciality at this time, usually done in a Pennsylvania Dutch motif, with Amish figures at the 12, 3, 6, and 9 positions of the clock's face. Her husband, Henry T. Fisher (1923 - 1978), installed an electric clock motor and fashioned the knife and fork hands, usually from a child's tea set purchased at one of Lewistown's 5 & 10s. Beside the volume of Amish work, Anne Fisher also took a serious interest in depicting Mifflin County's past. She completed several local projects, including a series from the life of Chief Logan for the Kish Valley Bank and a Bicentennial project with views of historic Brown Township, and a series of paintings for titled "Remember When" in celebrating local history. Anne and Henry had three sons, Forest K., Matthew H. and H. Scott, all of Reedsville.

5 - Logan, Chief of the Mingoes

For some two hundred years, stories about Logan's life have been told and retold in books and publications of all types, from histories to travelogs . This repetition has created a body of traditional material about Logan. The stories of William Brown's family, the first meeting, etc., can be found in Eli Bowen's *Sketch-Book of Pennsylvania Or Its Scenery, Internal Improvements, Resources, and Agriculture,* 1852; Sherman Day's *Historical Collections of the State of Pennsylvania, 1843;* and Franklin Ellis *History of the Susquehanna and Juniata Valleys,* 1886 and others.

* I. D. Rupp's *Early History of Western Pennsylvania* Harrisburg, Pa.: Daniel W. Kauffman, Publisher 1846. (Appendix, pp. 213-217. In a letter written by Devereux Smith in 1774 to Pennsylvania's governor shortly after the event, tells of the death of Logan's Family by a group led by Daniel Greathouse, not Michael Cresap, as asserted by Logan in his famous speech.)

* Anthony F. C. Wallace *Jefferson And The Indians: The Tragic Fate Of The First Americans* 1999. Wallace notes in his book, *"About the same time, a party led by Daniel Greathouse killed and scalped nine Indians, including Logan's kin, at Baker's Tavern, fifty-five miles down the river, across from the mouth of Yellow Creek (which enters the Ohio several miles above present Wheeling, West Virginia). It was these last murders and the mutilation of Logan's pregnant sister that spurred Logan to take revenge. According to Smith, Logan's attacks were directed particularly at settlements along the upper Monongahela River and in the neighborhood of Redstone Creek, whence Cresap's and Greathouse's men had come."*

* *Logan, Mingo Chief,* Belleville, PA: Kishacoquillas Valley National Bank, 1976. (Written and illustrated by Mifflin County artist Anne K. Fisher 1925 - 1977). The sketches accompanying the Logan article were pen and ink illustrations used in the 1976 KVB booklet. Other selected readings on Logan include:

* Allen W. Eckert *The Frontiersmen,* "The Winning of America" series, 1967
* Hale's *The Indian Wars of Pennsylvania*
* Norman Woods *Lives of the Famous Indian Chiefs*
* Henry W. Shoemaker *Indian Folk-Songs of Pennsylvania* 1927
* *Mifflin County Yesterday & Today* 1993

6 - The Seven Mountains

The interesting topic of buffalo hunting in the Seven Mountains was raised during research for this article and the next, Hunting in Mifflin County. Henry W. Shoemaker's *A Pennsylvania Bison Hunt* written in 1915 and his *More Pennsylvania Mountain Stories* tells of hunting bison in the "high table" area of the Seven Mountains. He details the last stand of the bison in nearby Snyder and Union Counties. Patrick M. Reynolds presents the same episode in Volume 11 of his *Pennsylvania Profiles Series* in 1987, recounting the death of a 2,000 lb. bison bull called 'Old Logan by local pioneers in 1799. Ted Franklin Belue in *The Long Hunt - Death of the*

Buffalo East of the Mississippi, Mechanicsburg, PA: Stackpole Books, 1996, generally discounts the possibility of any "vast" herds of Pennsylvania bison, while Robert B. Eckhardt argues the possibility of "Buffalo in Pennsylvania" in *Pennsylvania 1776* published by PSU Press in 1976. These are several sources for further reading on the Seven Mountain's buffalo.

    * *The State Book of Pennsylvania Containing an Account of the Geographical, History, Government, Resources, and Noted Citizens of the State; with A Map of the State and of Each County* published in 1846 has a map of Mifflin County on page 199 that identifies the " Seven Mts." It also mentions the area turnpikes.

    Other suggested readings on the Seven Mountains:

    * Jeffrey R. Frazier *Pennsylvania Fireside Tales (Origins and Foundations of Pennsylvania Mountain Folktales and Legends)*

    * Henry W. Shoemaker *Eldorado Found - The Central Pennsylvania Highlands, A Tourist's Survey*

    * Paul A. W. Wallace, *Indian Paths of Pennsylvania*

    * Stroup, J. Martin & Bell, Raymond M. *Genisis of Mifflin County*

7 - Hunting in Mifflin County

Juniata Huntress - the story of Dorcas Elizabeth Holt Stackpole's adventure can be found in Henry W. Shoemaker's *Pennsylvania Deer and Their Horns*. The 1915 edition has been out of print for many years. A reprinting was published in 1992 by the Lycoming County Historical Society, but even that volume is now difficult to find. However, a new revised 2002 edition, with a second part including commentary on modern deer management is available from Wennawoods Publishing, Lewisburg, PA 17837. Contact the publisher at 1-800-796-1702 or at their Website www.wennawoods.com

    * "The Last Panther Hunt" is described in *Historical Souvenir of Lewistown, Penna* Lewistown, PA: The Sentinel Company and Old Home Week Celebration Committee, 1925.

    * In addition, S. Duane Kauffman's *Mifflin County Amish and Mennonite Story 1791 - 1991* Chapter VIII , pages 203 - 206 titled "The Good Old Days" details many a good old fashioned yarn of hunting prowess aimed at supplementing the table or income among members of these conservative groups.

    * Mifflin County newspapers on microfilm found in the Mifflin County Historical Society archives include: The Lewistown Republican, The True Democrat, Democratic Sentinel, The Democrat and Sentinel, The Daily Sentinel and Lewistown Gazette. This resource holds a wealth of information for the persistent researcher.

    * *The Pennsylvania Game Commission 1895 - 1995 100 Years of Wildlife Conservation* by Joe Kosack tells the story of hunting in Pennsylvania. Chapter 1, A Land of Plenty, gives an excellent historical backdrop for this topic.

    * The Game commission's Website at http://www.pgc.state.pa.us/ is greatly expanded and well worth a visit.

8 - Fort Granville and the "Mysterious" French Letter

Roger J. Cuffey of the Dept. Geosciences, Penn State University, wrote this essay on the military significance of Fort Granville's placement for presentation at the North-Central Section (36th) and Southeastern Section (51st), GSA Joint Annual Meeting held April 3–5, 2002:

    Within the Appalachian Valley-&-Ridge Province, in a synclinorial valley underlain by Silurian shales, lay Fort Granville. Its probable site is 1.0 mi (1.6 km) W30ºS from the courthouse in downtown Lewistown (Mifflin County), 300 ft (100 m) NE from the intersection of Crystal Spring Avenue and Riverview Drive. The fort was apparently on the southwestern lip of the shallow ravine there cutting down into the north bank of the Juniata River. Grading for street and house construction since has disturbed the soil on the site so much that no clear-cut evidence remains of the fort.

    Fort Granville was built at the end of 1755 as one of a chain of forts to protect the northwestern mountain frontier settlers from Indian raids, a morale boost, but military failure because the forts were too widely spaced, given travel conditions at the time. The site, on a wide valley floor between high ridges, takes advantage of a topographic constriction narrowing the valley (enhancing visibility of forces moving past), a location midway between two water gaps (a principal overland route through the mountain ridges), and situation on the bank of a major river (ready access back to settled areas to the southeast). The valley was heavily forested (providing logs for construction), with alluvial soils or soft shale bedrock (hence stockade post-holes easily dug). Water could be supplied from either the river or an on-site small spring (which, like most in the region, was seasonal and thus was dry when needed in the siege in mid-1756).

In summary, some of the characteristics of the Fort Granville site had positive military value, but about as many, in actual practice, turned out to be negative instead.

Text can be found at http://gsa.confex.com/gsa/2002NC/finalprogram/ abstract_30149.htm Professor Cuffy can be contacted at cuffey@ems.psu.edu. or at Dept. of Geosciences, Penn State University, 412 Deike Bldg., University Park, PA 16802. For reading in more detail on the historical background of Fort Granville, see these publications:

* William A. Hunter's *Forts on the Pennsylvania Frontier, 1753 - 1758*, PHMC in 1960 and reprinted by Wennawoods Publishing, Lewisburg, PA in 1999. Pennsylvania historian William A. Hunter called the French letter "a puzzle in that day and a mystery in ours."

* *Frontier Forts of Pennsylvania*, Report of the Commission to the Pennsylvania Legislature in two volumes Harrisburg: Clarance M. Busch, State Printer of Pennsylvania 1896 (Location of Fort Granville and description of seige and capture with color map.)

* *Frontier Forts of Pennsylvania*, Report of the Commission to the Pennsylvania Legislature in two volumes Second Edition edited by Thomas Lynch Montgomery, Litt. D. Harrisburg: Wm. Stanley Ray, State Printer of Pennsylvania 1916 (Includes an extensive appendix with data on Fort Granville completed by the Mifflin County Historical Committee on determining the location of the fort.)

* McIlnay, Dennis P. *Juniata, River of Sorrows* Hollidaysburg, PA: Live Oaks Press First Edition 2002 (Excellent narrative of the event and its aftermath including the horrendous death of prisoner John Turner at the stake.)

* Rupp, I. D. *History and Topography of Northumberland, Huntingdon, Mifflin, Centre, Union, Columbia, Juniata and Clinton counties, Pa.* Lancaster: G. Hills 1847. (Appendix contains extensive transcript and discussion of the French Letter found at Fort Granville.)

* Patrick M. Reynolds also wrote about Fort Granville in a multiple part feature in *Pennsylvania Profiles* Volume XI Red Rose Studio, Willow Street, PA 17584, 1987. (Pages 7 - 16, details the Fort Granville episode and aftermath.)

9 - Mifflin County's First Drive-thru Window

Peacock Major's Tavern is discussed in *Historical Souvenir of Lewistown, Penna* Lewistown, PA: The Sentinel Company and Old Home Week Celebration Committee 1925.

* Also see *History of that part of the Susquehanna and Juniata Valleys, Embraced in the Counties of Mifflin, Juniata, Perry, Union and Snyder in the Commonwealth of Pennsylvania*, Published by Everts, Peck and Richards, Philadelphia two volumes, 1886. On p. 495 Major as noted as president of Lewistown Council in 1814 and his tavern is discussed on p. 506.

Peacock Major's tavern was referred to as "The Wayside Inn" by J. Martin Stroup in an article that appeared in the *Sentinel* in 1964. Stroup likened the venerable Peacock to the inn keeper in *Tales of a Wayside Inn* by Henry Wadsworth Longfellow. Stroup quoted the poet's inn keeper to Peacock Major. Stroup's quotes include:

> But first the Landlord will I trace;
> Grave in his aspect and attire;
> A man of ancient pedigree,
> A Justice of the Peace was he,

Known in all Sudbury as "The Squire."
And over this, no longer bright,
Though glimmering with a latent light,
Was hung the sword his grandsire bore
In the rebellious days of yore,
Down there at Concord in the fight.

Stroup notes Major, like the landlord of Longfellow, was "grave in his aspect and attire" and served himself against the British "In the rebellious days of yore." The complete work can be found in: Longfellow, Henry Wadsworth. *Tales of a Wayside Inn* New York: David Mckay, 1966.

10 - The Journal of Philip Vickers Fithian

Princeton President John Witherspoon was the father-in -law of Mifflin County Presbyterian minister James Sterrett Woods, who lived at Woodlawn in Lewistown, PA. In 1818, Rev. Woods married Marianne Frances Witherspoon, youngest daughter of Rev. Witherspoon, member of the Continental Congress from New Jersey, the only clergyman to sign the Declaration of Independence. During 1876, ceremonies associated with the US Centennial held that year in Lewistown, one of the Woods descendants commented that the family had a copy of the Declaration of Independence kept in a wooden box, along with a copy of the Stamps Acts brought from England in the box during the 1760s. What ever became of the rare documents is not known.

J. Martin Stroup, in his *Genesis of Mifflin County* recounts Fithian's local journey.

The "Laura" he referred to was Elizabeth Beatty, his future wife, whom he weds in October, 1775, a year prior to his death. She is the daughter of Rev. Charles Beatty mentioned earlier. In his journal, Fithian alternately calls her Eliza or Laura, according to Albion and Dodson.

John Fleming , 1734 - 1820, said to have settled in the valley in 1764, owner of Fleming's Mills, located between what is Milroy and Reedsville today. *Historical Register*, Vol. II (1884), pp. 114, 196.

Squire Brown was William Brown (1737 - 1825), Mifflin County's first presiding justice in 1789 and friend of Chief Logan. Brown was an early settler of the Kishacoquillas Valley in 1760. His home was on the site of present-day Reedsville. The creek mentioned "cutting through the mountain" would be Kishacoquillas Creek passing through Jack's Mountain via the Reedsville Narrows, eventually joining the Juniata River at Lewistown.

Dr. Samuel Maclay of Milroy, Pa., in the Kishacoquillas Valley, wrote in 1884: '*The road by which Rev'd Mr. Fithian entered our valley was no doubt the old Penn's Valley Road, which crossed the Seven Mountains a few miles north of this place, and is still plainly discernible. Historical Register*, Vol. II (1884), p. 196. Probably the present highway from Bellefonte southeast to Lewistown follows the same general course.

A century later, Frank Leslie's *Popular Monthly* described the same cave in the 1870s as not far from Perryville (Milroy's former name), accessible on the Milroy Branch of the Pennsylvania Railroad. The cave then was the object of excursions and outings, even band concerts were reportedly held in its cavernous halls. In 1884, the spot was termed "a large limestone hill," and described as "little altered except the absence of any arch or covering." - *Historical Record*, Vol. II (1884), p. 197.

This is considered the first recorded description of Alexander Caverns in Armagh Township, complete with the accurate location of the Alexander's stone house, which stood above the water opening until 2002, when it was disassembled, stone by stone, and moved to a location in Brown Township, Mifflin County.

11 - The Riot of 1791

History of that part of the Susquehanna and Juniata Valleys, Embraced in the Counties of Mifflin, Juniata, Perry, Union and Snyder in the Commonwealth of Pennsylvania ,Published

by Everts, Peck and Richards, Philadelphia two volumes, 1886 - pp. 460-463
    * Also, the *Historical Souvenir of Lewistown, Penna* Lewistown, PA: The Sentinel Company and Old Home Week Celebration Committee, 1925 recounts the event, among other county histories, like those of Cochran or Stroup and Bell's *Genesis of Mifflin County*.
    * Not directly related to The Riot, but a good source for the cultural and political feel for the colony prior to Independence is *Pennsylvania 1776* by Robert A. Secor (Editor), and Irwin Richman (Editor) , University Park Pennsylvania State University Press, 1975. Details many aspects of daily life in early Pennsylvania, including natural history, American Indians, religion, science and much more.

12 - Fifty Years in Chains - first published in Mifflin County

Slavery in America - The Life and Adventures of Charles Ball by Isaac Fisher and published by John W. Shugert of Lewistown in 1836. Another edition came out of New York published by John S. Taylor in 1837. Kraus Reprint Co., New York reproduced the Taylor edition in 1969.
    * American Slave Narratives:An Online Anthology is located at: http:// xroads.virginia.edu/~HYPER/wpa/wpahome.html This site describes its resources this way: *From 1936 to 1938, over 2,300 former slaves from across the American South were interviewed by writers and journalists under the aegis of the Works Progress Administration. These former slaves, most born in the last years of the slave regime or during the Civil War, provided first-hand accounts of their experiences on plantations, in cities, and on small farms. Their narratives remain a peerless resource for understanding the lives of America's four million slaves. What makes the WPA narratives so rich is that they capture the very voices of American slavery, revealing the texture of life as it was experienced and remembered. Each narrative taken alone offers a fragmentary, microcosmic representation of slave life. Read together, they offer a sweeping composite view of slavery in North America, allowing us to explore some of the most compelling themes of nineteenth-century slavery, including labor, resistance and flight, family life, relations with masters, and religious belief.*
    This web site provides an opportunity to read a sample of these narratives, and to see some of the photographs taken at the time of the interviews.
    The site's "Related Sources" offers Electronic Texts such as Sojurner Truth, *The Narrative of Sojurner Truth* or Booker T. Washington, *Up From Slavery* plus others online
    * The complete narratives can be found in George P. Rawick, ed., *The American Slave: A Composite Autobiography* Westport, Conn.: Greenwood Press, 1972-79. .

13 - Mifflin County reacts to Slavery

Additional reading on the Maclay House, in Milroy can be found in these sources: *Historic Homes and Buildings of Milroy and Armagh Township* and *Mifflin County Revisited Vol II* by Raymond Harmon ; Historic Sites Survey, Mifflin County, Pennsylvania by the Mifflin County Planning Commission 1978; The Sentinel Feb. 17, 1966 - Microfilm files at the MCHS Research Library. Harmon recounted an interview with the owners of the Maclay House, Dave and Sandy Goss. The Goss family knows of no records of actual Underground Railroad activity involving their house, however, according to Harmon's account. From 1928 to 1933 it served as American Legion Post # 287 and earlier it was a veterans' home and once served as a tavern on the stage line.
    Brief biography of William McClay taken from *US Congressional Biographies:*
    William Maclay (July 20 1737 - April 16 1804) was a politician from Pennsylvania during the eighteenth century. Maclay pursued classical studies, and then served as a lieutenant in an expedition to Fort Duquesne in 1758. He went on to serve in other expeditions in the French and Indian Wars . He studied law and was admitted to the bar in 1760. After a period of practicing law he became a surveyor in the employ of the Penn family, and then a prothonotary and clerk of the courts of Northumberland County in the 1770s. During the American revolution he served in the Continental Army as a

commissary. He was also a frequent member of the State legislature in the 1780s. During that period he was also the Indian commissioner, a judge of the court of common pleas, and a member of the executive council.

After the ratification of the Constitution Maclay was elected to the United States Senate and served from March 4 1789 to March 3 1791 . He received a two-year term instead of the usual six-year term for senators after he lost a lottery with the other Pennsylvania senator, Robert Morris . A similar issue was dealt with in each state, with one senator receiving a two or four year term rather than a six year term to determine the election cycle for senators in that state. In the Senate, Maclay was one of the most radical members of the Anti-Administration faction. In his journal, which is one of the most important records of the First United States Congress, he criticizes many of the Founding Fathers, including John Adams and George Washington . He also criticized many of their supporters who ran the senate and included particularly senators from the far north and far south, believing that their ways of running the Senate were inefficient. He was unsuccessful in his attempt to be re-elected by the state legislature of Pennsylvania.

Maclay retired to his farm in Dauphin, Pennsylvania, but was also a member of the State house of representatives in 1795, 1796 and 1797;. In addition, he was a presidential elector in 1796, a county judge from 1801 until 1803, and a member again of the State house of representatives in 1803. He died in Harrisburg, Pennsylvania and was interment in Old Paxtang Church Cemetery. Several of his relatives were also politicians, including his brother, Samuel Maclay and his nephew, William Plunkett Maclay.

Also see *American National Biography* ;*Dictionary of American Biography* ; Aurand, A. Monroe, Jr. *The Genealogy of Samuel Maclay, 1741-1811* . Harrisburg, PA: Aurand Press, 1938; Maclay, Samuel. *Journal of Samuel Maclay* . Williamsport, PA: Gazette & Bulletin Printing House, 1887.

Two additional publications on the Underground Railroad include:
 * *Hippocrene Guide to The Underground Railroad* by Charles L. Blockson   NY Hippocrene Books, 1994.
 * *Underground Railroad and Abolitionists of Pennsylvania* by Nilgun Anadolu Okur An article that is part of a series of slide-illustrated lectures sponsored by the Pennsylvania Humanities Council.
 * *Pennsylvania Dutch Genealogy...Underground Railroad Websites* at http://midatlantic.rootsweb.com/padutch/urailroad.html The Pennsylvania Dutch Family History Website is owned and maintained by FamilyHart (Don & Jeanine Hartman) The Hartman's write, "We love our heritage. We are the sons and daughters of the Pennsylvania Dutch. Some were Brethren, Reformed, Lutheran, Mennonite, Amish, Catholic or of other faiths. They came to America from Switzerland, Germany, and the eastern parts of France or wherever the German language was spoken before 1800. They came to Pennsylvania first. Some stayed and others went on to other places north, south, east and west. We seek to learn their history, their customs, their culture and their genealogy."

Underground Railroad links on the Pennsylvania Dutch site include: The National Geographic Online Presents The Underground Railroad, National Underground Railroad Freedom Center, Aboard the Underground Railroad, Taking the Train to Freedom, The Underground Railroad in Franklin County, Pennsylvania , The Valley Project and Slavery in Pennsylvania.

14 - 1861 Haiti Migration

The Mifflin County Historical Society's newspaper archives (1860s) contains *Lewistown Gazette* entries that detail the travelers who left the county for Haiti. It was not a successful venture, although there are descendants living in Haiti today with a Mifflin County connection. This was not the first migration to Haiti from the United States. The Website of The Haiti Program of Trinity College, Washington, DC, Dr. Bob Maguire, Director, presents some historical background of African-American migration to Haiti.:

In 1818, Jean-Pierre Boyer succeeded Alexandre Petion as President of Haiti. Two years later, upon the death of King Henri Christophe in Milot, near the northern city of Cap Haitian – at the time called Cap Henri, Boyer brought the Northern Province under his jurisdiction, reuniting the two separate sections of the former French colony. In 1822, Boyer expanded the national territory significantly, establishing Haitian control over the eastern half of the island of Hispaniola, the present-day Dominican Republic.

Throughout his political career, Boyer expressed a keen interest in the plight of African-Americans and in the idea of inviting them to immigrate to Haiti. One of the first African Americans to hear the call of Haiti was Henri Simonise, a mulatto born in South Carolina, and educated in England. Simonise migrated to Haiti in 1818 to escape the humiliation of daily life in the United States.

With the support of Boyer's Secretary of State, Joseph Balthazar Inginac, Simonise encouraged his countrymen to join him in Haiti. An unspecified number of African-Americans responded to the encouragement, moving to the Black Republic at their own expense. In 1820, President Boyer, seeking to reinforce this trend, extended this formal invitation to African Americans. The collapse of Boyer's government in 1843 and the turmoil that followed led to the secession from Haiti of the eastern part of the island, which proclaimed its independence as the Dominican Republic, and the isolation of that population from Haiti.

In 1847 Faustin Soulouque, whose 12-year reign was marked by failed attempts to reclaim the eastern province, became Haiti's President. Some African-Americans, most notably James Theodore Holly, an African-American clergyman of the Episcopal church, continued to explore interest in Haiti during Soulouque's notoriously corrupt and tyrannical rule. As a rule, however, significant migration of African-Americans from the US virtually ground to a complete halt during Soulouque's years in power, as other erstwhile settlers returned home.

Holly, who eventually became a leading proponent for migration to Haiti as well as the first African-American bishop of Haiti's Episcopal church, delayed his arrival to Haiti until 1861, two years after the demise of the Soulouque government. At that time, a second emigration of African-Americans to Haiti was gaining ground, in part as a result of the turmoil in the U.S. during its Civil War.

The Haiti Program site is located at: http://www.trinitydc.edu/academics/depts/Interdisc/International/Haiti_Program.htm

15 - Alamo Connections

The Mifflin County Historical Society's "Alamo" file includes J. Martin Stroup's materials on the subject. He was the editor of the local daily, "The Sentinel" for over thirty years and frequently published the results of his historical research in a column he authored on local history. He did an extensive multipart series in the 1960s on the county's Alamo locals, including Reynolds. In the 1830s and 40s (and later), Mifflin County had the traditional rival papers espousing opposite political opinions. There was "war talk" in the Lewistown Gazette concerning Texas, but the Lewistown Republican kept the local pro-Texas pot stirred with editorials and advertisements. Stroup used these actual newspapers in his sixties series, but since then the newspapers were placed on microfilm - both the Republican and the Gazette. The actual newspapers are also in the society's archives.

In March, 2000, Southwestern University of Georgetown, Texas displayed the medical legacy of Mifflin County native John Purdy Reynolds - his medical books. Their significance cannot be underestimated, as notes by Reynolds add to the picture of the young doctor's life beyond his home state of Pennsylvania.

The books were apparently abandoned by Reynolds in Tennessee - Mifflin, Tennessee. Handwritten notes in the books state that they were purchased at an estate sale in Mifflin, Tennessee in 1842. One of the books, Thatcher's American Modern Practice is inscribed: "Joseph J. McGee's book/Bought at Dr. Reynolds' dec'd sale in Mifflin, Tenn/July, 1842."

Several other books have a similar inscription. McGee signed his name in almost all of the books, which were all donated to Southwestern by his widow. Most have a plate which reads: "Presented by Mrs. McGee of Rice, Texas. Owned by Dr. John Reynolds who was killed at the Alamo."

The books were in the general circulation of the university library's regular book collection and bear the stamp, "may be kept out for two weeks only." In 1941, eight of the books were loaned to the Alamo, where they have been for over fifty years. At the time of the loan, they were deemed to have little value. Some of the books today are considered significant texts in the history of medicine and are valued in the thousands of dollars, as a check of prices at Barnes and Noble's Rare Books affirms.

All are early nineteenth century medical texts, except for a Greek/Latin Lexicon, which he would have needed in his medical studies. Most were published in Philadelphia, where Reynolds is thought to have studied. Two well-known American physicians, William Dewees and Caspar Wistar, taught at the University of Pennsylvania in the early 1800s, and their works are among Reynolds' books. John Purdy Reynolds' signature appears in most of the books, and several have notes indicating when he read particular books.

He completed his undergraduate studies, by some sources, at Franklin College in Lancaster County, and studied medicine in Philadelphia. Was he a practicing physician? His books indicate he was. The Reynold's family thought so and erected a marker at St. Marks Cemetery in Lewistown bearing this inscription: "My Brother, John Purdy Reynolds, M.D., March 14, 1806, killed in the Battle of the Alamo, Texas, March 6, 1836." In one of Reynolds' books, *Wistar's System of Anatomy* he inscribed in his own hand, "Commenced reading Anatomy Oct. 13th, 1832, Mifflin, Tenn." Perhaps his private practice wasn't in Mifflin County, Pennsylvania, but in Mifflin, Tennessee.

How did Reynolds reach Texas? Contemporary accounts in the local newspapers say that he went to Texas for the express purpose of aiding the Texans in their fight to win freedom from Mexico. It is entirely possible he did, as some accounts suggest, travel to Texas via Tennessee with the legendary Davy Crockett and his volunteers.

The Handbook of Texas states that Reynolds traveled from Tennessee to Nacogdoches, arriving in 1835. He joined the Volunteer Auxiliary Corps of Texas in January, 1836 and, according to the Handbook, went to San Antonio de Bexar with Crockett. Records from San Antonio refer to him as a private, with at least five other physicians or surgeons on the rolls. One argument: the books left in Tennessee indicate he wasn't going to Texas as a doctor. However, an equally strong argument can be made that any medical books he would have taken with him had no chance of surviving the destruction following the battle.

We'll probably never know, but Reynolds' books add to his story.

Suggested books on the Alamo are:

* Patrick M. Reynolds, *Pennsylvania Profiles Volume VI* Red Rose Studio, Willow Street, PA 17584 1982 (Page 315 the St. Marks' Cemetery and Reynold's monument are featured.)

* *A Time to Stand* by Walter Lord New York Pocket Books, 1963. (During his research, Lord conducted a correspondence with the Mifflin County Historical Society's J. Martin Stroup and discovered a third Mifflin Countian at the Alamo, William McDowell.)

* *Duel of Eagles* by Jeff Long William Morrow and Co. Inc. 1990. (Proposes the idea that Crockett survived the Spanish attack, only to be executed after the battle.)

* *Three Roads to the Alamo* by William C. Davis HarperCollins Publishers, 1998. (Details the lives of Crockett, Bowie and Travis leading to their deaths at the Alamo.)

* Daughters Of The Republic Of Texas maintain an outstanding Website at http://www.thealamo.org/main.html with links to almost two dozen sites in and around Texas. A brief biography of David P. Cummings and 31 other Alamo Defenders can be found on Sons of DeWitt Colony Texas Website at http://www.tamu.edu/ccbn/dewitt/dewitt.htm

16 - Four from Mifflin County Received the Medal of Honor

R. B. Wessel wrote biographies of the county's recipients Lilley, Davidsizer, Landis and Rankin titled *Medal of Honor Recipients of Mifflin County, Pennsylvania*, Lewistown, PA, 2001. Also, *Lewistown Sentinel*, April 28-29, 2001 "Civil War hero pictured in print" article describes an artist's print featuring MOH recipient William H. Rankin.

* *Medal of Honor: Profiles of America's Military Heroes from the Civil War to the Present* by Allen Mikaelian ,Mike Wallace , Commentaries by Mike Wallace , 2002 Published by Hyperion. Allen Mikaelian presents a stirring and patriotic look at eleven outstanding Americans who have earned the Congressional Medal of Honor. They include Lieutenant Ernest Childers, who, in his assault on a WWII German position, was reduced to throwing rocks at the enemy; and pacifist medic Desmond Doss, who saved more than 100 lives in a single day. *60 Minutes* icon Mike Wallace contributes an introduction.

* *Medal of Honor Recipients: 1863-1973* Washington, D.C.:Government Printing Office, 1973. Official Congressional listing of MOH Recipients.

The US Army Center for Military History maintains a Web site at http://www.army.mil/cmh-pg/moh1.htm The site notes: "The President, in the name of Congress, has awarded more than 3,400 Medals of Honor to our nation's bravest Soldiers, Sailors, Airmen, Marines, and Coast Guardsmen since the decoration's creation in 1861. For years, the citations highlighting these acts of bravery and heroism resided in dusty archives and only sporadically were printed. In 1973, the U.S. Senate ordered the citations compiled and printed as Committee on Veterans' Affairs, U.S.Senate, *Medal of Honor Recipients: 1863-1973* (Washington, D.C.:Government Printing Office, 1973). This book was later updated and reprinted in 1979. The breakdown (on the Web site) of these is a duplicate of that in the congressional compilation. Likewise, some minor misspelling and other errors are duplicated from the official government volume. These likely were the result of the original transcriptions."

The index of the full-text files by war.

* The Medal of Honor Website page located at http://members.aol.com/veterans/moh.htm is part of a site maintained by Vets for Vets. Downloadable indexes of MOH citations can be traced by Name, Actions between Post-Civil War to Pre-WWI, China (The Boxer Rebellion), The Civil War, Cuba, Dominican Campaign, Haiti, Indian Wars, Korea, 2d Nicaraguan Campaign, Philippines Actions, Somalia, Vera Cruz, Mexico, Vietnam War, World War I, Post World War I, World War II and Belated Awards.

17 - William Henry Harrison's Log Cabin

The story about Richard Smith Elliott and the log cabin was related in *Historical Souvenir of Lewistown, Penna* Lewistown, PA: The Sentinel Company and Old Home Week Celebration Committee, 1925 by George R. Frysinger.

Richard Smith Elliott expounded on his "log cabin" experience in his memoir, *Notes Taken in Sixty Years,* (printed in St. Louis, MO by R. P. Studley & Co., in 1883). Elliott recounts his attendance at the Whig Party Convention in December, 1839 when Harrison was nominated for the US Presidency, along with John Tyler in the second spot. He recalls in some detail the *Baltimore Republican* (a Democratic paper) lambasting Harrison's "cider drinking" and him being content to sit beside a "sea coal" fire in his log cabin studying "moral philosophy." Elliott explains how he became involved with the cabin symbol as follows, in part:

In January, Mr. Thomas Elder, a gentleman of three score in years, and a big score in the bank of which he was president, sent a request for me to visit him one evening at his mansion, fronting the Susquehanna river...Mr. Elder had noted the slur on Gen. Harrison by the Baltimore paper, and thought we ought to make use of it; build a cabin, or something of that kind, which would appeal to the eye of the multitude. He was a shrewd old gentleman, Mr. Elder was, who had excellent Madeira, and well knew that passion and prejudice, properly aroused and directed, would do about as well as principle and reason in a party contest.

We talked the matter over, and while we sipped our wine and gravely assured each other that the treatment of the old hero by the Baltimore editor was intolerable, I had my pencil at work, sketched an imaginary log-cabin with a coon-skin tacked on it, an outside chimney of sticks and mud, a wood-pile consisting of a log with an ax stuck in it, and other accessories; and on taking leave told him I would try to put his idea into operation. At home I completed my sketch much to the amusement of the family, who had no vary exalted notion of my skill as an artist. Next day I had a carriage painter confidently at work on a transparency.

174

On the 20th of January we had a mass meeting at Harrisburg to ratify the nominations. As soon as the chairman took his seat I addressed him, stating that our grand old hero, the soldier and statesman, had been insulted most infamously by the Baltimore Republican, and concluded by moving for a committee of seven to bring into the meeting, "the best representation to be got of Gen. Harrison's log cabin." (Carried by acclamation.) When our committee reentered, Sam Clark bearing aloft the lighted transparency, with the log cabin on one side, and flags and mottoes on the others...

Senator Frederick Farley from Philadelphia, the speaker at the time the illuminated log cabin image was ceremoniously paraded into the hall, ceased speaking and bowed to the image. He "rose to the occasion and seemed to draw it up with him and kept the assembly in a frenzy of enthusiasm," as Elliott puts it, that lasted for an hour. From that moment on, the log cabin and William Henry Harrison were wedded. Log cabins became floats in political parades around the country or the image was printed in newspapers. Songs described at the time as "doggerel ballads made for the occasion ' with titles like The Log Cabin Song or Log Cabin Rising made the rounds of political meetings, thanks to Mifflin Countian Richard Smith Elliott's inspiration in this pivotal campaign.

* James D. Taylor of the State Library of Ohio wrote concerning this campaign, "Historians have described the 1840 campaign as the first modern political campaign. Harrison broke with tradition and campaigned actively for president on the Whig ticket. The log cabin became the symbol of Harrison's campaign when his Democratic opponents ridiculed him, saying he would be content to spend his days in a log cabin drinking hard cider. Harrison's supporters turned this insult around to portray Harrison as a man of the people." Ohio Memory Project, Ohio Historical Society , 1982 Velma Ave., Columbus, OH 43211-2497

18 - The Lincoln Stone

A special thanks to the Mifflin County Historical Society's Research Librarian, Jean Suloff. The information presented here on Robert Hoover is the result of the extensive research and transcription of the Hoover letters. Her research is always meticulous and presented the writer with a workable, coherent set of transcripts from which to write.

* A comprehensive book on the burial sites of all United States Presidents by C-SPAN's Brian Lamb and staff, with contributions by historians Richard Norton Smith and Douglas Brinkley, is titled *Who's Buried in Grant's Tomb? A Tour of Presidential Gravesites* - 2000. This book also discusses the plot to steal Lincoln's remains..A more detailed account can be found in *The Great Abraham Lincoln Hijack* by Bonnie Stahlman Speer, which details how a counterfeiting ring plotted to hold Lincoln's corpse for ransom.

* Abraham Lincoln's coffin has been moved 17 times, primarily due to frequent reconstructions of Lincoln's final resting place and fears for the safety of the President's body. His coffin was opened 5 times: December 21, 1865, September 19, 1871, October 9, 1874, April 14, 1887, and September 26, 1901. This information appeared in *Abraham Lincoln Fact Book and Teacher's Guide* by Gerald Sanders.

The agreed facts concerning Lincoln's last exhumation, the one most relevant to Mifflin County's connection to the 16th President's tomb, are as follows:

In 1900 the monument at Abraham Lincoln's tomb had to be torn down and completely rebuilt, due to concerns about stability expressed by son Robert Lincoln. Construction of the tomb took 15 months, and during that time Lincoln's coffin was in a temporary grave nearby. In late August, 1901, Lincoln's body was moved to its new resting place. A month later, Robert Lincoln visited the tomb and insisted on some further changes. In 1876 thieves had failed in an attempt to steal Mr. Lincoln's corpse and hold it for ransom. Robert Lincoln wanted to prevent this from ever happening again. The coffin would be buried in a huge cage 10 feet deep and finally encased in concrete.

On September 26, 1901, a discussion arose among those present for the reburial about opening Lincoln's coffin. Some argued that the remains should be identified given the rumors flying about the country that Mr. Lincoln was not the body in the coffin. Others believed opening the coffin was a privacy issue. Finally it was decided to open the casket and identify the remains within.

Two plumbers, Leon P. Hopkins and his nephew, Charles L. Willey, chiseled an oblong piece out of the top of the lead-lined coffin. The piece these two men cut out was just over Lincoln's head and shoulders. When the casket was opened, a choking odor emanated. 23 people slowly moved forward to view the remains. Mr. Lincoln's features were totally recognizable. His face had a melancholy expression, but his black chin whiskers hadn't changed at all. The wart on his cheek and the coarse black hair were obvious characteristics of Lincoln's, though his eyebrows had vanished. The president was wearing the same suit he wore at his second inauguration, but it was covered with yellow mold. All 23 people were unanimous that the remains were indeed those of Abraham Lincoln.

The people who viewed the remains of Mr. Lincoln have long since died. One of the last was 13 at the time, Fleetwood Lindley died on February 1, 1963. Three days before he died, Mr. Lindley was interviewed in Life Magazine. He said, "Yes, his face was chalky white. His clothes were mildewed. And I was allowed to hold one of the leather straps as we lowered the casket for the concrete to be poured. I was not scared at the time but I slept with Lincoln for the next six months."

The other youth present, George Cashman, also remembered the event until his death and it made even more of an impression on him, even as an adult. The last years of his life, George Cashman was the curator of the National Landmark in Springfield called "Lincoln's Tomb." He particularly enjoyed relating his story to the more than one million visitors to the site each year. Mr. Cashman died in 1979, the last person to have viewed the remains of Abraham Lincoln.

* An excellent and expansive Internet source for these and further details is the Abraham Lincoln Research Site maintained by Roger Norton at http://members.aol.com/RVSNorton/Lincoln2.html. He cites Dorothy Meserve Kunhardt's article in Life, dated February 15, 1963 as the primary source for his page on the Lincoln exhumation..

* Also www.wordiq.com, an online encyclopedia, contains a wealth of facts about all US Presidents.

* One more item of note. The photo on page 158, bottom, seems to show two small children in the lower right corner, bent intently over the tracks looking at the results of what a trolley car could do to US coins. What do you think? At least in 1906 is wasn't Lincoln pennies the children were experimenting with.

Selected Bibliography

Sources citing locations, events, groups or individuals relating to Mifflin County history.

Albion, Robert G. and Dodson, Leonidas ,Edited by
Philip Vickers Fithian: Journal, 1775 - 1776 Written on the Virginia-Pennsylvania Frontier and in the Army Around New York Princeton: Princeton University Press 1934. (Description of pioneer life in Mifflin County during the 1770s.)

Atlas of Perry, Juniata and Mifflin Counties, Pennsylvania, Philadelphia: Pomeroy, Whitman & Co. 1877. (Reprinted 1975 by the Mifflin County Historical Society - 70 pages)

Aurand, Dr. Eleanor M. ed.
Mifflin Countians Who Served in the Civil War Compiled by George R. Frysinger as published in the Lewistown Gazette in 1905, Lewistown, PA: MCHS, 1996.

Bell, Dr. Raymond Martin
Families and Records Before 1800 - Mifflin Co Supplement
   ---- *Heads of Families in Mifflin County in 1790* 1958, Lewistown, PA: MCHS, Reprinted 1985, 1991
   ---- *Mifflin County, Pennsylvania in the Revolution 1775 - 1783* comp. by Bell, R. M. & Stroup, J. Martin

Biddle, Major General William S.
Major General Frank Ross McCoy 1874 - 1954 Soldier - Statesman - American Lewistown, PA: MCHS, 1956.

Copeland, Willis R.
The Logan Guards of Lewistown, Pennsylvania Our First Defenders of 1861 Lewistown, PA: MCHS, 1962.

Beyer, George R.,
Guide to the Historical Markers of Pennsylvania, Harrisburg: Commonwealth of Pennsylvania PHMC 2000. (Details the historical markers of the state in all 67 counties, including the 11 markers and one historic plaque in Mifflin County.)

Blardone, Chuck ed.
Lewistown and the Pennsylvania Railroad From Moccasins to Steel Wheels Altoona, PA: Pennsylvania Railroad Technical & Historical Society, 2000. 161 pages

Bowen, Eli
Sketch-Book of Pennsylvania Or Its Scenery, Internal Improvements, Resources, and Agriculture Philadelphia: Willis P. Hazaard 1852 (Part IV titled *Philadelphia to Pittsburg (sic)* contemporary travelog of the PRR route through Mifflin County by Eli Bowen.)

Bronner, Simon J.
Popularizing Pennsylvania - Henry W. Shoemaker and the Progressive Uses of Folklore and History University Park, PA Pennsylvania State University Press, 1996.

Burrows, Thomas H.
The State Book of Pennsylvania Containing an Account of the Geographical, History, Government, Resources, and Noted Citizens of the State; with A Map of the State and of Each County Philadelphia: Uriah Hunt & Son, 44 N. Fourth Street, 1846.

Climb Aboard! Celebrate Historic Mifflin County Lewistown, PA The Sentinel Company 1989 (This Mifflin County Bicentennial publication is an excellent resource covering the county's early history to preserving the past today.- 169 pages)

Cochran, Joseph
History of Mifflin County Its Physical Peculiarities, Soil, Climate, Etc. Harrisburg: Patriot Publishing Company, 1879.

Commemorative Biographical Encyclopedia of the Juniata Valley, comprising the Counties of Huntingdon, Mifflin, Juniata and Perry, Pennsylvania Chambersburg, PA: J. M. Runk & Co., 1897 2 volumes.

Cuffey, Roger J.
Geologic Considerations Relevant to Fort Granville (Central Pennsylvania; French and Indian War). 2002., Geographic Society of America, 29 July 2002.

Day, Sherman
Historical Collections of the State of Pennsylvania containing A Copious Selection of the most Interesting Facts, Traditions, etc. Philadelphia: Published by George W. Gorton, 56 North Third Street, 1843. (Shows etching of Mifflin County's third courthouse, see first page of the Preface of this book, plus a chapter on all 67 Pennsylvania Counties.)

D'Invilliers, E. V.
Report on the Geology of the Four Counties Union, Snyder, Mifflin and Juniata Harrisburg, Published by the Board on Commissioners for the Second Geological Survey, 1891. (Chapter VI, pages 219 - 296 detailed geology of Mifflin County by township.)

Dodge, William Logan,
The Last of the Race of Shikellemus, Chief of the Cayuga Nation. A Dramatic Piece by Dr. Joseph Doddridge. Reprint of the Virginia Edition of 1823 with an Appendix

Relating to the Murder of Logan's Family Cincinnati, Ohio: Robert Clarke & Co, 1868.

Donehoo, Dr. George P.,
A History of the Indian Villages and Place Names in Pennsylvania with Numerous Historical Notes and References Harrisburg, The Telegraph Press, 1928. Reprinted 1977, 1995 Baltimore, MD: Gateway Press for the Pine Creek Historian, Spencer L. Kraybill, Waterville, PA 17776 (Names in Mifflin County are found in this book. Ex. Kishacoquillas, a creek and a valley...)

Eckert , Allen W.
The Frontiersmen A Narrative, Boston and Toronto Little, Brown and Company "The Winning of America" series, 1967.
--- *Wilderness Empire* Boston and Toronto, Little, Brown and Company, 1969.
Eckert wrote about the Frontiersmen, "This book is fact, not fiction. Seven years of extensive research turned up written documents that brought the Colonial period to life."

Egle, William H. M.D.
An Illustrated History of the Commonwealth of Pennsylvania Harrisburg: De Witt C. Goodrich & Co., 1876 (Mifflin County data and revisions by Silas Wright and C. W. Walters)

Ellis, Franklin
History of that part of the Susquehanna and Juniata Valleys, Embraced in the Counties of Mifflin, Juniata, Perry, Union and Snyder in the Commonwealth of Pennsylvania, Philadelphia: Everts, Peck and Richard, 1886 (1602 pages in 2 vols. Reprinted Unigraphic, Inc. 1975 Juniata County Bicentennial Commission with extensive 173 page index compiled by Stella Benner Shivery and Shirley Garrett Guiser)

Elliott, Richard Smith
Notes Taken in Sixty Years St. Louis, MO. R. P. Studley & Co., Printers 1883. Memoir covers his life in Mifflin County until about eighteen. Includes how he was influenced to support William Henry Harrison on the election of 1840. Interesting recounting of life in Mifflin County just after the War of 1812. Rare book dealers also link Elliott to "Council Bluffs Indian Agent, 1834, with Doniphan's Expedition, 1846."

Fosnot, H. J.
Lewistown, Penna., As It Is, Lewistown, PA: The Lewistown Gazette 1894.
---- *Lewistown: Descriptive of A Progress Central City of Pennsylvania, of Its Possessions and Prospects, Its Advantages and Opportunities,*   Lewistown: The Lewistown Gazette, 1909. 58 pages

Frazier, Jeffrey R.
Pennsylvania Fireside Tales Old-time Legends and Folktales from the Pennsylvania Mountains Lancaster, PA Wickersham Printing Company, 1996. (Legends of the Seven Mountains, page 1)

Frontier Forts of Pennsylvania, Report of the Commission to the Pennsylvania Legislature in two volumes Harrisburg: Clarance M. Busch, State Printer of Pennsylvania, 1896 (Location of Fort Granville and description of seige and capture.)

Frontier Forts of Pennsylvania, Report of the Commission to the Pennsylvania Legislature in two volumes Second Edition Edited by Thomas Lynch Montgomery, Litt. D. Harrisburg: Wm. Stanley Ray, State Printer of Pennsylvania 1916 (Includes an extensive appendix with data on Fort Granville completed by the Mifflin County Historical Committee on determining the location of the fort.)

Harmon, Raymond E.
Historic Homes and Buildings in Reedsville and Brown Township from the 1800s Reedsville, PA: Brown Township Library and Museum Association, 1987.
---- *Historic Homes and Buildings in Milroy and Armagh Township from the 1800s* Reedsville, PA: Brown Township Library and Museum Association 1988.
---- *Mifflin County Revisited 1730 - 1990* in two volumes Reedsville, PA Brown Township Library and Museum Association 1990.

Historical Register: Notes and Queries, Historical and Genealogical, Relating to Interior Pennsylvania...V. 1-2; Jan. 1883-Dec,1884 Harrisburg, Pa.: L. S. Hart, Printer, 1883-84.

Historic Sites Survey, Mifflin County, Pennsylvania by the Mifflin County Planning Commission Lewistown, 1978.

Hodge, Frederick Webb ed.
Handbook of American Indians in Two Parts Smithsonian Institution, Bureau of American Ethnology Bulletin 30, Washington: Government Printing Office, 1912.

Hughes, Gene
A Pictorial History of Mifflin County, Lewistown, PA: MCHS, 1976.

Hunter, William A.
Forts on the Pennsylvania Frontier, 1753 - 1758 Harrisburg, Commonwealth of Pennsylvania PHMC, 1960 and reprinted by Wennawoods Publishing, Lewisburg, PA in 1999. Pennsylvania historian William A. Hunter in 1960 described the French Letter of Fort Granville as "a puzzle in that day and a mystery in ours."

Jones, U. J.
History of the Early Settlement of the Juniata Valley: Embracing an Account of the Early Pioneers, and the Trials and Privations incidents to the Settlement of the Valley Predatory Incursions, Massacres, and Abductions by the Indians During the French and Indian Wars, and the War of the Revolution, etc. Philadelphia: Henry B. Ashmead First Edition, 1856.

Jones, U. J. and Hoenstine, Floyd G.
History of the Early Settlement of the Juniata Valley: Embracing an Account of the Early Pioneer, and the Trials and Privations incidents to the Settlement of the Valley Predatory Incursions, Massacres, and Abductions by the Indians During the French and Indian Wars, and the War of the Revolution, etc. With notes and Extensions complied as a Glossary from the Memoirs of Early Settlers, The Pension Statements of Revolutionary War Soldiers, and Other Source Material by Floyd G. Hoenstine Harrisburg, PA: The Telegraph Press, 1940.

Kauffman, Henry J.
Early American Gunsmiths 1650 - 1850 New York: The Telegraph Press, 1952. (Details of a Dickert rifle.)

Kauffman, S. Daune
Mifflin County Amish and Mennonite Story 1791 - 1991 Belleville, PA: Mifflin County Mennonite Historical Society, 1991.

Lewistown Sentinel.
Climb aboard! Lewistown, Pa: The Sentinel, 1989.
(A booklet prepared to commemorate Mifflin County's Bicentennial, 1789-1989.)

Mayer, Brantz
TAH-GAH-JUTE; or Logan and Cresap, an Essay Albany, NY Joel Munsell, Publisher, 1867. (An essay aimed at vindcating Michael Cresap as murderer of Logan's family.)

McClenahen, Daniel
Compiled the extensive "Mifflin County Series" based upon archived local newspapers and available public records that can be found at the Mifflin County Courthouse. Should the researcher wish to access the original material, entries are abstracted from these listed sources. The writer cautions that publications are based on available material and are not claimed to be all-inclusive. The series is a monumental project, with additional volumes planned.
   Former Residents of Mifflin County 1832 - 1883 Vol. I
   Former Residents of Mifflin County 1884 - 1896 Vol. II
   Marriages of Mifflin County 1822 - 1885
   Naturalization Papers of Mifflin 1803 - 1906
   Obituaries of Mifflin County 1822 - 1880
   Obituaries of Mifflin County 1880 - 1896 Vol. II
   People in the News in Mifflin County (1822 - 1886)
   Surname Index for the 1860 Census - Mifflin County
   Wills of Mifflin County, Vol I, 1789 - 1860
   Wills of Mifflin County, Vol II, 1860 - 1900

---- *A Walk through Mifflin County History,* Video approx. 60 min. Commentary written by Daniel McClenahen, Lewistown, PA: MCHS, 1999.

McIlnay, Dennis P.
Juniata, River of Sorrows Hollidaysburg, PA: Live Oaks Press First Edition 2002 (Excellent description of the seige, capture and subsequent fate of the captives.)

McMullen, Edward
The Milkman Cometh...Home Milk Delivery Mifflin County,   PA 1900 - 1980 Mifflin County, PA: Privately published Aug., 1998.

McNitt, Richard P. ed.
Growing Up in Reedsville Privately published 4th Ed. 1991 (Outstanding firsthand accounts of growing up in an American small town in the late 19th and first half of the twentieth centuries. 171 pages)

Mifflin County Development Committee
A Survey of the Resources and Opportunities of Mifflin County, Pennsylvania, Mifflin County Development Committee, Lewistown, 1947.

Mifflin County School District
Projects and publications:
---- *Mifflin County Yesterday and Today,* Lewistown, PA: MCDS, 1993.
---- *History of Mifflin County* Lewistown, PA: Special Education Department, MCSD, 1976.

Meyers, Ben & Hattie
Birds and friends of Central Pennsylvania Mifflin County Lewistown, PA: Mifflin

County Printing Orb Rowden, Publisher, 1973.

Reynolds, Patrick M.
Pennsylvania Profiles Series Volumes 1 - 15 Red Rose Studio, Willow Street, PA 17584, 1978. (Presents episodes of Pennsylvania history related to Mifflin County including the Grasshopper War, Fort Granville and the Alamo Defenders from Mifflin County.)

Rupp, I. D.
Early History of Western Pennsylvania Harrisburg, Pa.: Daniel W. Kauffman, Publisher, 1846 and Reprinted in 1995 by Wennawoods Publishing, Lewisburg, PA. *Appendix, pp. 213-217. (Death of Logan's Family by Daniel Greathouse)*
---- *History and Topography of Northumberland, Huntingdon, Mifflin, Centre, Union, Columbia, Juniata and Clinton counties, Pa.* Lancaster: G. Hills 1847 (Appendix contains extensive transcript and discussion of the French Letter found at Fort Granville)

Secor, Robert A. (Editor), and Richman, Irwin (Editor)
Pennsylvania 1776 University Park Pennsylvania State University Press, 1975

Sentinel Company
Historical Souvenir of Lewistown, Penna Lewistown, PA: The Sentinel Company and Old Home Week Celebration Committee 1925.

Seven Stories of Early Mifflin County History for Elementary Grades. A Teachers' Curriculum Report. Lewistown, PA: Mifflin County Historical Society, 1954. The seven stories are: The Early Indians, Ohesson, the Indian Village, Fort Granville, The Story of Captain Jack, The Story of Freedom Forge, The Story of George Sigler, The Mann Axe. Includes a few illustrations, suggested activities and references.

Shoemaker, Henry W.
Eldorado Found - The Central Pennsylvania Highlands A Tourist Survey Altoona, PA Altoona tribune Publishing Co., 1917. Reprinted by the Pine Creek Historian, Waterville, PA by Gateway Press, Baltimore, 1993.
---- *Indian Folk-Songs of Pennsylvania* Ardmore, PA Newman F. McGirr, 1927. (Page - Death and burial of Chief Logan, as retold to Shoemaker by his great nephew Jesse Logan at the so called 'Pennsylvania Indian Reservation' in 1917.)
---- *In the Seven Mountains* Reading, PA The Bright Printing Co., 1913 (Hunting tails, like "Dan Treaster's Nights, The Story of the Wolf Knob.)
---- *Juniata Memories* Philadelphia, John Joseph McVey, 1916. (Page 139, Birth of Nita-nee on the banks of the Juniata River near Newtown-Hamilton... General category of the Legend of Bird Rock.)
---- *Pennsylvania Deer and Their Horns* 1915 edition, reprinted 1992 by the Lycoming County Historical Society, new revised 2002 edition, with a second part including commentary on modern deer management, Wennawoods Publishing, Lewisburg, PA.

Sipe, C. Hale
The Indian Chiefs of Pennsylvania Butler, PA Ziegler Printing Co. 1927.
---- *The Indian Wars of Pennsylvania* Harrisburg, PA 1929 Reprinted by Wennawoods Publishing, 1995. (Location of Fort Granville and Lord Dunmore's War.)

Stroup, J. M. Lewistown, PA: MCHS,
---- *The People of Mifflin County* 1755 - 1798   Lewistown, PA: MCHS,
---- *The Genesis of Mifflin County Pennsylvania,* Lewistown, PA: MCHS, 1957. (Reprinted in 2003 with name index)

Two Hundred Years - A Chronological List of Events in the History of Mifflin County, Pennsylvania 1752 - 1957 Lewistown, PA: MCHS, 1957.

Van Diver, Bradford B.
Roadside Geology of Pennsylvania Missoula, Montana: Mountain Press Publishing Company, 1990. (A nice layman's description of the geology found along Mifflin County highways.)

Wagner, Orren R.
The Main Line of the Pennsylvania Canal through Mifflin County, Lewistown, PA: MCHS, 1963.

Wallace, Anthony F. C.
Jefferson And The Indians: The Tragic Fate Of The First Americans, Ann Arbor, Michigan: Scholarly Publishing Office, University of Michigan Library, 1999.

Wallace, Paul A. W.
Indian Paths of Pennsylvania Harrisburg, PA, Commonwealth of Pennsylvania PHMC, 1987.

Wessell, R. B.
Medal of Honor Recipients of Mifflin County, Pennsylvania Lewistown, PA Privately Published, 2001.

Wirt, George H.
Joseph Trimble Rothrock: Father of Forestry in Pennsylvania Lewistown, PA: MCHS, 1956

Woods, Norman B.
Lives of Famous Indian Chiefs Aurora, Ill. American Indian Historical Publishing Company, 1906.

Photographic Sources

Mifflin County Historical Society Archives - Extensive photo archives cover the history of Mifflin County from the Civil War era to the present, including both negative files and photographic images.

In addition, the vertical files of the Society contain newspaper images, engravings, advertisements and other art work. A photo example one might find: 1895 Lewistown Centennial Parade on E. 3rd St., Lewistown shown at left.

The Kepler Studio Collection - The Kepler Studio was owned and operated for sixty years by Luther F. Kepler, Sr. and his brother James A. Kepler, from 1925 until it discontinued operation in the mid-1980s. The business first operated on Chestnut Street, and later at 127 E. Market Street, on Dorcas Street beside the YMCA and lastly on the corner of Third and Dorcas Streets across from the Catholic Church, Lewistown, PA. The Kepler Studio Collection consists of negative files from the 1920s (some earlier) through the 1960s. The collection is owned by the author. The Kepler Studio Camera Room at 127 E. Market Street, Lewistown, PA shown below.

APPENDIX 1 - Mifflin County Internet Histories

1. A Website titled *Keystone Heritage - A Site for People Researching the Settlement of Pennsylvania's Juniata Valley* is a valuable, developing resource with extensive bibliography for counties Bedford, Blair, Huntingdon, Juniata, Mifflin and Perry. Prepared and maintained by Janet Eldred, a student at the University of Pittsburgh, it contains sections on transportation, periodicals past and present, research locations, maps and atlases, and church histories, to mention a few. Impressive site!

The site can be reached at http://www.keystoneheritage.com/index.html

2. Selected chapters from Franklin Ellis' *History of That Part of the Susquehanna and Juniata Valleys Embraced in the Counties of Mifflin, Juniata, Perry, Union and Snyder* Philadelphia, 1886 are available at the USGenWeb Project page for Mifflin County at http://www.rootsweb.com/~pamiffli/ellis/ellis-toc.htm

Here is an excerpt:
HISTORY OF MIFFLIN COUNTY - CHAPTER I.
Civil History - Erection of Mifflin County - Location of Seat of Justice - Public Buildings - Provision for the Poor - Rosters of Officials 1789 to 1885 - Population.
THE territory embraced in Mifflin County at the time of its erection was in that part of Cumberland County which was contained in the great tract or "Purchase," the title to which was secured from the Indians at Albany July 6, 1754. Settlements were made so rapidly during that season that petitions were sent in to the court of Cumberland County from settlers in Sherman's Valley, along Buffalo Creek and in Tuscarora and Path Valleys setting forth "their great distance from the county-seat and asking for the erection of new townships, that they might better transact the necessary business to facilitate the improvement and good government of the new settlements." These petitions were presented to the court at its August term in that year, and, in accordance with their prayer, four "new townships to the side the N. Mountain" were erected. One of these was "Lac," whose territory was thus stated: "And we do further errect the settlement called the Tuskerora Valey into a sepparate Township and nominate the same the Township of LAC, and we appoint John Johnston to act therein as Constable for the remaining part of the current year." It embraced all of the county of Juniata lying west of the Juniata River. Its territory was reduced by the erection of Milford, November 7, 1768.

3. The "Mifflin County" selection from Sherman Day's 1843 *Historical Collections of the State of Pennsylvania* is available at www.rootsweb.com/~pamiffli/day-sherman.htm

Here is an excerpt:
MIFFLIN COUNTY was formed from Cumberland and Northumberland counties by the act of 19th September, 1789. Length 39 miles, breadth 15; area about 360 sq. miles. Population in 1790, 7,562; in 1800, 13,80; in 1810, 12,13; in 1820, 16,618; in 1830, 21,690; in 1840, (after the separation of Juniata Co.) 13,092. The county forms a long irregular figure, stretching in a southwest and northeast direction, traversed longitudinally by a series of rugged mountain ranges, of nearly uniform height. These mountains are separated by soft undulating valleys of slate and limestone, of exceeding beauty and fertility. The lovely vale of Wyoming has been more distinguished in history and song; and yet it is only a specimen - a rare one, it must be conceded - of many similar valleys that adorn the apparently rugged Appalachian formation, both in Pennsylvania and Virginia. The valley in which Lewistown is situated bears a striking resemblance to that of Wyoming, and if in some points inferior, it has the advantage in the possession of limestone, that inexhaustible element of fertility. The mountain ranges, commencing on the S. E., are Blue ridge, and Shade, Jack's, Stone, and Path Valley mountains. The latter is sometimes called the Seven Mountains.

NOTE - These files has been transcribed and contributed for use in the USGenWeb Mifflin County Genealogy Project by Judy Banja .

APPENDIX 2 - Selected Anniversary Histories of Mifflin County Boroughs and Townships

Armagh Township, The History of - "Strike the Great Valley Off" 1770 - 1995 Milroy, PA: Armagh Township Historical Book Committee 1995.

Brown Township Area, History of 1776 - 1976 Reedsville, PA: Brown Township Bicentennial , Committee 1976.

Burnham, Pennsylvania Historical Book Golden Jubilee 1911 - 1961 Burnham, PA: Burnham Golden Jubilee Executive and Steering Committee 1961.

Burnham Fire Company Centennial Celebration 1902 - 2002 - United We Stand Burnham, PA: Centennial Booklet Committee, 2002. 96 pages

Historical Souvenir of Lewistown, Penna Lewistown, PA: The Sentinel Company and Old Home Week Celebration Committee, 1925 162 pages

Logan, Mingo Chief, Belleville, PA: Kishacoquillas Valley National Bank, 1976. (Written and illustrated by Mifflin County artist Anne K. Fisher 1925 - 1977).

McVeytown, Bratton and Oliver Townships, A History of McVeytown, PA: McVeytown Area Bicentennial Book Committee, 1976. 112 pages

Mifflin County Heritage - In Celebration of Mifflin County's Bicentennial Lewistown, PA: Mifflin County Broadcasting Company 1989. 46 pages

Our Heritage from Ohesson Russell National Bank 125th Anniversary Booklet, Lewistown, PA: Russell National Bank, 1974 48 pages

Souvenir Booklet on the History of Lewistown, Pennsylvania and the Greater Lewistown Area Lewistown, PA: Quasquisesquicentennial Celebration Committee, 1970.

Yeagertown, Pennsylvania Past & Present 1842 - 1992 Yeagertown PA: Yeagertown Sesquicentennial Committee, 1992 126 pages

Index

189

190

About the Author

Forest Fisher's interest in history came at an early age. Raised in a household with an extended family, including a great-grandmother and a set of grandparents, he heard stories of a bygone era almost from birth. Commenting on this point recently, he noted:

"When you live with older relatives, you often heard stories about their youth and to me it was interesting stuff. I was probably five or six, when my great-grandmother Kepler told about traveling from Juniata County through the Lewistown Narrows in a buckboard with her parents, sometime around 1870. A trip of minutes now took all day back then," Fisher recalled, "the road was so rough and rocky."

"She also knew the Lewistown couple who rode their house down the Juniata River during the Great Flood of 1889," Fisher continued, "Grandma told me that story one day while she was baby-sitting me and it was raining like heck outside. I was wide-eyed waiting for the creek to lift OUR house off the foundation! The rain passed, and we were safe. But when you're five, you never know! Stories like that tend to stick in one's mind."

Fisher was born and raised in Reedsville, Mifflin County, Pennsylvania. He attended the old Reedsville Elementary School and graduated from Kishacoquillas High School in 1967. Fisher graduated from Harrisburg Area Community College and then transferred to University Park where he earned a B.S. in Elementary Education at Penn State. He's been an elementary teacher with the Mifflin County School District since 1975. "Elementary age students still want to learn and are eager to hear the stories of history that involve real people, like area pioneer Dorcas Buchanan," Fisher commented.

His work with the Mifflin County Historical Society began in 1996, when he joined the board of directors. The next year he began editing the society's newsletter, a job he's held ever since, dubbing the publication *Notes from Monument Square*. Fisher served as society first vice-president, then a term as society president that ended in 2004 and now serves as the board's second vice president. He also chairs the Scholarship Committee plus develops the society's annual calendar and collector post card sets.

In addition to his writing for the MCHS newsletter, his articles on Mifflin County history have appeared in Common Ground Magazine, the Lewistown Sentinel and the County Observer. He is a contributor to the Mifflin County School Districts local history, *Mifflin County Yesterday and Today*, and the Pennsylvania Railroad Technical & Historical Society's *Lewistown and the Pennsylvania Railroad From Moccasins to Steel Wheels.*

Fisher and his wife Dot, a physical education teacher in the Mifflin County School District, live along Honey Creek in his family home, Raven Roost, shown at left in a 1940s photo.

195

"PRESERVING THE PAST FOR THE FUTURE"

Founded in 1921, the Mifflin County Historical Society operates under this motto, endeavoring to conserve the heirlooms of a county established in 1789.

- OFFICIAL COUNTY HISTORICAL SOCIETY -

The Society's museum, the Mc Coy House, is located at 17 North Main Street, Lewistown, Pa. The house was the birthplace of soldier-statesman Major General Frank Ross McCoy. The 1841 McCoy House was acquired and restored by the Pennsylvania Historic and Museum Commission. McCoy House is host to periodic special exhibits and is the permanent home of the society's collections.

McCoy House is listed on the National Register of Historic Sites and the Pennsylvania Trail of History.

Seasonal Hours from mid-May through mid-December: Every Sunday 1:30 to 4 PM Call the Society office for arranging group or special tours.

McCoy House - 17 North
Main Street, Lewistown, Pa.

Mifflin County Historical Society Office& Library
Historic Mifflin County Courthouse
1 West Market Street, Lewistown, PA 17044
Office: (717) 242 - 1022
E-mail: mchistory@acsworld.com

Office: Open every Tuesday & Wednesday - 10 AM to 4 PM
Library: Open every Tuesday & Wednesday - 10 AM to 4 PM
The 1st & 3rd Saturday of each month - 10 AM to 3 PM

SOCIETY MEMBERSHIP

Your membership in the Mifflin County Historical Society supports the preservation of the county's past through the daily operation of the society's office, research library and through exhibits at the McCoy House Museum.

The society's newsletter, *Notes from Monument Square*, arrives five time each year and is your connection to society happenings and special programs.

The twelve page publication includes: Society News & Notes, Membership Updates, The Picture Page, Mifflin County Trivia, Genealogists Corner, The Editor's Desk, plus an article in every issue on Mifflin County history.

The newsletter has been described as "the best historical society newsletter in the state!" Support local history by becoming a member of the Mifflin County Historical Society and judge our newsletter for yourself.

Annual Dues Structure	
-Individual membership	$10
-Family membership	$15
-Supporting membership	$35
-Civic club membership	$50
Life Membership	
-Individual membership	$150

Mifflin County Historical Society Research Library
(Partial list of materials available)

* complete set of published Pennsylvania Archives

* many area and family histories and genealogies in book form, including two biographical encyclopedias, one in 1897 and in 1913.

* U. S. Census records, 1790 – 1930, for Mifflin County and many surrounding counties on microfilm

* the printed index to the 1790 – 1850 Pennsylvania census and the 1860 – 1870 census for Central Pennsylvania

Research volunteer Margaret Spahr, above, at the reception desk in the renovated Research Library. Volunteers Peggy Goss and Winona Simmons below in the expanded library.

* collection of area newspapers for 1822 to present (not complete) on microfilm

* Deed and Mortgage Index, Orphan Court Index, Quarter Sessions Court Records and other miscellaneous county records on microfilm

* several volumes of cemetery records for Mifflin County, compiled in 1977 from research and field surveys

* two volumes containing names and other genealogical information abstracted from wills recorded in the Mifflin County courthouse, 1789 through 1860

* vertical files of family research done by Society members or others who have shared work

* three volumes of Genealogical Abstracts of Revolutionary War Pension Files

Call the Society office for questions or for more details about research or becoming a society member.

Community Outreach

* Annual Scholarships for Mifflin County High School Seniors

* Free annual distribution of MCHS calendars to area elementary students

* Special group guided tours at McCoy House

* Historical slide program to club, church and civic groups

Volunteers are always welcome to help out with the traveling slide show or at the McCoy House Museum. Contact the MCHS at (717) 242 - 1022 or E-mail- mchistory@acsworld.com.